Musical Theatre Song

Musical Theatre Song

A Comprehensive Course in Selection, Preparation, and Presentation for the Modern Performer

STEPHEN PURDY

Foreword by Hunter Foster

methuen | drama

LONDON · NEW YORK · OXFORD · NEW DELHI · SYDNEY

METHUEN DRAMA
Bloomsbury Publishing Plc
50 Bedford Square, London, WC1B 3DP, UK
1385 Broadway, New York, NY 10018, USA

BLOOMSBURY, METHUEN DRAMA and the Methuen Drama logo
are trademarks of Bloomsbury Publishing Plc

First published in Great Britain 2016
Reprinted 2016, 2017, 2018, 2019 (twice)

A catalogue record for this book is available from the British Library.

A catalog record for this book is available from the Library of Congress.

ISBN: PB: 978-1-4725-6656-0
ePDF: 978-1-4725-9510-2
ePub: 978-1-4725-9511-9

Series: Performance Books

Typeset by RefineCatch Limited, Bungay, Suffolk
Printed and bound in Great Britain

To find out more about our authors and books visit
www.bloomsbury.com and sign up for our newsletters.

For my family
and my family of students

CONTENTS

ACKNOWLEDGMENTS

I would like to extend my deepest gratitude and heartfelt thanks to the staff at Bloomsbury, especially to my editor and friend Anna Brewer, for her immeasurable wisdom and unwavering enthusiasm throughout. Thanks as well go to Tim Howard and Emily Clark, my colleagues at Marymount Manhattan College in New York City, who were instrumental in getting this book on the path toward publication. Finally, a huge thank you to Andrea Palesh for her inexhaustible efforts to obtain rights to reprint the lyrics contained herein.

I am extremely grateful to my family, my wife Kendall, and sons Caden and Rowan, for being understanding of my "other" job, that of writing this book, and especially to my mother, Jacquelyn Purdy James, who worked diligently readying this book. Without her, it would not have happened.

ABOUT THE AUTHOR

Stephen Purdy is on musical theatre faculty at the American Musical Theatre Academy, the American Musical Theatre Academy of London, Marymount Manhattan College in New York City, and is the founder and principal coach at the New York Vocal Coaching Studio. His students have been cast in the Broadway and Broadway touring companies of nearly every major musical of the last fifteen years. He regularly delivers master classes and seminars to musical theatre students around the globe, and has conducted and accompanied numerous Broadway show companies in New York, nationally, and in Europe. He is married to actress and fellow voice pedagogue Kendall Purdy, and they have two sons, Caden and Rowan.

MUSIC CREDITS

"Separate Ways" (Worlds Apart)
Words and music by Steve Perry and Jonathan Cain.
Copyright © 1982 Love Batch Music (ASCAP) and Twist And
    Shout Music, a division of Weed High Nightmare Music
    (ASCAP).
All rights for Weed High Nightmare Music, administered by
    Wixen Music Publishing Inc.
International copyright secured.
All rights reserved.
Reprinted by permission of Hal Leonard Corporation.

"Soliloquy" (from *Carousel*)
By Richard Rodgers and Oscar Hammerstein II.
Copyright © 1945 by Williamson Music (ASCAP), an Imagem
    Company, owner of publication and allied rights throughout
    the World.
Copyright renewed.
International copyright secured.
All rights reserved.
Used by permission.

"Sweet Liberty" (from *Jane Eyre*)
Music and lyrics by Paul Gordon.
© 1995
All rights reserved.

"The Beauty Is" (from *The Light in the Piazza*)
Music and lyrics by Adam Guettel.
Copyright © 2003 by Matthew Music, administered by
    Williamson Music (ASCAP).
International copyright secured.
All rights reserved.
Used by permission.

"Who I'd Be" (from *Shrek the Musical*)
Words by David Lindsay-Abaire.
Music by Jeanine Tesori.
Copyright © 2008 DWA Songs (ASCAP).
Worldwide rights administered by BMG Rights Management (US)
 LLC.
International copyright secured.

FOREWORD

What is more American than a musical? Whether we know it or not, the American musical, as an art form, is woven into the very fabric of American society. Everyone has at least seen or heard of a musical; and I am sure most people have performed in a musical at one time or another, most likely in high school or community theatre, or have children, nieces, and nephews who have donned a costume, put on makeup and danced a box step to a classic tune. Some of the most beloved films of all time are musicals: *The Sound of Music*, *My Fair Lady*, and *The Wizard of Oz*, to name but a few. And now, musicals are more popular than ever. When I first came to New York City, there were eight Broadway shows running. Eight! That was musicals *and* plays. It was a sad time for the art form, but this past year, we have had an abundance of new musicals and revivals open on Broadway—more than any other year that I can remember.

So, what does it take to be a Broadway performer? It's not an easy task. Being on Broadway is hard work. Sure, it's ultimately a rewarding profession with opening night parties, award shows, and camaraderie with other actors, but it also can be strenuous work. On Broadway and in most major regional theatres, there will be eight shows a week. The job involves performing at Christmas, on Thanksgiving, on every weekend in the summer when everyone else is at the beach. In a lot of ways, it's a sacrifice; and even though it's only two to three hours of work every night, those are intense hours in front of a live audience that can leave a performer drained physically and emotionally at the end of a long week.

So, in many ways, performers must train themselves like an athlete. It's making sure that you are ready to perform every single time you go out on that stage, and replicating the same performance even when you are sick, tired, or dealing with the ups and downs of life. You have to have training and technique. You have to have a solid foundation on which to build your performance and character. Just like a basketball player has "fundamentals," performers have to have a toolbox of technique: things that are so ingrained in their bodies and minds that they don't have to think about them on stage.

The one question I am asked the most by young performers is what they should concentrate on as they train themselves to be a musical theatre performer. I always say that there is no substitute for good acting. As a director, I sit and watch many an audition in which very talented singers and dancers come through the door, but they are not good actors. Even at dance calls, I look for the dancers who can act. My number-one mantra in directing and writing shows is "storytelling." As theatre artists, the basis of everything we do is telling a good story, and good actors can help tell that story.

The other thing I tell young performers is to be a kind human being. Be a team player. Jerry Zaks, the acclaimed Broadway director, once told me that in every scene on stage, you should always make the other person more important than yourself. And if everyone on stage did that, we would all be working like a team. We would all be lifting up each other. I see many shows in which you can tell that actors are going "rogue," thinking only of themselves and not giving the other actors what they need so that the entire company can all share in the experience. More often in this business, that happens. Let's face it, we all want some sort of acclaim, some sort of validation for the things that we do. We all want our "moment," our chance to shine, our name singled out in the papers. But, I must tell you, after over twenty years of performing on Broadway, there is nothing more rewarding than to be a part of a cast that is in total harmony with one another.

The other thing that is most important for young performers is knowing the world around you. If you are only immersed in the world of the theatre you are limiting yourself as an artist. Every day, you should read the paper or browse news sites on the Internet. Keep up with the world. As artists, we are in charge of helping to change and shape the future of humanity. What new things do we have to say? How does our performance make an audience member rethink the world in which they live? Enrich their lives? Move them so that what we do as artists stays with them days after the performance?

The importance of this was never more evident than when we opened *Urinetown* in September 2001—one week after 9/11. In fact, we had to go back to work two days after the towers fell. The smoke still lingering in the air, Air Force jets still flying over the city; but, Mayor Giuliani said it was important for us to go back to work, to help inspire hope to a devastated city. And I still remember that night and all the audience members who waited for us after the show, all of us hugging and crying, strangers coming together, and the appreciation that for two-and-a-half hours, they could forget the terrible events of that fateful day.

Lastly, it's books such as this by Stephen Purdy that are essential in helping instruct the young performer. Books by professionals in this business who understand what it's really like and how things really work. I've learned the most by listening to the professionals around me who have the experience and knowledge of the past, and are helpful in passing down this knowledge to younger generations so that they can become theatre artists themselves. And that's what we all are: artists—creators of new and wonderful things.

I remember one time, as a young performer, I was in rehearsal and struggling with a particular monologue and I just couldn't crack it. I just couldn't remember the lines. An older actor came up to me and said, "Remember why you do this; it's because you love it." Nothing could be more true. Through all the struggles, rejections, heartbreaks that you will face—and trust me, there will be many—always remember the joy that being a performer brings you, and the love that you bring to others; believe me, in the end, that's all that really matters.

Hunter Foster
June 2015

PREFACE

Anyone can be a star, or so the ubiquitous so-called contestant "talent-driven" television programs of the early twenty-first century would have you believe. With offerings ranging from riveting expressions of prodigious talent to those that might be best described as inane, this pop-culture phenomenon of the fresh-faced newbie with precisely the perfect measure of appeal and "wow" factor can impress judges both in person and across the airwaves, and a celestial catapult can result. With what might be characterized as no less than pandemic, anyone within the proximity of a television transmission or Internet video-sharing site may view these nobody-becomes-somebody narratives any time and nearly any place. After a passionate and protracted contest, the resulting message from the winner's corner is: "Yes, viewer, this can happen to you, too." Indeed, it seems that no matter the country or the continent, that particular populous has undeniably "got talent."

Despite the presence of these mass media, it remains true (perhaps in equal number, but this crosses wits with the more cynical me) that many of today's would-be performers were struck with an irrepressible urge to perform and enticed by the prospect of a career onstage the old-fashioned way. Adrenalin-charged visceral reactions brought on from watching live stage performances of musicals or their filmed counterparts have fired up human pistons for generations, so why shouldn't they still? The enduring presence (and in recent years, the re-emergence of the latter after a period of all but disappearing) of these pillars of entertainment ensures us of the fortitude of the musical theatre and the live, context-driven stage performance in general. It also happily reassures us that the stage musical remains an ever-evolving presence in our culture of live entertainment. This is true whether that musical takes place on a Broadway or West End stage, or any regional, community, or school stage in any country or on any continent.

For the modern professional and aspiring professional theatrical singing actor (both to whom this book is directed), whatever the means of first and subsequent encounters, the path to stage worthiness and "truth" in performance (whether those come by presentations intended as pure entertainment or drawn from the headier, heartier contemplations of the human condition) remains a magnificent and beguiling life-long endeavor. It is still the mysterious concoction of labor and love that it has always been to dyed-in-the-wool devotees. But now, for the contemporary musical theatre stage performer, it is one that also requires the heavy lifting of a newly emerging set of burdens to bear—the highest degrees of versatility and wherewithal. The reasons for this are twofold. First is that the emerging performers of today are no longer competitive simply by being skilled in only one or two disciplines. You, if one of them, must now be the whizz-kid of the get-it-done, multi-tasking agenda both on stage and when managing your career. The second is more succinct. There are just too many of you competing for the same jobs. You can no longer disregard the reality of the ever-shrinking stable employment odds of the entertainment industry and hope for the best. In short, you have to, for artistic survival, arm yourself with as formidable an arsenal as possible.

To compete, you must have the skills to not only put over with fervor the many singing and dancing performance styles in use today, but you must also be thoroughly immersed in the performance customs of your chosen genre's history. The ability to do so is often the deal maker or deal breaker in getting the job, keeping the job, and winning over your audience. Most importantly, and unlike ever before, at the root of all this facility there must be a steely resilience and a white-hot resolution to carry on for the love of the art.

It's no wonder that this fire-in-the-belly craving to perform on stage finds its way into so many. We could speculate that this occurs in large part because of the culture's obsession with the above-mentioned talent television. Perhaps this is why would-be performers are emerging in astonishing numbers, more than ever before in the history of show business. The true reason, however, may be mostly an organic one. It is an undeniable fact that few career choices enjoy the kind of mutual satisfaction and reciprocation that a performer exchanges with his audience. (I use the pronoun *his* throughout this book for convenience only; clearly, I am also referring to *her* as well.) The "take" or the "get" affirmation in return for the "give" can be an addictive, potent intoxication; and the resulting euphoria that a performer feels while engaging with his audience in acknowledging his audiences' esteem may well lead to the repeated desire to give, and thus, get more. The dream of the life of a performer is born.

I don't pretend to be smarter than or speak more truthfully than someone else's dreams, but I have seen firsthand that the gaps among desire, wherewithal, and successful outcome may be extensive. Moreover, whereas "popular" music, and screen and film performances make extensive use of manipulative editing magic tricks to render a perfect performance, live musical theatrical performers have no such luxuries. There is no overdubbing, no auto tune, and no stunt double to substitute for the two-left-footed leading lady. There is only the naked performer with no place to hide, his technique and training his best line of defense.

It is the quality of content within what transpires during this critical time of training and preparation that will first determine the performer's merits and then that individual's value and marketability in the theatre marketplace. Success in the business of show business is built on the bedrock of an ironclad performance and audition technique, a highly evolved sense of self, a keen business savvy, an infallible work ethic, good fortune, and of course, talent. You, the modern musical theatre performer, should consider yourself forewarned: Wanting it alone, while key, is not an adequate setup for success; and the process of training should never be sacrificed in order to arrive at an accelerated and hasty result.

This book is intended to guide you, the singing actor, through a great number of strategies and exercises toward optimized performances by filling the aforementioned lapses, if present. Its equally important mission is to provide you with a "Who am I and where did I come from?" context in order to inform your work. This writing is not intended as a wholesale across-the-board substitute for live training itself; no book alone can provide that. More specifically, this publication is intended to navigate you through the song selection, preparation, and presentation process in order to optimize your audition performances and your onstage performances. Meeting these objectives does not occur through or with a singular method, but instead through the means of an amalgamated number of them in concert. "Get It Done" exercises, which are aimed at utilizing the concepts presented and putting them in motion within your song work, will guide you along the path. The thoughts, ideas, instructions, and exercises that are expressed and appear here represent not only a sort of road map for readying you for stage worthiness, but also serve to arm and embolden you with practical advice so that you will be as fortified as possible in the dizzying world that is the modern musical theatre.

Portions of this book are designed to lead the performer at the genesis of his journey, and I invite the nonneophyte to feel at liberty to move on to the portions of the book that are allocated for everyone. Whatever your classification and situation, the purpose of these pages is to help close your gaps as succinctly and efficiently as possible, and to provide you with momentum in today's challenging, fractured, and still wonderful musical theatre.

SECTION ONE
Song Selection

CHAPTER ONE

Introduction to Song Selection and Historical Context:

What You Should Know (and Why You Should Care)

Introduction

The theatre is full of surprises. Anyone who has ever sat saucer-eyed in a darkened theatre, aghast as the chandelier hurtles earthbound to the chromatic crescendo of the Phantom's theme or felt goose bumps on their arms as Eliza Doolittle descends the stairs on her way to the ball or even felt unapologetically child-like when Peter Pan asks the audience to clap their hands without restraint to save Tinkerbell's life knows the matchless thrill of those ineffable moments. The theatre, unlike recordings and film, materializes in the here-and-now, carrying the audience to multitudes of fanciful, exotic, and even daunting places. On any given day, a musical theatre-goer may find himself transplanted to France during revolutionary times as in *Les Misérables*, the *South Pacific* ocean, a shoddy lower-Eastside New York apartment in *Rent*, or the craggy,

Dickensian streets of London in *Oliver!* Wherever the locale, the
theatre makes us feel as if we have been magically, as though by a
time-and-distance traveling machine, transported to places both
past and present that we might otherwise never have expected to
visit in an ordinary lifetime.

But stagecraft, locale, and dramatic convention aside, the theatre
can only embody itself as a flesh-and-blood affair with actors,
those blessed, can-do, gritted-teethed wonders of the universe. This
slightly batty band of folks, as characters on the stage, open their
worlds to us, confide in us, confess their failings to us, and invest
their unique stories in us. We, in turn, listen and empathize with
them, laugh with them and *at* them, hum along with them, and
reveal ourselves *to* ourselves through them, becoming willing
audience participants as they solve the problems of their lives. In
doing so, we become well acquainted with their circumstances, and
we discover what they want in that particular context and what or
who is standing in the way of their having it. All the while, knowingly
or not, we are being led to a greater, more richly defined
understanding of what it is to be human and alive. From the moment
that the house lights are darkened, the wheels of theatre have begun
to turn, and we're on our way.

The musical theatre, as we think of it, utilizes a course of not only
"acting" through speech and gestures to accomplish these means, but
also the disciplines of dance and song to enliven, enrich, and propel
its storytelling. The artistic union of these elements appoints the
musical theatre as a stand-alone entity; opera comes close, and
operetta probably closer, but in these genres, the principal storytellers
rarely dance (there is a separate ensemble for that) and a well-ordered
delivery of the text is often a distant second to delivering an ideally
formulated sound. By contrast, the actors of today's musical theatre
sing, act, and dance, often simultaneously, and the circumstances of
the characters are often far more accessible than those of the opera,
which routinely tends to inhabit mythical and long-ago places and
circumstances and sometimes doesn't even involve mere mortals.
Indeed, in the modern musical theatre, the performers do it all, and
the theatre at large—whatever the form and on whatever continent—
is a far more exhilarating and enlightened place for it.

Anyone requiring evidence that singing, dancing, and acting
make natural bedfellows in theatrical storytelling and character
realization and who can't readily attend a well-produced musical

production is urged to view one of any number of stellar performances captured on film and video. Watching these, we can barely imagine the marvels that must have pervaded the theatre as Yul Brynner preened and prowled about the stage like a tiger uncaged in *The King and I* or the electric energy bouncing madly around as Chita Rivera belted out her exaltation to the wonders of "America" (*West Side Story*). And what about the collective audience astonishment during Jennifer Holliday's gut-heaving, banshee-wailing pleas and defiance in her rendition of "And I Am Telling You I'm Not Going" (*Dreamgirls*) or even the uproarious reaction to witnessing the scarecrow-legged Dorothy Loudon hamming it up as the boozy Miss Hannigan in "Easy Street" (*Annie*)? The parallel universe of Theatreland London has been equally astonished watching some of these performances that originated on Broadway, and a remarkable number of home-grown ones such as Robert Lindsay relishing "The Lambeth Walk" (*Me and My Girl*), Michael Ball camping and dragging it up in *Hairspray*, or Elaine Paige stirring the stardust in her seemingly endless line of star turns. While readers of a certain age might recall seeing these performances live, present-day audiences no doubt recall the same pleasures watching Idina Menzel defy gravity, Bertie Carvel channel Miss Trunchbull, and Norbert Leo Butz's charm-laced swindle game in *Dirty Rotten Scoundrels*. *Getting and having* these species of too-wonderful-for-words moments are the reasons we go to the theatre, and conversely, *giving* them is why you are an actor.

The above-referenced performances, along with a host of others, should be requisite viewing for the musical theatre performer, always a warrior of his present and a steward of his past. He should also pore over the Hollywood renditions of both many classic and contemporary musicals. While not all of the film renditions of Broadway musicals hit their mark as compelling filmmaking and/or in being entirely faithful to the stage musical upon which they were based, many did, and some of Broadway's most astounding performers and performances translated well onto the big screen. The big-budgeted, extravagantly produced MGM (and others) 1930s and 1940s movie musicals should factor in as well to this viewing curriculum as they consistently delivered treasure troves of movie musical moments not to be missed.

All of the above-mentioned hallmarks add up to a rendering of the lengths that singing, acting, and dancing together may go to tell the sort of gripping tale you want to stick around for a couple of hours with, particularly when told by skilled storytellers. To enlighten the point on the three disciplines operating and functioning together in service of the story being and getting told, I only need to point out that it's all but impossible to imagine *West Side Story* without dance as a critical storytelling device, *In the Heights* with the music or singing removed, or *My Fair Lady* devoid of dialog. Moreover, these reveal how singing-and-dancing actors are at the innermost workings of the theatre machine not as meager cogs, but rather as the propulsion itself. Although the nature of this writing prevents detailed narratives and descriptions of all the great performances and productions of theatrical musicals, it is reassuring to know that these performances and shows can and will forever be defined as seminal ones. We can, though, however humbly, summarize the broad-stroked history of the Broadway[1] musical and characterize the readers' familiarity with it as a necessary, fundamental component of what lies ahead in these pages. We, as theatre folks, must, after all, know from where we came if we are to know where we are. This requisite information must figure prominently in your trajectory toward becoming the most formidable version of yourself in the modern musical theatre universe, for to be without it is to sail a rudderless boat.

Accordingly, what follows should be understood as a condensed backward glance into the historical context of musical theatre for the musical theatre performer as a practitioner of all that has preceded him. It is no substitute for hands-on training, studying, and performing these shows and their respective songs and vocal performance styles, but it will provide historical reference and overview. Likewise, it should not be read as a substitute for a great number of texts on the history of the musical theatre, many of which provide this information in a more comprehensive and developed way. Much of the emphasis of this modest history is placed upon the songs that drive these shows, many that still steer much of our musical theatre culture. Space is also allotted to the principal points of the storylines of many shows as a means of reference, particularly when choosing to perform a song from the show and/or auditioning for that particular show. As a means to ground the discussion, invention and climate change in the musical theatre (this includes historical, societal, and cultural trends and events) throughout the past 100-plus years are the signposts that dictate the direction.

Additionally, the Broadway musical (in this context as a geographic reference) is at the heart of this discussion because the origins of the musical began as many different theatrical and musical cobblestones that, in time, paved a road to a new form of entertainment in America.[2] This is not to subvert any contributions to its inventions and advancement made elsewhere; these are noted accordingly over the course of the discussion as keystones that have led us to this point. Great Britain, for example, has made enormous contributions to the musical theatre, and the vast popularity of musicals in many European countries (and more recently, much more far-reaching global locales) has happily led to its perpetuation and longevity for a larger populous. These are noted appropriately in what follows. The present discussion, purely for convenience, is set (as a play would be set) on Broadway (see Endnote 2).

This chapter began with a remark regarding how surprising the nature of the theatre can be. In 1927, an audience attending *Show Boat* certainly understood that before them was an offspring of musical "comedy" with a variety of content that had likely never before been experienced, or for that matter contemplated for the escapist musical stage. And that, of course, required pause to digest for the average escapist entertainment-Joe. The show, which provided a vigorous (and given audience expectations, mandatory) dose of lighthearted entertainment as well, aimed openly at addressing, grappling with, and inviting discussion of such taboo topics for the musical stage as racial and cultural unrest and miscegenation, a first for the heretofore relatively frivolous Broadway musical. As visionaries no longer possessing a willingness to churn out boy-meets-girl fluff, the playmakers of *Show Boat*, Oscar Hammerstein II and Jerome Kern, did not just press the boundaries of conventional content allowances of the musical and the form and structure of it—they gave them a weighty, off-the-cliff shove. The team also wrote a bouquet of incandescent, timeless songs for the show that blissfully persist and endure today: "Ol' Man River," "Make Believe," and the revelatory "Bill" are all pristine examples of the "classic" show song. But appealing songs and the musical stage had always taken one another for granted, although often occurring in a pastiche, this and that, catch-as-catch-can format. Prior to *Show Boat*, the songs of a musical comedy were largely written independently of any serious integration with plot line, if there was one to speak of. The remainder of the creation—storyline and script—was by and large affixed around the songs. With *Show Boat*, the libretto (Oscar Hammerstein II) and the score (Jerome Kern) moved in a linear fashion, signifying that the songs' relevance was pinned to the libretto, and the libretto was pinned to the songs. This, in structural terms, was a giant leap forward for the Broadway musical. When *Show Boat* arrived on the Broadway stage, the first cannonball of the revolution of the musical theatre's aspirations toward social and political themes was lobbed over the bow of the Great White Way, the West End, and musical theatre showplaces everywhere.

In today's musical theatre, even as content and aesthetics have dramatically evolved, *Show Boat* is still performed with some regularity, in spite of the fact that nearly 100 years have passed. This fact is bullet-proof evidence that the knowledge and comprehension of the shows and styles of yesteryear are of immense consequence for those who carry them forward. When styles change or fall from favor, they may take along with them certain prior convention. Even so, the former style remains and is performed with a high degree of repetition. (Think of summer stock or regional theatre, which will often present the latest, trendiest shows to be released for production soon after a mainstream closing and follow it or precede it by a week of a classic show written some sixty-plus years earlier.) The theatre is a cumulative workplace; and the enlightened and most marketable performer is not only adept at as many styles as possible, however antiquated he might think the styles may be, but is also a willing and gracious envoy and custodian of them. It may solidify the point by stressing that *Oklahoma!*, another early pioneering musical, is still one of the most often-performed musicals worldwide. Indeed, the old-school style of musical theatre is still very much with us; and most successful, often-working actors willingly confess that fluency in these styles is a matter of necessity and even of *survival*.

Prior to (and to an extent even after) *Show Boat*'s trailblazing arrival, the American musical theatre had been a hodgepodge of offerings rooted in light opera and variety-type revue productions often reflecting the vast melting pot of immigrants and cultures present in New York City in the nineteenth and early twentieth centuries. In those days, the cacophony of sounds heard from the tenement buildings and in the streets of the Lower East Side of Manhattan would have been a mottled symphony unique to each ethnic group. The musical, and musical entertainment in general, have nearly always mirrored the common interests of both the topical and the broader nature. American culture and music (and by extension, the musical theatre) have nearly always run hand-in-hand, although Broadway has occasionally proven itself a laggard in catching up to the cultural flavor and social issues of the times.

The minstrel show, the saloon revue, and the first "musical"

Glancing back nearly two centuries, we see a wildly popular form of entertainment widely accepted as one of America's first indigenous musical theatre formats. The so-called minstrel show (or minstrelsy) was in fashion as far back as the 1830s and endured until the early 1900s as a mainstay of American and (very peripherally) British entertainment. Incredible as this may seem, these shows were performed by white people in blackface makeup (and later, by black people in blackface), and the content of these assembly-kit creations, formulaic and predictable, was of several varieties: comic vignettes, song-and-dance numbers, and comedic monologues, most of which depicted blacks in an unflattering, denigrating fashion.

By the 1870s, Negro spirituals such as "Nobody Knows the Trouble I've Seen" and "Deep River" began to enter the proceedings. Spirituals (or "shouts") dated back to the early days of American slavery, with the early spirituals sung in church or worship meetings in the slaves' plantation houses and in the farming fields. The inclusion of them in minstrel shows proved significant as they must have provided a measurable quantity of legitimacy to the black voice and experience (even under the circumstances) versus the usual defamatory mockery of the minstrelsy. Perhaps even more significant, other musical inclusions were the contributions of venerable songwriter Stephen Foster, who wrote some of the most beloved and defining songs in the legacy of early American popular music. Many of these, which ran the gamut from knee slappers to the stylishly iridescent, were written for and included in minstrel shows, and encompassed the ever-enduring "Camptown Races," "Swanee River," and the lovely "Jeanie with the Light Brown Hair." Foster's contribution to the minstrelsy extended beyond his songs, however; he also openly encouraged existential commentary in the context, a fact so significant that he might also be credited with being perhaps the first musical *theatre* writer of consequence. Should you, as a song seeker, find yourself in need of crafty, early popular music well-endowed with character and frequently witty folksy narratives, the Foster songbook supplies many fine options from which to choose.

In Great Britain, the Industrial Revolution of the middle nineteenth century gave rise to the new urban working class. A direct effect of the further emphasis on class structure pluralism were the more than 300 music halls that sprouted in London by 1875, producing squeakish variety shows appropriate to all ages (and both genders) on that side of the Atlantic. The saloon-based, low-brow, variety show revue, the unsanitized American version of the British music hall show, was said to have been born in the bowels of Lower Manhattan, but soon extended to any location in the United States where crowds of men could congregate, fraternize, and booze. As historian Douglas Gilbert (1963) summed it up, "The audiences (all male) were none too bright, a mental condition hardly improved by alcoholic befuddlement. Jokes had to be sledge-hammered home. The days of personalities, subtlety, wit, expert dancing, and superb technique were to come" (p. 26).

Songs about political and military events were sometimes included, often as parody in a satirical manner, and dance numbers were included as stage derivatives of popular dances of the day; but, generally speaking, given the clientele, we would rightfully speculate that much of the entertainment was directed toward the working class, echoing experiences and the goings-on in their daily lives. Most of these were unremarkable and disposable ditties that probably evaporated soon thereafter, but other, more substantial songs (such as "Golden Slippers" and "Old Folks at Home") often heard in the saloon variety show endured and are still well remembered today by some.

The lewd content, ripe with sexual innuendo and off-color humor, another mainstay of the saloon variety show, may not have been heard verbatim since, but it did prove to be the ancestor of another popular entertainment form yet to fully emerge—burlesque. Prior to its far seedier, fleshier offshoots, burlesque was originally highly physical comedic satire and a not-to-be-underestimated craze of popular entertainment.

The seeds of the yet-to-materialize musical insofar as a vehicle inclusive of music, drama, and dance *combined* are generally agreed to have been unwittingly planted by *The Black Crook* and later sown elsewhere. Theatre historians sometimes butt heads in their estimations of the show's calculable contributions to the evolution of the musical comedy form itself, but documented historical accounts reveal that a European dance troupe arriving in New York was stunned to learn that the theatre in which they had been scheduled to perform had burned and closed prior to their arrival. There are varied accounts with wide deviations of what transpired next, but certain is that the dance troupe, which now needed a theatre, and a separate New York dramatic troupe that had a theatre but whose next production hadn't piqued a great deal of ticket-buyer interest, and therefore, needed a boost, forged an alliance of genres. A deal was struck, and an embryonic theatrical formulation was concocted that incorporated dancing into the dramatic and musical storytelling. This was a new kind of conception because, unlike opera and operetta, the entity that resulted from the two troupes' fortuitous alignment relied heavily on the spoken word and also used dancing, not only by the chorus, but also by the full cast, to accompany the action, and even to some extent, move the storyline along.

The variety show and vaudeville in America

The vignette-driven, "slice-of-life"-type vehicle passed through several incarnations of format and content, but had a resolute stronghold in entertainment. With the saloon show having proven itself dependable to make a buck (or several), the variety show eventually found its way, courtesy of opportunistic entrepreneur presenters, off the barroom stage and onto the more "legitimate" ones. What had begun in Great Britain as family fare and in the United States as entertainment intended for and directed toward besotted, pie-eyed men in tiny sawdust-carpeted beer halls was evolving into what would become the young country's most popular form of entertainment for the next fifty years.

The advent of rail travel made it possible to move throngs of people around at unheard of rates of speed, and ticket sellers doled out admission billets as quickly as the trains moving patrons in to see the shows. Importantly, rail travel, light years speedier and less cumbersome and arduous than horse-and-wagon travel, also enabled the shows to come to the general populace with ease as touring companies. Show material was, predictably, now being presented in a more family-oriented, G-rated fashion. This meant that the admission price for a family of five was far higher than the shows intended for the men folk alone; and a new title was adopted for this revised brand of variety show, perhaps to avert suspicions of tawdry, lampoonish content. It was called "vaudeville," and it was, in essence, as evolution would have it, the American version of the British music hall, that mainstay entertainment in Britain.

Family entertainment in the form of an excursion to a vaudeville show in those days was the future's equivalent of a working class family's night at the movies, and if you were of a higher station, you might have enjoyed these evenings as much as, or possibly more than, your evenings at the opera, stuffy as it could be.

In 1904, a major revolutionary milestone in American theatre history, and in America itself, occurred as the underground subway became operational. By the time it opened at 42nd Street, the Grand Central terminal, a few blocks east, had undergone extensive structural renovations, and now it was possible to travel with relative ease through the borough of Manhattan liberated from the hassles of surface transportation over grubby city streets rife with stifling fragrances of heat-simmering refuse and carriage horse excrement. The theatre district was now officially situated in and around the area formerly known as Longacre Square, and on April 9, 1904, it was officially monikered "Times Square." This meant that, whereas formerly the epicenter of American vaudeville had been at and around the perimeter of Tony Pastor's (who is widely credited with sanitizing the variety show so that women and children could attend) 14th Street theatre at Union Square, audiences could now easily travel a few stops north to 42nd Street to shop, dine, and attend live entertainment events, the spectrum of which increased with nearly slap-happy rapidity. These dramatic upticks in the business end of show business meant that new theatres needed to open their doors quickly, and theatres began popping up at alarming tempi nearly overnight, many in the new area known as "the crossroads of the world," or in entertainment parlance, "Broadway," the main thoroughfare running down Times Square and through the theatre district. The most glittering jewel (in esteem, at any rate) in the crown of these ornate, fastidiously built new Broadway theatres was still a few years away from opening its doors, but "playing the Palace" (Theatre) would become the gold standard of vaudeville entertainment, in that sense akin to London's Palladium. One of the few theatres in the Broadway theatre district that is positioned on or faces Broadway (the street) itself, the Palace would, in time, become vaudeville's most revered house.

The typical vaudeville program (or "bill," as it was known) would include a mishmash variety of acts from instrumentalists, singers, and comedians to animal acts, magicians, acrobats, and dancers. The stars (headliners) of the shows were as recognizable and celebrated in the United States (many also abroad) as their United Kingdom counterparts were in Great Britain. Names such as Sally Rand, Sophie Tucker, Jack Benny, Ray Bolger, Harry Houdini, and Fanny Brice were to popular entertainment in American vaudeville what Marie Lloyd, Florrie Forde, George Robey, and Harry Champion were to British music halls. Even though the mercurial nature of theatre styles and favored popular entertainment eventually merged to bring an end to vaudeville and the music hall, no show business epoch has ever been as referred to and repeatedly referenced post-mortem. Modern-age performers encounter the era regularly in musicals as show business characters dwelling within the era or by reference—directorial, choreographic, or verbal.

Tin Pan Alley and Irving Berlin

It was Israel Baline who penned the words to "Marie from Sunny Italy," but due to a printer's spelling error the name was inadvertently changed on the published sheet music and that name would stick; that fellow would forever be called Irving Berlin. A Lower East Side Manhattan Russian Jewish refugee, Berlin would later be responsible for the words and music to one of the best-selling songs of all time, and go on to add hundreds more to his already formidable lot, many of which would become synonymous worldwide with popular music itself. "Alexander's Ragtime Band" was that song, and it was popularized partly because of its catchy and clever melodic strain, but in at least equal part, because ragtime music, with its jagged and jolty rhythms, had become a bona fide craze. Whether or not some claimed that ragtime music was doing the devil's bidding, you might have heard the song, along with countless others, all rickety racketing, each trumpeting bolder than the next from storefront windows while walking through West 28th Street in Manhattan. In the early years of the twentieth century, this was the popular music publishing epicenter of the world, and the place where popular songs were hawked, test-driven, and sold. The notion of "popular" or "fad" music had begun as early as 1891 when the song "After the Ball" had emerged independently, but had eventually been included in the musical *A Trip to Chinatown* for popular exposure (it worked), and sheet music publishers required a central marketplace for buyers. Those who bought ranged from the vaudeville star shopping for his next song vehicle to your average enthusiast from one of the countless households that owned a piano and played and sang along to the middleman music retailer who shopped for the stack loads of sheet music he would sell back in Dubuque. Tin Pan Alley, as it came to be called, bolstered many a soon-to-be-famous songwriter and song "plugger" (Berlin among them in his early years) who attended to these potential buyers, playing and often singing the latest and greatest hits from the nearly endless parade of user-friendly songs. If the customer liked the song, the sale was made and the plugger, or salesman, earned a small commission.

Today, many of the greatest hits of Tin Pan Alley are no longer widely performed, but do occasionally make appearances on the musical theatre stage, sometimes within revues and sometimes as the musical subjects of them, but by and large, the songs now languish in long-receded memory, referred to or heard periodically by the present generation only in films and referred to in literature set in the period. The sheet music for songs such as "Sweet Adeline," "The Sidewalks of New York," "The Band Played On," "Bill Bailey Won't You Please Come Home?," and "Come Josephine in My Flying Machine" may have long been relegated to the bottom of your great-grandmother's piano bench, but at the time, they were all spectacular hits of the day, alongside still occasionally heard titles such as "Sweet Georgia Brown," "Ain't She Sweet," and the often-heard "God Bless America" by Irving Berlin.

The songs of Tin Pan Alley were regularly heard on Broadway and on the West End in those days with sometimes as many as a dozen or more songwriters contributing to the score. Berlin was the first Tin Pan Alley writer to pen a Broadway musical score entirely on his own, and by 1914, his music, which introduced, among others, "Play a Simple Melody," had moved uptown from 28th Street in Manhattan to the New Amsterdam Theatre with *Watch Your Step*. He also made regular contributions to the *Ziegfeld Follies* extravaganza shows (which were short in substance, but long in towering, beaded, and bangled chorus girls and a miscellany of variety acts) that were first produced in 1907 in spare-no-expense and show-every-penny opulence by showman Florenz Ziegfeld, Jr., and then after his death, intermittently by others.

By the 1920s, Great Britain's André Charlot and Charles Cochran were producing Ziegfeld-type shows in the United Kingdom, although Charlot tempered the spectacle and emphasized the talent. Among the headliners there was Gertrude Lawrence, who would soon become the toast of the town in New York, too. As though Ziegfeld himself had made an everlasting covenant with theatre yet to come (and certainly as a testament to the allure of the era), the Ziegfeld style and the prototype of the Ziegfeld showgirl persist in today's musical theatre. Shows such as *The Will Rogers Follies*, *Funny Girl*, and *Crazy for You* would exist as altogether less recognizable and certainly less categorical entities if the ghosts of Ziegfeld and those who emulated him weren't on those stages as well.

George Gershwin, the revue, and cultural crossovers

"Swannee" had been kicking around Tin Pan Alley for a while, but had not generated much interest until Al Jolson heard it. Jolson was, in modern cultural terms, the superstar "it" guy of his day—a boisterous hellcat of a performer—who, between his New York stage appearances, touring engagements, and gramophone record sales, was earning a king's ransom at about $10,000 a week by 1922. Jolson went certifiably crazy for "Swannee" when he heard it, and immediately began using the song in his touring edition of *Sinbad*, later recording it. It was an instant hit, and the sheet music and record sales were astronomical—two million record sales alone, which created a nearly indistinguishable distinction between man and song.

George Gershwin, the up-and-coming composer of the song, had been working as a rehearsal pianist for the *Ziegfeld Follies*, had a few songs being performed in revue shows around town, and was earning steady pay as a song plugger on Tin Pan Alley. But now, with the success "Swannee" had shored up, he was a songwriter under many a watchful eye. Gershwin could not have known at the time that, in the years to come, he (along with his brother Ira and other lyricists) would go on to rethink, reformulate, and reshape the alchemy of the musical language of both Broadway, America, and much of the world's popular music.

At midnight on January 16, 1920, widespread Prohibition of alcohol began, and until further notice, booze was outlawed in the United States, although most large cities were lax, at best, at enforcement. Manhattan nightlife flourished, and New York partied louder and harder, liquor and all, most notably in its Harlem nightclubs and speakeasies. This was amid an abundance of kickbacks and bribery in one form or another among club owners, the mob, and law enforcement that guaranteed no interruption of the rowdiness. New York City was still a place where you could find a good time, and the "hootch" could be easily enjoyed with only a moderate amount of effort. The 1920s were indeed roaring.

With the unprecedented demand for entertainment nearly combustible, there was an enormous onslaught of ever-the-opportunist producers, writers, backers, and theatres all looking to get in on the lucrative game of entertainment as commerce, grabbing at low-hanging fruit. In one season alone, 264 plays and musicals, many of them revues, were produced on Broadway, an unheard of number and the most of any single season to date, and twenty new theatres were built. As the revue shows were flourishing in Harlem, where cheap booze was readily available, and downtown as well, the revue show was thriving by day, and especially, by night. As the West End was being practically overrun by American imports and the urbane wit of Noël Coward in the 1920s, the revue format dominated New York and Broadway (although operettas were still in fashion) and became fertile ground for songwriters, many from Tin Pan Alley. *George White's Scandals*, *The Blackbird Revues*, *The Garrick Gaities*, the *Earl Carroll Vanities*, and of course, the *Ziegfeld Follies* were all suffused with the songs of both established and aspiring songwriters, many of whom were writing songs at that time that would become part of what history would eventually term the "Great American Songbook," and the songs that would now occupy even an elevated rank in what we might call the "mainstream" of theatre songs. George and Ira Gershwin ("Stairway to Paradise," "Somebody Loves Me"), Richard Rodgers and Lorenz Hart ("Mountain Greenery," "Manhattan"), Jimmy McHugh and Dorothy Fields ("I Can't Give You Anything But Love," "I Must Have that Man," "On the Sunny Side of the Street"), Arthur Schwartz and Howard Dietz ("Dancing in the Dark," "Alone Together"), and Irving Berlin ("A Pretty Girl Is Like a Melody," "What'll I Do?," "All Alone") were all making regular contributions to the shows, and Berlin even opened a theatre as a home for showcasing his songs (the Music Box and the *Music Box Revues*). George Gershwin alone wrote the entire score for *George White's Scandals* of 1920 and would go on to write forty-five songs for the White shows over the next five seasons.

Gershwin's theatre songs and, perhaps especially, his concert music would swiftly become nearly interchangeable with New York City itself, bringing the syncopated beat of "Jazz" into the mainstream and symbolizing the "Jazz Age" itself for many in America and throughout Europe. Moreover, his modern music double-dared listeners not to wriggle and jostle their bodies with abandon, shaking off any remnants of what once was taboo and inadmissible in a polite, mannered society.

The musical comedy in the 1920s and 1930s

Despite the immense popularity of the quickly assembled variety show, the musical comedy was still holding court nightly in Broadway theatres, just as it was on the West End. Rife with mostly paper-thin and feather-weight plotlines easily transferable to any number of other shows and circumstances, many nevertheless held some of the richest musical offerings of the twentieth century that almost effortlessly found their way to the status of "standards." While most shows of the period accepted their fate as mere vehicles, a few are noteworthy because of the songs therein and their creators.

During the period between 1924 and 1934, George and Ira Gershwin's *Lady, Be Good*; *Oh, Kay!*; *Funny Face*; *Strike Up the Band*; *Girl Crazy*; and *Let 'em Eat Cake* were all seen and heard on the Broadway stage, and with the exception of *Let 'em Eat Cake*, were appreciable hits, certainly by the standards of long runs in those days. *Funny Face*; *Lady, Be Good*; and *Oh, Kay!* were also wildly applauded in London, numbering performances in the hundreds. One show of George and Ira Gershwin (*Of Thee I Sing*), although not a runaway hit, nonetheless garnered a Pulitzer Prize for its salty and satirical take on American politics.

Some of these Gershwin creations fared far better as source material for much later musicals performed now with regularity, including *Crazy for You*, *My One and Only*, and *Nice Work If You Can Get It*, titles that should be on any musical theatre performer's radar.

Irving Berlin's *Face the Music* (another political satire); Cole Porter's *Fifty Million Frenchmen*; Richard Rodgers and Lorenz Hart's *A Connecticut Yankee*; B.G. DeSylva, Lew Brown, and Ray Henderson's *Good News*; and of course, *Show Boat*, with its pioneering content, also deserve worthy mention as notable shows during that period. Along with *Show Boat*, Cole Porter's *Anything Goes*; Kurt Weill and Bertolt Brecht's *The Threepenny Opera*; and Irving Caesar, Otto Harbach, and Vincent Youman's *No, No, Nannette* should all be recognized for being included in the collection of only a handful of shows still performed, while *Anything Goes*, with its string of revisionist retakes, is credited with being one of the most often-performed musicals worldwide (for other notable shows and songs from this time period see chart on p. 19).

Before there was Richard Rodgers and Oscar Hammerstein II, that most awe-inspiring of collaborations, there was Richard Rodgers and Lorenz Hart, also that most awe-inspiring of collaborations; and it's next to impossible, even negligent, when tracing the journey of the musical through time, not to pause along the way and admire the scenery they gave us. Despite their notoriously contrary work ethics (Rodgers was famously disciplined, mannered, and efficient, and Hart was a reckless, indolent alcoholic seemingly hell-bent on self-destruction), we never fail to be astonished at the success and longevity their yin and yang union generated. From around 1925 to the early 1940s, Rodgers and Hart were the golden boys of musical comedy, turning out one great song

Other notable shows and songs from 1924 to 1934

Show, Year, and Songwriters	Notable songs	Also of note
Lady, Be Good (1924, New York; 1926, West End) George/Ira Gershwin	"Oh, Lady Be Good," "Fascinating Rhythm," "Little Jazz Bird"	The Gershwin brothers' first Broadway collaboration starred brother and sister vaudeville duo Fred and Adele Astaire.
No, No, Nanette (1925, New York; 1925, West End) Irving Caesar/Otto Harbach/Vincent Youmans	"I Want to Be Happy," "Tea for Two"	The revised 1971 New York revival version is generally credited as precedent-setting for Broadway's revival "craze." The London production of the original played twice as many performances as its Broadway counterpart.
Oh, Kay! (1926, New York; 1927, West End) George/Ira Gershwin	"Someone to Watch over Me," "Clap Yo' Hands," "Do, Do, Do"	Gertrude Lawrence starred and was the first British stage actor to headline a Broadway musical.
Good News (1927, New York) B.G. DeSylva/Lew Brown/Ray Henderson	"The Best Things in Life Are Free," "Button Up Your Overcoat" (1993), "You're the Cream in My Coffee" (1993), "Life Is Just a Bowl of Cherries" (1993)	The 1993 revised production was first seen in the United States at the Music Theatre of Wichita (Kansas) and received subsequent productions with some regularity.

(continued)

Table Continued

Show, Year, and Songwriters	Notable songs	Also of note
Strike Up the Band (1927, 1930 revised, New York) George/Ira Gershwin	"The Man I Love," "Strike Up the Band"	Original 1927 production closed in Philadelphia, but a revised version had a relatively brief Broadway run in 1930, minus "The Man I Love."
A Connecticut Yankee (1927, New York) Richard Rodgers/Lorenz Hart	"Thou Swell," "To Keep My Love Alive" (1943 revival), "My Heart Stood Still"	Based on Mark Twain's novel entitled *A Connecticut Yankee in King Arthur's Court*, the show is a never-performed dinosaur, but oh those songs!
Funny Face (1927, New York) George/Ira Gershwin	"Funny Face," "'S' Wonderful," "He Loves and She Loves," "My One and Only"	One of the primary sources from which the 1983 Tommy Tune/Twiggy hit *My One and Only* was derived. The original (once again) starred Fred and Adele Astaire.
Girl Crazy (1930, New York) George/Ira Gershwin	"Embraceable You," "I Got Rhythm," "But Not for Me"	Starred Ethel Merman in her inaugural Broadway role, and turned both her and Ginger Rogers into overnight stars.
As Thousands Cheer (1933, New York; 1935, West End under the title *Stop Press*) Irving Berlin	"Easter Parade," "Heat Wave," "Suppertime"	Ethel Waters, an African American, sang "Suppertime," a lament to her husband who had been lynched in the context of the show. Waters also received top billing alongside her white costars, a first.

| *Anything Goes* (1934, New York; 1935, West End) Cole Porter | "I Get a Kick Out of You," "Easy to Love," "It's De-lovely," "Anything Goes," "Blow, Gabriel, Blow" | Several revisions exist of both the libretto and song list, most notably the 1987 Lincoln Center revival starring Patti LuPone in a Tony-winning turn. The well-received 2011 revival starred Sutton Foster, who received a Tony Award for her portrayal of Reno Sweeney. Perhaps the most notable U.K. production, a concoction unto itself, was Trevor Nunn's 2003 outing. |

after the other. The sparkling wit and winning melody of the song "Manhattan" wasn't the team's opus one, but it was the first to spawn the kind of widespread accolades every writer or writing collaboration requires as a bon voyage to success. As it was for Charles Lindbergh, who was making his celebrated solo nonstop flight from New York to Paris about this time, the sky, it seemed, was the limit for Rodgers and Hart. With runaway hits such as "You Took Advantage of Me," "My Funny Valentine," "Where or When," and "Bewitched, Bothered and Bewildered" to their credit, the team was a buttress of American popular songs of the era, and their songs are ever-present in the sphere of musical theatre today. From 1925 to 1930, Rodgers and Hart wrote scores to eighteen shows, not all of them gems, but most with the traits of the team's hallmark—to dispense with the "formula" musical that had long held sway over musical comedy. This was timely. When the U.S. stock market crashed in 1929, the Depression set in two-fold. New York theatres were still open for business even amid the shantytowns along the East River of Manhattan, and some days and nights there appeared to be more people in the breadline at Duffy Square (where the TKTS booth stands nowadays) than there were in the seats of the Broadway houses. Theatre audiences fled their daily lives for the escapism of the make-believe world of Broadway, but many theatre artists and writers of Broadway simply fled, many migrating to the lure of Hollywood with its sunny skies, easier lifestyle, and fat paychecks. The advent of the "talkie," or "talking picture," a few years earlier had, and remains so today, arguably the single greatest economic impact upon the stage musical and stage show in general. Popular entertainment could now be found just about anytime and anywhere, and wasn't only ubiquitous, but also more affordable in the "Brother Can You Spare a Dime?" Depression era. Scores of Broadway theatres closed to become movie houses, and Hollywood was literally churning out (often tacky and ludicrously unfaithful to the source material) movie adaptations of the Broadway musicals. Within the first few years following the 1929 stock market crash, nearly every major Broadway songwriter (George Gershwin, Jerome Kern, Cole Porter, Irving Berlin, and Richard Rodgers among them) had forged some commercial alliance with Hollywood.

Within a few years' time, the notion that substance trumps flash, one initiated by Richard Rodgers and Lorenz Hart, Jerome Kern, Oscar Hammerstein II, and others perhaps having grown weary of the writers' Hollywood celluloid, began to fully take hold. This philosophy would eventually spread like wildfire to the stages of the world as many of these émigrés returned from where they came. *Show Boat* had proven that Broadway audiences were amenable to hefty topical matters onstage, but after the 1929 Crash, trends moved decidedly toward feel-good entertainment. It was nearly impossible to predict whether a return to "serious" topics would bolster or further debilitate the musical in an escapist entertainment era, and creators approached that matter gingerly at first. Eventually, however, they found that Broadway and the West End proved themselves to be an ever-durable forum and platform for expression and social commentary, and social issues began to re-emerge as standard fare on the musical stage. Escapist entertainment such as Cole Porter's *Anything Goes* remained a fixture, to be sure, but now Broadway also freely satirized American politics (*Of Thee I Sing* and others), openly sang of class relations as never before (*As Thousands Cheer*), and generally wasn't tepid about confronting whatever didn't fall on deaf ears. There also began to be a decided movement toward truth of character and characterization; and the musical would soon be used to deliver, compete, and reinvent, perhaps as a response to the Hollywood invasion, perhaps in spite of it. Soon, and in a more deeply felt and more meaningful way, Richard Rodgers and theatrical titan Oscar Hammerstein II would become the engineers and missionaries of the "new" Broadway musical and a new era of musical theatre (for other notable shows and songs from this time period see chart on p. 24).

The "fully integrated" musical

In 1943, when Richard Rodgers and Oscar Hammerstein II crafted *Oklahoma!*, the musical seemed to be in crying need of wholesale overhaul. Their creation of a musical format that directly addressed the relationships and psyches of its characters, as told through the medium of dialog, song, and dance, procured the sacred model that became the standard by which others were judged. There was nary an inclusion of any element that existed for its own sake alone; all were embedded as a means of telling the story and dutifully serving the storyline. From the outset, Rodgers and Hammerstein intended that this brand of musical would devote itself entirely to this end, never

Other notable shows and songs from 1935 to 1942

Show, Year, and Songwriters	Notable songs	Also of note
Porgy and Bess (1935, New York; 2006, West End) George/Ira Gershwin/DuBose Heyward	"Summertime," "I Got Plenty O' Nuttin'," "There's a Boat Dat's Leavin' Soon for New York"	Gershwin's celebrated "masterpiece" distorted the line between musical and opera, but George Gershwin himself determined that it should play a Broadway house rather than an opera house in its original New York incarnation.
Jumbo (1935, New York) Richard Rodgers/Lorenz Hart	"The Most Beautiful Girl in the World," "My Romance," "Little Girl Blue"	An unorthodox Broadway incarnation that mixed the musical and the circus, complete with animal acts (including a live elephant) that played the 5,000 seat Hippodrome Theatre (no longer standing).
On Your Toes (1936, New York; 1937, West End) Richard Rodgers/Lorenz Hart	"There's a Small Hotel," "Glad to Be Unhappy," "Quiet Night"	The musical included "Slaughter on Tenth Avenue," an extended dramatic ballet sequence (one of the first of its kind for the Broadway musical) choreographed by George Balanchine.
Babes in Arms (1937, New York) Richard Rodgers/Lorenz Hart	"Where or When," "My Funny Valentine," "The Lady Is a Tramp," "Johnny One Note," "I Wish I Were in Love Again"	The original run was modest in number of performances (289), but the score spawned many of Rodgers and Hart's greatest hit songs.

Show	Songs	Notes
The Boys from Syracuse (1938, New York; 1963, West End) Richard Rodgers/Lorenz Hart	"Falling in Love with Love," "This Can't Be Love," "Sing for Your Supper"	The first of several musicals to be based on a Shakespearean play (*The Comedy of Errors*).
Pal Joey (1940, New York; 1954, West End) Richard Rodgers/Lorenz Hart	"You Mustn't Kick It Around," "I Could Write a Book," "Bewitched, Bothered and Bewildered"	The show that probably best preceded the "fully integrated" musical. The original production was praised for the manner in which it so fully fleshed out its characters, but despite this and a crackerjack score, a long run did not ensue; it ran only 374 performances. A 1952 New York revival was praised, and West End audiences embraced the show, some more and some less, in 1954 and 1980.
Lady in the Dark (1941, New York; 1997, West End) Kurt Weill/Ira Gershwin	"My Ship," "The Saga of Jenny," "Tschaikovsky (and other Russians)"	Kurt Weill's first American hit starred Gertrude Lawrence and Danny Kaye in which all of the music (except the last song, "My Ship") was heard in three separate psychoanalytic dream sequences.
By Jupiter (1942, New York) Richard Rodgers/Lorenz Hart	"Everything I've Got," "Wait Till You See Her"	Starred Ray Bolger, who was by now enjoying acclaim and wide recognition as the actor who played the Scarecrow in *The Wizard of Oz* film, released in 1939.

separating the dancer from the dance, the singer from the song, the song from the story, and the story from its mission—one which could function and exist entirely on its own merits—the "integrated" musical. The credo, something of a long shot in this World War II era, worked, and audiences devoured and adored it. Whereas previously a show had been determined a "hit" if its performances numbered in the hundreds, *Oklahoma!* ran a whopping 2,212 performances in New York and created a worldwide brand (although the "branding" of a show would reach unheard of proportions forty years later). The show also trumpeted a new movement in dance as a vehicle for the telling of the story and propelling its linear motion. Before *Oklahoma!*, never before had the plotline been so fully supported by the dance routines, and also the reverse. Agnes deMille, the venerated choreographer, crossed well beyond even that notion by imagining and implementing an extended ballet sequence, commonly known as the "Dream Ballet," at the close of the first act. In this conception, the show's lovelorn Laurey falls asleep and dreams of being wed to Curly, the show's leading man, but her bliss is quickly interrupted by the scowling Jud Fry, the farmhand obsessed with the notion that Laurey will be his alone. The dreamscape quickly turns hellish as Jud murders Curly, and Laurey awakens with a start and an affirmed certainty that Curly should be her betrothed, the one for whom she is intended. This leap in storyline in order to propel the story exists devoid of any dialog as the dance is employed in its stead. It was a remarkable achievement for a musical production.

An uncommon seed creates an uncommon harvest, and the modern musical steadily evolved in this fashion and with this mission following *Oklahoma!*. In the early and middle 1940s, as much of the United States and Europe were engulfed in World War Two, New York City was a hotbed of war-related activity that unsurprisingly found its way onto the Broadway stage. As it had been during World War I, when Irving Berlin (*This Is the Army*, "God Bless America") and others were depicting wartime life on U.S. shores and themes of nationalism, the Broadway musical galvanized the country's collective consciousness and portrayed and commented on its manifestations into daily life. Choreographer Jerome Robbins received a wall of bravos for his short ballet entitled *Fancy Free*, a tale involving three sailors on shore leave, and thereafter, the idea emerged to develop the ballet into a full-length Broadway musical. Robbins and Leonard Bernstein, the ballet's composer, rounded up pals Betty Comden and Adolph Green to assume the duties of writing the libretto and lyrics (also actors, the two craftily wrote roles for themselves), and with a nod to *Oklahoma!*'s original title *Away We Go!*, away they went. With songs such as "New York, New York (a helluva town)," "Lonely Town," "Lucky to Be Me," "I Can Cook, Too," "Ya Got Me," and "Some Other Time," the resulting *On the Town* was a smash. Jerome Robbins, who had an uncanny flair for choreographic storytelling that was steeped in human psychology and everyday behavior, was, in many ways with *On the Town*, previewing his own artistry and colossal contributions yet to come.

Among other significant musicals of the era between *Oklahoma!* and the early years of the next decade was *Carmen Jones*, a retelling of Georges Bizet's opera *Carmen* in which Oscar Hammerstein II fashioned a modern take on the libretto, changed the story's setting, and set new lyrics to the opera's thrilling music that featured an all-black cast. *Finian's Rainbow* (1947) boasted the songs "Old Devil Moon," "When I'm Not Near the Girl I Love," and "How Are Things in Glocca Morra?," and took a satirical stab at race relations, setting the story in the fictitious U.S. state of "Missitucky" and spun in part the saga of a bigoted white senator who, through the casting of a spell, is rendered black. The enduring *Annie Get Your Gun* (1946), which starred Ethel Merman, centered on the story of sharpshooter Annie Oakley and featured a knockout score by Irving Berlin that included "They Say It's Wonderful," "Anything You Can Do," and the love letter to the stage, "There's No Business Like Show Business."

Expect songs from *On the Town*, *Finian's Rainbow*, and *Annie Get Your Gun* to make ongoing appearances in your theatrical world and to bounce cheerfully around inside your head as pristine exemplary Golden Age show music craft.

The Richard Rodgers and Oscar Hammerstein II catalog in the years following *Oklahoma!* grew to include an assemblage of hits that also gently reminded the human race of its own humanity and built-in lessons of reversing social and racial dissonances. Themes such as cultural exchange (*The King and I*, its score packed with Rodgers and Hammerstein hits such as "Hello Young Lovers," "I Have Dreamed," "Something Wonderful," and "Shall We Dance?"), topped with racism and prejudice (*South Pacific*, which won the Pulitzer Prize for Drama in 1950 and included the Rodgers and

Hammerstein standards "A Cockeyed Optimist," "Some Enchanted Evening," "There Is Nothin' Like a Dame," "I'm in Love with a Wonderful Guy," and "This Nearly Was Mine"), were of frequent interest to the duo who also grappled with spousal abuse and class structure (*Carousel*, which yielded the much-loved songs "Mister Snow," "If I Loved You," "You'll Never Walk Alone," and the watershed "Soliloquy") and often included still other extended musical dance and movement sequences as narrative, most notably "The Carousel Waltz" (*Carousel*) and "The Small House of Uncle Thomas" (*The King and I*).

Rodgers and Hammerstein's inclusion of these themes was of more-than-meets-the-eye consequence. A high percentage of post-World War II audiences were again seeking "escapist" entertainment, and the duo managed to provide feel-good family entertainment while airing open debate over topics of social concern, even if the presence of discussion was to some degree subconscious for the audience. Unlike other musicals, the era of Rodgers and Hammerstein shows came but never went. The shows mentioned above, along with *The Sound of Music*, that chestnut of a household name, in part because of the astonishingly popular film version, come to life as frequently in musical theatre houses as does Verdi in opera houses. Musical theatre performers should expect to encounter the shows with regularity (for other notable shows and songs from this time period see chart on p. 29).

Musical theatre in the 1950s

By the early 1950s, Broadway had more serious competition as did theatre in Britain and nearly worldwide, and radio and movies had a mighty cohort. Television sets were in more than half of U.S. households by 1954, up from only a half of a percent of households as recently as 1946. In spite of the perturbation, musical theatre pressed on and did so even amid shrinking attendance. Although bereft over the continued mass exodus of performers and creative staff to Hollywood, it used the popularity of television to its benefit, regularly transplanting its performers from the theatre stage onto the television studio stages and transmitting across the airwaves the sights and sounds of the "modern" musical. Theatre songs topped the charts of the greatest hits of the day, and musical

Other notable shows and songs from 1943 to 1951

Show, Year, and Songwriters	Notable songs	Also of note
One Touch of Venus (1943) Kurt Weill/Ogden Nash	"I'm a Stranger Here Myself," "Speak Low," "That's Him"	Firmly established the venerable Mary Martin as a Broadway star singing a first-rate Weill musical score.
St. Louis Woman (1946) Harold Arlen/Johnny Mercer	"Any Place I Hang My Hat Is Home," "I Had Myself a True Love," "Come Rain or Come Shine"	A much discussed, deeply troubled show with a firecracker of a score, but one that couldn't save the famously troubled (onstage and off) show.
Brigadoon (1947) Alan Jay Lerner/Frederick Loewe	"Waitin' for My Dearie," "Almost Like Being in Love," "The Heather on the Hill," "Come to Me, Bend to Me," "There But for You Go I"	The third time was the charm for Lerner and Loewe, having written two shows prior that suffered cruel Broadway fates.
Allegro (1947) Richard Rodgers/Oscar Hammerstein II	"Know It Can Happen Again," "So Far," "You Are Never Away," "The Gentleman Is a Dope," "Come Home"	The third time was *not* the charm for Rodgers and Hammerstein, who delivered a show with a sterling score, but which was reportedly virtually impossible to stage. Audiences were tepid and stayed at bay.

(continued)

Table Continued

Show, Year, and Songwriters	Notable songs	Also of note
Where's Charley? (1948) Frank Loesser	"Make a Miracle," "Lovelier than Ever," "Once in Love with Amy"	The original production had a respectable run at 792 performances, and Ray Bolger won a Best Actor in a Musical Tony Award. The show did not run until 1958 in the West End, where it was a moderate hit, although it ran only about half the number of performances as the Broadway original.
Kiss Me, Kate (1948) Cole Porter	"Another Op'nin', Another Show," "Why Can't You Behave?," "So in Love," "Too Darn Hot," "Always True to You in My Fashion," "Brush Up Your Shakespeare"	A mammoth hit in the United States, Cole Porter penned the score as much a staple as a staple can be in the musical theatre. The show won the first Tony Award presented for Best Musical in 1949. London enjoyed it, although perhaps not as much, in 1951, clocking 400 performances. The 2001 Michael Blakemore production, however, was a piping hot West End ticket for some time.
Gentlemen Prefer Blondes (1949) Jule Styne/Leo Robin	"I Love What I'm Doing," "Diamonds Are a Girl's Best Friend," "Just a Little Girl from Little Rock"	A huge hit with a charming score that introduced the equally charming Carol Channing starring in her first Broadway show.

Show / Composer	Songs	Description
Call Me Madam (1950) Irving Berlin	"The Hostess with the Mostes' on the Ball," "It's a Lovely Day Today," "The Best Thing for You (Would Be Me)," "You're Just in Love"	Irving Berlin's next-to-final outing, with the last being *Mr. President* (an abysmal failure); he surely wished he had stopped with this one. A hit that starred (once again) Ethel Merman.
Guys and Dolls (1950) Frank Loesser	"I'll Know," "Adelaide's Lament," "If I Were a Bell," "I've Never Been in Love Before," "Luck Be a Lady," "Sit Down, You're Rockin' the Boat"	A chapter all its own in Musicals 101; it is the perennial of perennials based on Damon Runyon stories of the seedy and the righteous in New York City circa 1930–1950.
Paint Your Wagon (1951) Alan Jay Lerner/Frederick Loewe	"I Talk to the Trees," "They Call the Wind Maria"	The story about gold miners failed to strike gold on Broadway, but a couple of musical gems panned out.

stars stood toe-to-toe with Hollywood greats jockeying for the public's entertainment dollars. The 1950s into the 1960s introduced some of the theatre's most revered creative talent, and to this day, the era remains as being the height of Broadway's Golden Age, with many of its offerings one and the same with the idea of Broadway itself. This naturally held forth in London's West End as the musicals regularly made their way across the Atlantic.

Because both leisure and business travel were now commonplace, due in part to expanded and much improved rail and airways, New York City and London began to enjoy an influx of tourists arriving en masse weekly. The publicity that "hit" records, popular songs heard on radio, and the television variety show provided was a producer's pot of gold, and many Broadway shows of the time were decidedly shaped and bent to appease the "everyman."

Two shows, in particular, seemed to happily reach right into the tired businessman's wallet and pluck the price of admission right out, pegging the tried and true formula of the "integrated" musical with stories and themes easily related to by average, middle-class audiences. *The Pajama Game* and *Damn Yankees* were immense hits opening in 1954 and 1955, respectively, both with scores written by Richard Adler and Jerry Ross, direction by Broadway behemoth George Abbott, and produced, in part, by an up-and-coming Harold Prince. The young, indefatigable Bob Fosse's choreography proved to Broadway audiences that not only was he tireless, but peerless as well, and both shows held prosperous musical offerings. *The Pajama Game*, a show centering on a labor dispute at a pajama factory and the jumbled romance of an employer and employee, sang out with hits such as "Hey There," "A New Town Is a Blue Town," "I'm Not at All in Love," "There Once Was a Man," "Hernando's Hideaway," and "Steam Heat," the latter inclusive of Bob Fosse's trademark Derby hats. *Damn Yankees*, which turned the red-headed siren Gwen Verdon into a genuine Broadway star, included the Broadway song standards "Heart," "A Little Brains, A Little Talent," "Whatever Lola Wants (Lola Gets)," and "Those Were the Good Old Days." Songwriter Ross, at the age of 29, died suddenly six months after the show's opening. Given the awe-inspiring output that the team of Richard Adler and Jerry Ross gave us, we can only imagine what treasures would have been in store had he lived. More notable than the popularity with audiences of the shows themselves is the torrent of hit songs that resulted.

In 1956, *My Fair Lady* was not only Broadway's first demonstrable blockbuster post-*Oklahoma!*, but it was also one of the greatest selling cast albums of all time, being the first to pass the three-million mark. The story of an arrogant, set-in-his-ways linguist who accepts a bet that he can convert a "guttersnipe" Cockney flower girl into a proper lady of society became the longest-running Broadway show of all time up until that point, with a through-the-ceiling total of 2,717 performances, turning its stars, Rex Harrison and Julie Andrews, as well as its creators, Alan Jay Lerner and Frederick Loewe, into brand names. Two years after its New York bow, the show created much the same stir in London with the original stars in tow and ran nearly as long as in New York. The score was loaded with hits: "Wouldn't It Be Loverly," "On the Street Where You Live," "Get Me to the Church on Time," "I've Grown Accustomed to Her Face," and of course, "I Could Have Danced All Night" sung by a radiant young Andrews well before her celebrated movie musical career began.

Meredith Willson's *The Music Man* opened on Broadway in 1957 to thunderous bravos and remained a Broadway staple for many seasons to come, hitting American mid-western sensibilities right between their heartstrings, and proffering a score crammed with hit songs—"Seventy-Six Trombones," "My White Knight," "Ya Got Trouble," and "Till There Was You." The show won the 1958 Best Musical Tony Award, having been nominated alongside a show that would, as time would tell, help usher forth a new epoch of musical theatre storytelling device and verisimilitude.

In September 1957, when *West Side Story* came to life at the Winter Garden Theatre in New York, a cultural and theatrical eruption was created. The show, a modern-day musicalized retelling of the story of Shakespeare's *Romeo and Juliet*, went much further afield than any musical that had preceded it. It not only addressed tough localized social issues of the time (as it had been for years, gang warfare was common in New York in those days) and the prejudice associated with them, it left the audience with two dead bodies lying on the stage at the end of the first act. Death, particularly violent death, and the musical had been skittishly keeping a safe distance from one another for some time. Perhaps most revolutionary of all was the absence of the convention that audiences were programmed to await and expect—a happy ending.

The musical theatre was becoming gritty.

Other notable shows and songs from the 1950s

Show, Year, and Songwriters	Notable songs	Also of note
Wonderful Town (1953) Leonard Bernstein/Betty Comden/Adolph Green	"Ohio," "One Hundred Easy Ways," "A Little Bit in Love"	The Tony Award winner for Best Musical of 1953 with a terrific score, but a show that generates only tepid audience interest nowadays.
Me and Juliet (1953) Richard Rodgers/Oscar Hammerstein II	"That's the Way It Happens," "No Other Love," "We Deserve Each Other"	The sixth stage collaboration of Rodgers and Hammerstein, and an abysmal failure, but several sparkling and enduring songs resulted.
Peter Pan (1954) Mark "Moose" Charlap/Jule Styne/Carolyn Leigh/Betty Comden/Adolph Green	"Neverland," "I'm Flying," "Distant Melody"	Starred Mary Martin in one of musical theatre's few "trouser" roles, playing the boy who wouldn't grow up.
Bells Are Ringing (1956) Jule Styne/Betty Comden/Adolph Green	"It's a Perfect Relationship," "I Met a Girl," "Long before I Knew You," "Just in Time," "The Party's Over"	The original production starred a Tony-winning Judy Holliday. Another knockout score within a musical too rarely produced.

Show	Songs	Commentary
The Most Happy Fella (1956) Frank Loesser	"Ooh! My Feet!," "Somebody, Somewhere," "Joey, Joey, Joey," "Big D," "Warm All Over," "My Heart Is So Full of You"	Another foggy distinction (like *Porgy and Bess* before it and *Sweeney Todd* after it) as to the question "Is it an opera or is it a musical?"—Loesser acknowledged the great number of songs and limited spoken dialog, but warily refrained from coining the show as an opera.
Gypsy (1959) Jule Styne/Stephen Sondheim	"Some People," "Small World," "You'll Never Get Away from Me," "If Momma Was Married," "All I Need Is the Girl," "Everything's Coming Up Roses," "Together Wherever We Go," "Rose's Turn"	One of the most popular and often-produced musicals of all time. Many musical theatre arbiters say it's also among the craftiest.
The Sound of Music (1959) Richard Rodgers/Oscar Hammerstein II	"The Sound of Music," "My Favorite Things," "Do-Re-Mi," "Sixteen Going on Seventeen," "So Long, Farewell," "Climb Ev'ry Mountain," "Edelweiss"	Rodgers and Hammerstein's final collaboration, and a show so beloved and often produced that it certainly needs no further commentary here.
Once upon a Mattress (1959) Mary Rodgers/Marshall Barer	"Shy," "Happily Ever After," "Yesterday I Loved You"	Among the talented creators was another composer Rodgers—Richard's daughter, Mary.

Further, there was an interesting paradox afoot in *West Side Story*. For all its nervous, clanking, seething musical elements coupled with the disturbing goings-on in the story, the score was, at its heart, wildly romantic and passionate, a trait that left a strong foothold in the closing of the door to the old-fashioned Broadway musical. The singing requirements placed near-operatic demands on the show's young stars, and the score was full of well-earned hit songs. "Somewhere," "Tonight," "One Hand, One Heart," "A Boy Like That/I Have a Love," and "Maria" are all traditional, "legit" musical theatre at its very essence, and together with songs that infused Latin and edgy rhythmic elements such as "America," "Something's Coming," and "Cool," the score by Leonard Bernstein, with lyrics by Stephen Sondheim, rightfully are at the forefront with the most innovative and inventive work on the musical stage.

West Side Story changed the landscape of the musical in another key way. For the first time, the dance numbers were ingeniously woven by Jerome Robbins into the fabric *throughout* the story and became a much more central part of the storytelling. Some would argue that, in fact, it became in a sense a metaphorical character unto itself, that of the restlessness and rebellious nature of youth or even symbolic of New York City itself. What other shows (e.g., *Oklahoma!*) had done brilliantly, skillfully, and innovatively, Robbins did exponentially (for other notable shows and songs from this time period see chart on p. 34).

Musical theatre in the 1960s

By the time *Bye Bye Birdie* wiggled and swiveled its hips on Broadway's Martin Beck Theatre stage in April 1960, the popular culture in the United States and much of Europe was emphatically moving to its own new beat, and rock and roll was, as the saying went, here to stay—a fact that was either celebrated or lamented by your point of view. But the old guard of the musical theatre would soon labor to subvert it in its own backyard, making no apologies. Ever since Elvis Presley gyrated, shook, and spun on *The Ed Sullivan Show*, a one-time landmark of American television, a cultural phenomenon of musical expression and sexual liberation had begun to take hold as had a psychological one. The squeaky-clean, sparkle-toothed youths and the obey-the-rules conventions of yesteryear were dissolving in American cultural terms, although *Ozzie and Harriet* (another landmark) and company would hold steadfast weekly for another six years to remind television audiences what wholesome American values looked like. Later in the decade, hair would get longer, social taboos would fall away, racial issues and relations would become inflamed, and young people (young women, in particular) would begin to enjoy freedoms of expression and liberal thinking as never before in American culture. The nation at large was undergoing a sea change as well in the early 1960s, and post-World War II America felt hopeful, optimistic, and renewed. U.S. President John F. Kennedy's inaugural address on January 20, 1961, seemed to engender these sentiments tenfold and led a charge as he urged America and the nations of the world to eradicate the "common enemies of man: tyranny, poverty, disease, and war itself."

If Elvis and the Beatles, in the late 1950s and mid-1960s, had reimagined and reinvented the sound of popular music, Broadway during this time preferred to remain insulated from it. After *Bye Bye Birdie*, audiences managed to escape from the post-*Birdie* clutches of rock music, eventually to be reclutched, but not in time to capture nearly an entire generation of would-be theatre-goers. Through whatever changes popular culture was undergoing, musical theatre, too, was undergoing a potent transformation of its own. The luminary creators of the Broadway theatre had nearly vanished overnight or were fading. Oscar Hammerstein II died in 1960, Irving Berlin's last new hit musical was long past with *Call Me Madam* in 1950, Alan Jay Lerner and Frederick Loewe's partnership had essentially evaporated after the turn of the decade, and Cole Porter had all but stopped writing (he died in 1964). New writing teams such as Charles Strouse and Lee Adams, John Kander and Fred Ebb, Sheldon Harnick and Jerry Bock, Jerry Herman, and of course, Stephen Sondheim were now carrying, or soon would be, the torch of invention of the Broadway musical. A generation of hit musicals had congealed the trend of the adaptation musical, and writers and producers continued plundering any and all available source material and the lives and times of historical and literary figures for their next hit show. King Arthur and the Knights of the Round Table, Don Quixote, Oliver Twist, and others all inspired Broadway renderings in the 1960s, some in more successful artistic outings than others, and all with mostly traditional musical theatre soundscapes. Through the schism that existed among Broadway, popular music, and social issues of those days, certain other progressive and relevant topical matters did emerge, however fleetingly. Richard Rodgers penned both the music and the lyrics of *No Strings* (his only Broadway score written without a collaborator) that approached, however gingerly, the topic of interracial marriage, and by extension, race relations. Curiously, however, no mention was made in the show of the leading lady being black, outside of an off-the-cuff remark that she grew up "north of Central Park" (presumably as a reference to Harlem). Other scant references were made of this topical matter of the day, most notably (and more effectively) Sammy Davis, Jr.'s turn in Charles Strouse and Lee Adams's *Golden Boy*. With its head firmly sand-bound in those days, Broadway seemed reluctant to fully embrace the show (it ran a modest but respectable 568 performances); and certainly not broached with any regularity on Broadway stages were the proverbial elephants in the room—the sexual revolution and the term coined the "generation gap."

Indeed, commercial musical theatre by and large preferred to remain a reliable source as an entertainment-driven entity rather than a journey too far afield into more complex subjects of the 1960s, and the musical, as Broadway had come to know it, flourished. *A Funny Thing Happened on the Way to the Forum*, a Stephen Sondheim/Burt Shevelove/Larry Gelbart romp for which Sondheim wrote the entire splendid score himself provided rowdy, belly-laugh entertainment derived from the farces of an Ancient Roman playwright. *Hello, Dolly!* (1964), another show that derived its material from a literary source (in this case, Thornton Wilder's play *The Matchmaker*), was terrifically popular, and a string of Dollys, including Carol Channing, Ginger Rogers, Mary Martin, and (in a twist of the unexpected when producer David Merrick changed the cast to an all-black one for a time) Pearl Bailey, strutted down the staircase, red feathers aloft, to the title tune nearly 3,000 times on Broadway, almost 800 in London, and countless others on the road. Composer Jerry Herman had a fantastic showing, generating some of the musical theatre's most beloved songs, including "Before the Parade Passes By," "It Only Takes a Moment," and "Put on Your Sunday Clothes" as well as the everlasting title song. Barbra Streisand was nominated for a Tony for her indomitable performance as Fanny Brice in *Funny Girl* (1964), also originating the role in London, belting out "I'm the Greatest Star," "Don't Rain on My Parade," and "People," with a score by Jule Styne and Bob Merrill.

Fiddler on the Roof was a gigantic hit and the last in Jerome Robbins's illustrious track record as a mega-hit Broadway director and choreographer. (Broadway and London would later see a revue of his work with *Jerome Robbins' Broadway* in 1989.) With a score by Jerry Bock and Sheldon Harnick, the show did breach a portion of the palpable divide that existed between Broadway and the times, with much of its subject matter centering on the generation gap between parents and children, and about women making nonconformist choices and breaking "tradition," albeit in a faraway Russian peasant village. But the real star of the show was Robbins. The score included "If I Were a Rich Man," "Sunrise, Sunset," "Matchmaker," and "Far From the Home I Love." The show was produced by one of Broadway's newest golden boys, Harold Prince, who would become a producing and directing behemoth in seasons to come. His *Cabaret* opened in 1966, and the musical would never be the same. Central to the conundrum he faced by embarking on the milestone musical was exactly how to most effectively tell the story that took place during the height of the sweeping changes and their horrific result that Nazism brought to Germany in theatrical language and musical theatre fare, let alone the treatment of such heart-weary, downer subjects as abortion and substance abuse. What resulted was a wonder of theatricality and theatrical invention wherein two playing arenas existed—one was the space in which most of the scenes that drive the narrative were played, and a separate, more conceptual one in which the manifestations of the Nazi era were played out and commentary offered on the stages of the Kit Kat Club. Of the many songs, "Don't Tell Mama," "Two Ladies," "The Money Song," and "Cabaret" are standouts. The show, like so many others of the 1960s mentioned here, is ripe fruit picked often by producers of theatre seasons both professional and amateur, and musical theatre folks should know them well and expect to encounter them with frequency.

In 1967, American producer Joseph Papp chose a new, edgy, and controversial show to launch his newly acquired Public Theatre space in New York's East Village, and one that smacked of everything, both topical and aesthetic, which had been un-Broadway in recent years. *Hair* later made the uptown move to Broadway

Other notable shows and songs from the 1960s

Show, Year, and Songwriters	Notable songs	Also of note
Camelot (1960) Alan Jay Lerner/ Frederick Loewe	"The Simple Joys of Maidenhood," "Camelot," "How to Handle a Woman," "If Ever I Would Leave You"	Widely acknowledged as a far from perfect musical, the show received an unlikely boost in the weeks following the assassination of U.S. President John F. Kennedy when his widow, Jackie Kennedy, revealed in an interview that the president had often listened to the cast album. From then on, *Camelot* and the fallen JFK would be linked with one another.
The Fantasticks (1960) Tom Jones/Harvey Schmidt	"Try to Remember," "Much More," "Soon It's Gonna Rain," "I Can See It"	The story of two fathers who pretend to despise one another in order to trick their children into falling in love is the longest-running (and one of the most often produced) musical on the planet.
Bye Bye Birdie (1960) Charles Strouse/Lee Adams	"The Telephone Hour," "How Lovely to Be a Woman," "Put on a Happy Face," "One Boy," "A Lot of Livin' to Do"	A musical that was reportedly in part inspired by (of all things) Elvis Presley's draft into military service in 1957.
Carnival! (1961) Bob Merrill	"Mira," "Yes, My Heart," "Love Makes the World Go 'Round"	A show, perhaps, that is at its most effective when heard and not seen.

Show / Lyricist / Composer	Songs	Description
How to Succeed in Business without Really Trying (1961) Frank Loesser	"Happy to Keep His Dinner Warm," "Coffee Break," "I Believe in You," "Brotherhood of Man"	The winner of the 1962 Pulitzer Prize for Drama, the show thrives as a star vehicle for the right charismatic leading man. A popular favorite with school thespian troupes.
Oliver! (1963) Lionel Bart	"Where Is Love?," "Consider Yourself," "As Long as He Needs Me"	A musical version of Charles Dickens's *Oliver Twist* with a whole probably greater than the sum of its parts is nevertheless an omnipresent favorite with family audiences.
She Loves Me (1963) Sheldon Harnick/Jerry Bock	"Tonight at Eight," "Will He Like Me?," "Dear Friend," "Vanilla Ice Cream"	An under-appreciated candy box of a musical with a luscious score. It is included on many pundits' list of the "perfect" musicals.
Man of La Mancha (1965) Mitch Leigh/Joe Darion	"What Does He Want from Me?," "The Impossible Dream," "Aldonza"	Inspired by Miguel de Cervantes's seventeenth-century *Don Quixote*, the show is a heavyweight evening out with a strong left hook.
On a Clear Day You Can See Forever (1965) Burton Lane/Alan Jay Lerner	"Hurry! It's Lovely Up Here," "On a Clear Day You Can See Forever," "She Wasn't You," "What Did I Have That I Don't Have?," "Come Back to Me"	A show that concerned itself with the unusual topics, for musical theatre certainly, of ESP and reincarnation. The script was troubled, but the score was sterling.

(continued)

Table Continued

Show, Year, and Songwriters	Notable songs	Also of note
Sweet Charity (1966) Cy Coleman/Dorothy Fields	"Big Spender," "If My Friends Could See Me Now," "Too Many Tomorrows," "Baby," "Dream Your Dream," "Where Am I Going?," "I'm a Brass Band"	Bob Fosse directed and choreographed Gwen Verdon in this musical drenched with 1960s-isms about a lovelorn dance hall hostess with a heart of gold. Despite being (wonderfully) dated in many respects, the show is, nevertheless, a frequent visitor to professional and amateur stages.
Mame (1966) Jerry Herman	"It's Today," "We Need a Little Christmas," "Mame," "Bosom Buddies," "If He Walked into My Life"	Angela Lansbury will never be forgotten for her performance as the elegant, eccentric Mame Dennis whose life is somersaulted by her appointment to raise her recently deceased brother's only child. Even if the show never peaked at nearly the popularity of Jerry Herman's other two most beloved offspring (*Hello, Dolly!* and *La Cage aux Folles*), it is nonetheless a noted presence in musical theatre and is produced with some frequency.

from the Public in 1968, and did tremendous business from not only free-thinking, liberal-minded New Yorkers, but also from perplexed parents who were anxious to close the generation gap between themselves and their long-haired, radical-thinking rebels at home and elsewhere. Eventually, as the music received radio airplay and gained popularity, the kids themselves were populating the seats, if they could get one, at the Biltmore Theatre on Broadway. Finally, "counterculture" (as it had become known) and individual freedom in thinking to challenge the "establishment" had a voice in the theatrical mainstream. Beat-driven music, like the kind that had been playing everywhere except Broadway for more than ten years, was, at last, a fixture on the Great White Way. If *Hair* had been a flash in the pan (as some hoped), all of this loud, drum-heavy music accompanying the *R*-rated subject matter would soon be an unpleasant memory as they settled into their seats to watch shows more decorous in nature like *1776*, the 1969 best musical winner centred around the signing of the American Declaration of Independence. *Promises, Promises* promised that it would not be however. Where *Hair* had been presented in what amounted to a loosely strung format, the Burt Bacharach and Hal David show, based on the 1960 Jack Lemmon/Shirley MacLaine film *The Apartment* about a corporate climber who "loans" his apartment to friends as a meeting location for their extramarital trysts, proved that popular music of the day could also serve the interests of the more conventional Broadway structure. Rock-and-roll and pop music, the evil stepchildren of musical theatre music, had gotten the last laugh, and, it seemed, had fired the parting shot from Broadway in the 1960s (for other notable shows and songs from this time period see chart on p. 40).

The 1970s: The doldrums . . . and then *that* happened

The arrival of *A Chorus Line* and *Annie* in New York could not have been more welcome. In the early 1970s, it was hard to say which was more depressed—Broadway people or Broadway itself. Those years, already tainted in the United States by the bitter-sweet homecomings of the Vietnam War veterans and the cynicism and deep mistrust brought about by the scandalous so-called Watergate era, were not kind to the Broadway musical in New York City itself. This was due, in part, to the bevy of pornographic movie theatres and strip clubs that littered 42nd Street and wound their way up and down the avenues as well. Their presence was disastrous for Broadway. Who in their right mind would opt to weave through the seething, poisonous milieu that surrounded the Broadway theatres, let alone with a family in tow? Contributing to the slump in attendance was the fact that the musical was dueling it out harder than ever for an audience share with television, widespread releases of feature films into multiplex cinemas, and changing popular trends, especially with the younger demographic. Inevitably, theatres at large found their attendance numbers shrinking mercilessly and rapidly. Outside of a few beacons of originality and forward thinking, little of what was in the musical theatre world was truly new. The world of nostalgia was Broadway's world (and to some extent, the West End's) for much of the early 1970s with shows such as *Grease, No, No, Nanette* (revival), *Over Here*, and later in the decade, *Irene* (revival) and *Sugar Babies* all drumming up remnants, themes, songs, and song styles of bygone eras. Here again, only *Grease* has any really notable presence nowadays. The *Grease* songbook included "Summer Nights," "We Go Together," and "There Are Worse Things I Could Do," and if the show was the most commercially successful of the lot in the early years of the 1970s, then *Follies*, which beckoned back to the days of the Ziegfeld era, was probably the most artistically successful, winning more than a handful of Tony Awards in New York in 1971 and inclusive of many Stephen Sondheim signatures such as "Broadway Baby," "I'm Still Here," "Losing My Mind," "Buddy's Blues," "Could I Leave You?," and "Too Many Mornings." Interesting to note is that although a sometimes lengthy period of time from a New York production to a commercial London showing is not at all unusual, the West End did not experience *Follies* until the middle of the 1980s. The show, helmed by Cameron Mackintosh and Mike Ockrent, prompted one critic to note that it "was worth the 16-year wait." Sondheim preceded and followed *Follies* with *Company* and *A Little Night Music*, respectively, and collectively, they represent one of the most artistically fruitful periods of his career. The show also made impacts in other ways. *A Little Night Music* revived the bygone era of the European operetta told in high style, and *Follies* and *Company* ushered in a new era of hold-nothing-back, tell-the-truth musicals that, for some, hit close to home, but nevertheless changed how musical theatre got many of its stories told.

The "black" musical and black artists, for years deserving of their due for musical theatre treatment, did get it, but mostly with nostalgia-related fare. Of them, one of the freshest and most inventive was *The Wiz*—a soulful retelling of *The Wizard of Oz* that offered songs such as "Ease on Down the Road," "Be a Lion," "Believe in Yourself," and "Home,"—that opened in 1975 and ran for four years, garnering a Best Musical Tony Award and others. Several other shows that featured black performers were presented in revue formats, most notably *Ain't Misbehavin'*, a smash that also won the Best Musical Tony Award later in the decade and featured the songs of Thomas "Fats" Waller. Other revue shows such as *Eubie!* (which featured Eubie Blake's and others' music) and *Bubbling Brown Sugar*, which featured the music of black artists popular during the Harlem Renaissance, also played but fell short of *Ain't Misbehavin*'s popularity. Far more successful was *Sophisticated Ladies*, a revue of Duke Ellington music that opened a few years later in 1981 and ran more than 700 performances.

Jesus Christ Superstar, the first of the many significant London-to-New York Andrew Lloyd Webber exchanges whose songs included "I Don't Know How to Love Him," "Everything's Alright," "Gethsemane," and the well-known title song, opened in New York in 1971 to reviews ranging from lukewarm to blistering. It managed to run more than 700 performances in New York, a diminutive number against the eight years it ran in London. *Evita* opened at the opposite end of the decade and included such songs as "Don't Cry for Me Argentina," "Rainbow High," "The Money Kept Rolling In," "Another Suitcase in Another Hall," and "High Flying, Adored," and was hugely successful. If *Jesus Christ Superstar* foreshadowed Broadway's version of the "British Invasion," then *Evita* sealed the deal.

With regard to American shows, when *A Chorus Line* and *Annie* opened in 1975 and 1977 (1976 and 1978 in London), respectively, Broadway attained what it needed at that time to resuscitate itself—gigantic hits, and in the case of *Annie*, the return of the family audience. After *A Chorus Line*'s sold-out run at the Public Theatre and opening on Broadway to unanimously rave reviews, director and choreographer Michael Bennett (who had earlier choreographed *Promises, Promises* and *Company* and co-directed *Follies* with Harold Prince) knew he had a hit, but did not realize how far-reaching the effects of it would be, commercial or otherwise. The show, about a group of dancers competing for roles at a Broadway audition where they are placed in the unorthodox positions of not only revealing their talents, but their personal lives as well (often resulting in uncomfortable, prickly coughs and uneasy twitching from audience members even more so than *Company* had induced a few years prior), was nonetheless a conventional, integrated structure but with highly unconventional subject matter. The show discussed and dealt openly with the limited shelf life of dancers because of physical constraints, aging, and the limited choices they face with regard to their futures. But the show also grappled with identity issues—the life of the chorus dancer who somewhat anonymously supports the star onstage, teenage angst, and sexuality and homosexuality. It was a new type of construct, and audiences took the bait. To boot, the show was a producer's dream. It was relatively inexpensive to run as there were no "over-the-title" stars to pay and whose outlandish demands had to be met, it traveled easily as a touring production because of its comparatively compact physical production elements, and it had a title that sold itself because it was a smash hit and had a Best Musical Tony Award. Marvin Hamlisch and Edward Kleban's first-rate 1970s pop score includes "At the Ballet," "Nothing," "Dance Ten, Looks Three," "One" (the show's glittering finale), and "What I Did for Love," a hit musical "standard" song from the get-go.

Annie was more old fashioned and unadventurous in nature, but hit the bull's-eye. It was the golden child of "feel good" musicals with a sprightly score, kids, a dog, villains, Christmas, and an impossible-to-resist (if to some, saccharine and mawkish) story about the eternally optimistic red-headed orphan Annie who melts Daddy Warbucks's money-hardened heart. Charles Strouse and Martin Charnin, the felicitous songwriters, won the 1977 Tony Award for both Best Musical and Best Score, with songs that included "Maybe," "It's a Hard Knock Life," "Easy Street," and of course, "Tomorrow." Both *A Chorus Line* and *Annie* remain staples of every conceivable sort of theatre troupe, whether professional or not.

At the opposite end of musicals of the "feel good" sort was *Sweeney Todd*, a mesmeric, ingenious, and odd Broadway property opening in March 1979. The story, about a barber who was wrongfully transported from London and falsely imprisoned on trumped-up, fixed charges by a lustful, morally bankrupt man of the law, seemed to attract mismatched audiences. One faction was the crowd that revered Sondheim and director Harold Prince's work as revolutionary was not sure if what was on stage in *Sweeney Todd* was an opera or a musical theatre piece. They knew the degree of sophistication and artistry the duo had achieved earlier with the likes of *Company*, *Follies*, and *A Little Night Music*, but were flabbergasted to see the creation onstage at the Uris Theatre (now renamed the Gershwin). The other faction was the rubbernecking crowd that wanted to find out firsthand what all the fuss was about. And there was a lot of fuss. Still others bought the show through group sales and theatre parties on the name recognition of Sondheim and Prince or stars Angela Lansbury and Len Cariou, and were entirely unprepared for the throat-slitting, grave-digging, blood-gushing macabre goings-on and left the theatre not entirely sure what to make of the whole gory shebang. The incomparable and complex score, most of which is entirely sung, includes "The Worst Pies in London," "Green Finch and Linnet Bird," "Johanna," "Not While I'm Around," and a trifecta of songs that end Act One utterly unmatched by any writer before or since: "Pretty Women," an achingly beautiful song set against the juxtaposition of imminent murder; "Epiphany," dissonant and deeply disturbing to hear, during which Todd broadens his revenge plot to include all of those motivated to oppress and take advantage of the less fortunate; and "A Little Priest," during which Todd and Mrs. Lovett, his accomplice, "cook" up the plan to do so. The latter's lyric is one of Sondheim's most inventive, imaginative, and inspired.

Despite eight Tony Awards, including one for Best Musical as well as Best Score and Best Direction, the show, because of its unusual subject matter and despite its magnitude as a theatre piece and a piece of theatre, shuttered after 557 performances. Opening in London the following year, it was all but a box office catastrophe after mixed reviews. But, as in many of Sondheim's outings, reception and ticket sales did not necessarily parallel artistic achievement. The show won the Olivier Award for Best New Musical that year. These days, the show enjoys a richly deserved presence not only in professional, regional, and educational settings

Other notable shows and songs from the 1970s in New York

Show, Year, and Songwriters	Notable songs	Also of note
You're a Good Man, Charlie Brown (1971) Clark Gesner (Andrew Lippa contributed material for the late 1990s revival)	"The Kite," "Suppertime," "Happiness" ("My New Philosophy" was added for the 1999 revival)	The original off-Broadway production was a smash, lasting 1,597 performances. The Broadway transfer, however, fell off the doghouse and closed after 32 performances.
Sugar (1972) Jule Styne/Bob Merrill	"We Could Be Close," "What Do You Give to a Man Who Has Everything?," "It's Always Love"	Based on the 1959 Jack Lemmon, Tony Curtis, and Marilyn Monroe film *Some Like It Hot*, the Broadway version left many cold.
Pippin (1972) Stephen Schwartz	"Magic to Do," "Corner of the Sky," "No Time at All," "With You," "Extraordinary"	Ben Vereen starred in the show, which many believe first denoted Fosse as "Fosse."
A Little Night Music (1973) Stephen Sondheim	"You Must Meet My Wife," "Liaisons," "Every Day a Little Death," "Weekend in the Country," "Send in the Clowns," "The Miller's Son"	Best Musical Tony winner 1973; composer Stephen Sondheim also won the Tony for the score, but director Harold Prince was bested by Bob Fosse, who won the Tony Award for *Pippin* that year.

Mack and Mabel (1974) Jerry Herman	"Look What Happened to Mabel," "I Won't Send Roses," "Wherever He Ain't," "Tap Your Troubles Away"	Despite being a flop that only ran for two months, Herman's score was poignant, snappy, and memorable; David Merrick produced. Years later, London was determined to give it a go in 1995 with a new, revised book that yielded a respectable run at the Piccadilly Theatre and an Olivier Award for Best New Musical nomination. A 2006 John Doyle staging was replete with the director's custom of self-musical accompanying actors.
Chicago (1975) John Kander/Fred Ebb	"All That Jazz," "Cell Block Tango," "When You're Good to Mama," "All I Care about Is Love," "Roxie," "Mr. Cellophane," "Razzle Dazzle," "Class," "Nowadays"	One of the few cases where the revival has played longer than the original in New York and then some . . . a heap of some. The original ran 936 performances, and the revival is the longest-running revival in Broadway history to date. It also jazzed up London for years.
Godspell (1976) Stephen Schwartz	"Day By Day," "Learn Your Lessons Well," "Turn Back, O Man"	Composer Stephen Schwartz arrived off-Broadway and eventually found his way uptown to Broadway with this succession of parables based in part on the Gospel of Matthew. A frenetic busy-bee revival in 2011 closed in New York after a few months.

(continued)

Table Continued

Show, Year, and Songwriters	Notable songs	Also of note
On the Twentieth Century (1978) Cy Coleman/Betty Comden/Adolph Green	"I Rise Again," "Veronique," "Never," "Our Private World"	A troubled, bulky show directed by Harold Prince and starring Madeline Kahn who withdrew after a small number of Broadway performances to be replaced by Judy Kaye and Rock Hudson starred in the U.S. national tour. These days, the show is most favorably remembered because of a richly appointed score, which is worthy of a listen.
The Best Little Whorehouse in Texas (1978) Carol Hall	"Twenty-four Hours of Lovin'," "The Aggie Song," "Hard Candy Christmas," "The Bus from Amarillo"	A guilty-pleasure hit with Tommy Tune at the helm as co-director and co-choreographer.
They're Playing Our Song (1979) Marvin Hamlisch/Carole Bayer Sager	"If He Really Knew Me," "They're Playing Our Song," "Just for Tonight," "I Still Believe in Love"	A 1970s ballad-heavy show, it was reportedly loosely based on Marvin Hamlisch and Carole Bayer Sager's on-and-off, sweet-and-sour romance.

worldwide, but also frequently scares the wits out of opera house crowds, too.

For the theatre scene in the seedy 1970s, even if *A Chorus Line* and *Annie* had not already done so, *Sweeney Todd* went many miles toward assuring that musical theatre was not dead, even if some of the characters on its stage were (for other notable shows and songs from this time period see chart on p. 48).

The 1980s—the wave of the mega-musical—and the 1990s

If the 1970s congealed the trend of the source material as the basis for "new" American musicals, the 1980s and the 1990s were a contagion of derivatives. With the backdrop of the end of the Cold War and the Berlin Wall falling in 1989 and the AIDS crisis that had a decimating effect on musical theatre and theatre in general, an avalanche of subject matter was siphoned from nearly every conceivable tap-able source, and all were fair game. Many wondered if the well had ostensibly run dry for the original musical in the United States, but the driving reason for these musical draw-froms and appendages, besides a still ever-increasing competition with Hollywood, which was pumping out mega-spectacular films with brain-bending special effects, was pure economics. There were other factors. In the first few years of the 1980s, besides an already lousy economy, along with high unemployment numbers, the labor unions' influence on New York producers was creating skyrocketing labor costs, and the cost of running and operating shows as well as surges in theatre rental fees was squeezing producers toward investing only in sure-fire pay-back hits. As an inevitable result, Broadway saw a mishmash of offerings that piggy-backed on already proven appeal material (much of it short-lived), including sequels (*Bring Back Birdie*, a 1981 follow-up to *Bye Bye Birdie*, which ran only four performances, and *A Doll's Life*, a 1982 contemplation of what resulted after Nora left her doll's house, which ran only five performances); more revues of music from earlier eras (*Tintypes* in 1980 and *Leader of the Pack* in 1985); more comic strip fare hoping to capitalize on the success of *Annie* (*Doonesbury* in 1983 and off-Broadway's *Snoopy* in 1982); magic shows hoping to capture the success of the earlier *The Magic Show* from the 1970s (*Blackstone!* in 1980 and *Merlin* in 1983); and an extraordinary number of revivals. The dramatic escalation in the number of revivals even prompted a new Tony Award category beginning in 1994 for Best Revival of a Musical. While some of the revivals (particularly in the 1980s) were assembly kit, off-the-road scuff that came and went without much fanfare and frequently induced "wake me when it's over" reactions, many were first-class re-imaginings of the originals, and even revised versions of them (prompting the term "revisals") that were particularly resonant: Lincoln Center Theatre's *Anything Goes* (1987); a scaled-back *Sweeney Todd* (1989); Harold Prince's racially focused *Show Boat* (1993); Nicolas Hytner's grittier *Carousel* (1994); *Chicago* (1996), which transferred to Broadway from the New York City Center *Encores!* Series; and a shocking, sexually charged *Cabaret* (1998), based on the 1993 Sam Mendes London Donmar Warehouse production, which excised songs from the original ("Sitting Pretty," "Why Should I Wake Up?"), reinstated a song ("I Don't Care Much") cut from the original production, and added two songs written for the film version ("Mein Herr" and "Maybe This Time"). The show also featured a score accompanied, in part, by actors in the production, a foretelling of a trend yet to come. London was moved by the revivals as well (save *Sweeney Todd*) as productions opened there subsequently.

Most of the blockbuster original musicals of the two decades were also derived from source material. By 1980, producing powerhouse David Merrick hadn't had a smash hit musical open in a decade. He got one with *42nd Street* in the summer of that year, which commenced a wave of Hollywood film-turned-Broadway outings in an exact reversal of the trend that had occurred some fifty years prior. *42nd Street*, with an illustrious score by Harry Warren and Al Dubin, included songs that had been around for decades, such as "Young and Healthy," "We're in the Money," "Lullaby of Broadway," "42nd Street," "About a Quarter to Nine," "You're Getting to Be a Habit With Me," and "Shuffle Off to Buffalo," and was directed and choreographed by the inimitable Gower Champion, who had also helmed some of Merrick's biggest earlier hits such as *Hello, Dolly!* Billed as a "Song and Dance Extravaganza," and still produced frequently by theatre companies the world over, the show became nearly as famous for what occurred offstage on opening night as what occurred onstage on opening night: Champion had died that morning, and Merrick famously announced the fact to a devastated crowd and sobbing cast after the multiple uproars of ovations at the curtain calls.

42nd Street was a standout example of a show that translated beautifully from screen to stage, and was richly rewarded with a run of more than 3,400 performances on Broadway and a lengthy London run featuring a fresh-faced Catherine Zeta-Jones; but others, in the years to come, were clunky and ill-fitting. *Singin' in the Rain* in 1985 imported songs from the film version, such as "Make 'em Laugh," "You Are My Lucky Star," the title song, and others from the Arthur Freed/Nacio Herb Brown songbook. *Footloose* opened in New York in 1998 and incorporated radio hits of Tom Snow, Dean Pitchford, and Kenny Loggins, such as "The Girl Gets Around," "Holding Out for a Hero," "Footloose," "Almost Paradise," and "Let's Hear It for the Boy" as well as other far more forgettable ones written for the stage version. Then there was *Saturday Night Fever*, which had cost a reported four million pounds to mount in London and discoed on Broadway in 1999 relying on a reservoir of Bee Gees songs used in the film, such as "Stayin' Alive," "Boogie Shoes," "More Than a Woman," "You Should Be Dancin'," "Jive Talkin'," and "How Deep Is Your Love." The latter two, despite respectable Broadway runs, were generally scrutinized as misfits of artistic integrity. That aside, the titular familiarity and nostalgia for the music of the era have made guilty pleasures of the shows, often produced in commercial, yet less scrutinized, situations. In the United Kingdom alone, both shows have racked up a number of national tours in the intervening years since the West End runs. Other shows that musicalized the Hollywood version of films ranged from the extremely well crafted (*Grand Hotel* in 1989, which included songs by Robert Wright and George Forrest, such as "We'll Take a Glass Together" and "Who Couldn't Dance with You?" and had additional music and lyrics by Maury Yeston who contributed, among others, "I Want to Go to Hollywood" and "Love Can't Happen") to the absurd, like *Carrie* in 1988 (following a month-long stint in the United Kingdom), which was based on the Stephen King novel about a girl with telekinetic powers dominated by a religious zealot of a mother, but whose score did include some likeable tunes by Michael Gore and Dean Pitchford, including "Open Your Heart," "It Hurts to Be

Strong," and "I'm Not Alone." *Carrie* closed after only a handful of performances and has become the poster child of the big-budget Broadway bomb. With the benefit of hindsight, a 2012 off-Broadway revised version fared far better.

Tommy Tune, who directed and choreographed *Grand Hotel*, seemed chosen to be the heir apparent to Michael Bennett, who had been at the front and center of the new generation of Broadway directors and choreographers (and whose last Broadway musical was the glitzy *Dreamgirls*). Bennett died of complications related to AIDS in 1987; and Tune made good, dreaming up a string of hits in the 1980s and 1990s. Shows included *Nine*, a 1982 Maury Yeston tuner that included the songs "My Husband Makes Movies," "A Call from the Vatican," "Unusual Way," and "Simple"; *My One and Only* in 1983, which utilized Gershwin songs with fresh and innovative stagings; and *The Will Rogers Follies*, a splashy 1991 production that fashioned the life and times of the namesake character as Ziegfeld himself would have imagined it and had a score by Cy Coleman, Betty Comden and Adolph Green that included "My Unknown Someone," "No Man Left for Me," and "Never Met a Man I Didn't Like."

La Cage aux Folles, originally intended to be directed and choreographed by Tommy Tune, but which instead fell into the arms of Arthur Laurents, offered a frank and unapologetic look at gay relationships, gay liberation, and gay pride. In those days, increasing amounts of theatrical fare relating to the gay lifestyle began to appear on New York, and to a lesser extent, English stages, much of it off- and off-off-Broadway, on fringe stages, and some in the mainstream. Among them, *La Cage* in 1983 was yet another musicalization of a film (this time derived from a French play) that kept the audience guessing which of the svelte, willowy chorus "girls" were actually, well, *girls*, but the heartbeat of the show was as old-fashioned and traditional as an MGM-esque romance—only with two men as the romantic leads. Jerry Herman's Tony Award-winning luscious score included "Song on the Sand," "Look over There," "The Best of Times," and "I Am What I Am," which became the anthem of gay pride. London wasn't so moved; the show ran only a fraction of the time on the West End as it had on Broadway, and lost nearly all of its financial investment.

Stephen Sondheim, deeply let down by the Broadway failure in 1981 of *Merrily We Roll Along* (among Sondheim's most memorable scores that included "Old Friends," "Like It Was," and "Not a Day Goes By"), had come back newly energized with newfound collaborator James Lapine, and the two seemed predestined for one another. Lapine's presence as a bookwriter and director gave Sondheim's work not only a new directing force after the relationship with Harold Prince had run afoul during and after *Merrily*, but Lapine's talent as a librettist profoundly invigorated Sondheim's own work. It was, it seemed, just what the doctor ordered not only for Sondheim, who had reportedly foresworn Broadway for the time being, but also for the future of the musical. The first oeuvre to emerge from the pair was the 1984 *Sunday in the Park with George*, motivated by the painting (and largely fictionalized personal life for the musical) of French pointillist Georges Seurat, and the outcome was as finely conceived and abundantly detailed as the painting itself. Sondheim's score included the indeed beautiful "Beautiful," "Sunday," "Putting It Together," "Move On," and Sondheim's vivid account of the obsessive and even tortured plight of an artist in "Finishing the Hat." On Tony night in 1984, when Jerry Herman took the stage to accept the Tony Award for Best Original Score for *La Cage aux Folles*, he stated that there had been a rumor around "that the simple, hummable show tune was no longer welcome on Broadway. Well, it's alive and well at the Palace" (Theatre). Many considered the remark bad sportsmanship and just plain rude as Herman might have been thumbing his nose at Sondheim. Sondheim and Lapine had the last laugh, though. *Sunday in the Park with George* won the Pulitzer Prize for Drama the following year.

In 1987, Stephen Sondheim and James Lapine gave Broadway *Into the Woods*, an ingenious concoction of characters from the Grimm fairy tales in pursuit of everything from a slipper as pure as gold to an elusive cow, and an exploration and reflection on and of the consequences of actions taken in order to get them. The show is probably Sondheim's most commercially successful as evidenced by the generous number of productions presented regularly by regional, stock, amateur, and school groups, especially in the United States and the United Kingdom. The score included "I Know Things Now," "Giants in the Sky," "Stay with Me," "On the Steps of the Palace," "No More," and "No One Is Alone," giving Sondheim a Best Original Score Tony Award (as well as Lapine for Best Book). The duo also conceived *Passion*, a troubled (and troubling) but enthralling creation from 1994 that also won Tony Awards for

Sondheim and Lapine, and included a wealth of Sondheim wonders such as "Happiness," "I Wish I Could Forget You," "Loving You," and "No One Has Ever Loved Me."

If *A Chorus Line* had been a tectonic shift for the musical theatre at large a mere seven years earlier, the opening of *Cats* in 1982, after a year on the West End, began an all-out Richter-scale levitating earthquake. The theatre of Andrew Lloyd Webber was not new on Broadway; *Jesus Christ Superstar* had stirred up the soup in the early 1970s, and *Evita* was still packing them in nightly in New York as it had been since 1978 in London and continuing for seven years. But *Cats*, whose score included "Jellicle Songs for Jellicle Cats," "The Rum Tum Tugger," "Mungojerri and Rumpleteazer," "Skimbleshanks: The Railway Cat" (the latter three are character names of cats in the show), and the hit "Memory," was different in that it was, in every sense of the word, a spectacle. The premise of the show based itself on T.S. Eliot's poetic musings of the lives and times of a litany of stealthy felines, some aged and wise, some mischief-making and odd-ball, from the pages of his *Old Possum's Book of Practical Cats* and strung together onstage as a series of vignettes. Before transferring to Broadway, the show was already enjoying a sold-out run in London, and was a hit even before it opened on the Great White Way with the largest advanced ticket sales in Broadway history up until that time—6.2 million dollars. From the moment that theatre-goers entered the theatre to John Napier's gargantuan set, abundant with articles that you would find in a larger-than-life junkyard, the audience knew it was about to witness something curious. The set was to scale with how a cat would see it, and in this case, dance around, on, over, and through it.

In a sense, *Cats*, a show about a kitty pack that assembles annually to determine which of the bunch will pass into the next of its nine lives, many revealing biographical data over the course of the conclave, did share a strand of DNA with *A Chorus Line*. By the time the show was over, the audience knew well the lives of the characters on the stage, each revealing himself one after the other in the course of the narrative. But *Cats*, oversized in nearly every conceivable way, overabundant in pastiche, and inclusive of human actors playing animals and not other humans, was at best adversarial and at worst hostile to the brand of theatre that *A Chorus Line* had introduced and championed, or so some argue. As it evolved, perhaps far more significant than *Cats* the show was *Cats* the brand, which was unlike any live entertainment property before it and became a worldwide juggernaut. *Cats* nearly singlehandedly, for a time, trend-set the wowza, behemoth, mega-produced show that gives the audience (particularly the tourists) maximum bang for their buck, and the show continues to be a hot ticket in regional and stock houses the world over, in part, due to name recognition alone.

Other Cameron Mackintosh-produced extravaganzas followed *Cats*. *Les Misérables,* based on Victor Hugo's novel of the same name, arrived in 1987 (two years after opening in London) and remained for sixteen years. The show was a revolution of its own, written by the French twosome Claude-Michel Schönberg and Alain Boublil, and eventually had record-setting simultaneous productions running around the world. The iconic emblem of the waif-like child set against the backdrop of the French flag was (and is) as recognizable and familiar worldwide as that of any major worldwide brand, and many of the songs in the show, such as "I Dreamed a Dream," "On My Own," and "Bring Him Home," are staples in the world of theatre music. The same can be said for *The Phantom of the Opera*, the Harold Prince-directed jumbo-sized show based on the French novel by Gaston Leroux with music by Andrew Lloyd Webber and lyrics by Charles Hart and Richard Stilgoe. The show opened on Broadway in 1986, shortly after its London bow, and the score included "Think of Me," "The Music of the Night," "All I Ask of You," and "Wishing You Were Somehow Here Again." In 1991, *Miss Saigon* was the Claude-Michel Schönberg/Alain Boublil (with additional lyrics by Richard Maltby, Jr.) follow-up to their earlier success and had an appealing popp-y score containing "The Movie in My Mind," "Why God, Why?," "Sun and Moon," "Last Night of the World," and "I'd Give My Life for You." As *Les Misérables* had on Broadway in 2014, so, too, did *Miss Saigon* get a London revival that year, both once again produced by British titan Cameron Mackintosh.

The AIDS crisis that was on everyone's mind in the 1980s and 1990s became Broadway topics with a number of shows, most notably William Finn's 1992 *Falsettos*, whose rich contemporary score included "The Games I Play," "What More Can I Say?," "Something Bad Is Happening," and "Holding to the Ground," and the hard-driving, edgy, rock music-inspired score of *Rent* that opened on Broadway in 1996.

Rent loosely adapted the storyline of the Puccini opera *La Bohème* and transplanted its inhabitants from Paris to the glory days of the East Village in New York City, where everyone was young and trying to pay it (rent) amidst the atmosphere of drug use and addiction, homosexuality and homophobia, anarchy, and HIV. Jonathan Larson's (who died just days shy of age 36 and one day before *Rent*'s off-Broadway debut) score was loaded with memorable material such as "One Song Glory," "Out Tonight," "Seasons of Love," and "Take Me or Leave Me." In the scheme of things, the show proved seminal. Due to its astonishing success (Tony Award for Best Musical, Tony Award for Larson for Best Book and Best Score, an array of other "outstanding" awards, and the 1996 Pulitzer Prize for Drama) and longevity (a twelve-year run on Broadway and countless productions worldwide, but a comparatively meager London excursion), it provided proof that audiences were willing to gulp, square their shoulders, and park nose to nose with very disquieting subject matter in the musical theatre yet again.

For those who still wished to beckon their inner child (or share the theatre experience with their children), there was Disney on Broadway and in London. Disney films, ripe for musicalization, first came a-knockin' on Broadway's door in tandem with New York Mayor Rudy Giuliani's hard-lined effort to clean up 42nd Street, that den of iniquity, and banish its seedy, immoral ways that had given Broadway and New York City a black eye for the longest time.

Beauty and the Beast opened on Broadway in April 1994 (London in 1997, winning the 1998 Olivier Award for Best New Musical) and invited the crowd to be its guest nearly 5,500 times, holding the record for the highest number of performances at Broadway's Palace (where it opened) and Lunt-Fontanne Theatre (where it eventually transferred). The show, visually resplendent with dancing utensils, singing teapots, and eye-popping effects, featured a tuneful, endearing score inclusive of many songs in the film version. For the stage, the film songs of Alan Menken and Howard Ashman were supplemented with new ones by Menken, Ashman, and Tim Rice to complete the score, which included "Home," "Be Our Guest," "If I Can't Love Her," "Something There," "Human Again," and "Beauty and the Beast." The show is, and likely will be even years out, a favorite of regional, community, and school theatres.

Other notable shows and songs from the 1980s and 1990s in New York

Show, Year, and Songwriters	Notable songs	Also of note
Barnum (1980) Cy Coleman/Michael Stewart	"There's a Sucker Born Every Minute," "The Colors of My Life," "One Brick at a Time," "Bigger Isn't Better," "Out There"	A musical that loosely chronicles the life of circus showman P.T. Barnum starred Jim Dale and featured all the whirligig fun you'd find in the three rings, and had heart to boot.
Little Shop of Horrors (1982) Howard Ashman/Alan Menken	"Grow for Me," "Somewhere That's Green," "Dentist!," "Suddenly Seymour"	The musical about an enormous plant with a thunderbolt voice that feeds on human flesh and is gardened by a nebbish flower shop worker was just right to become a hit off-Broadway and in London. It eventually became, and remains, an absolute kernel of small-size shows, making it popular with many thespian troupes.
Baby (1983) David Shire/Richard Maltby, Jr.	"What Could Be Better?," "I Want It All," "At Night She Comes Home to Me," "I Chose Right," "The Story Goes On," "Patterns," "Two People in Love"	A charming, if flawed, musical small in stature about three couples at different stages of their lives.
Big River (1985) Roger Miller	"Waitin' for the Light to Shine," "Muddy Water," "Leavin's Not the Only Way to Go," "Free at Last"	Based on the Mark Twain classic *The Adventures of Huckleberry Finn* and a hoedown of a good time.

(continued)

Table Continued

Show, Year, and Songwriters	Notable songs	Also of note
The Mystery of Edwin Drood (1985) Rupert Holmes	"A Man Could Go Quite Mad," "Moonfall," "Don't Quit while You're Ahead"	Based on the Dickens novel in which the audience votes on how the evening will end, the original production shortened its title to simply *Drood* about halfway through its Broadway run.
Nunsense (1985) Dan Goggin	"Turn Up the Spotlight," "Tackle that Temptation with a Time-Step," "I Just Want to Be a Star"	Stage-struck nuns puttin' on a show (featuring themselves), this popular fluff has been an international mainstay since it premiered.
Me and My Girl (1986) Noel Gay/Douglas Furber/L. Arthur Rose	"Me and My Girl," "Once You Lose Your Heart," "The Lambeth Walk," "Leaning on a Lamp Post"	A comic romp directed by British wunderkind Mike Okrent and starring Robert Lindsay was a big hit in New York and packed them in for eight years in London.
City of Angels (1989) Cy Coleman/David Zippel	"What You Don't Know about Women," "With Every Breath I Take," "Lost and Found," "You're Nothing without Me," "You Can Always Count on Me," "Funny"	Wonderfully original and smartly written in which two separate stories are interwoven—one in "real life" and one in film noir style. Accordingly, the former's scenes are played in color, and the latter's in black and white. Coleman's jazz score may well be his most appealing, and Zippel's witty lyrics are first class all the way.

Show	Songs	Description
The Secret Garden (1991) Lucy Simon/Marsha Norman	"Winters on the Wing," "A Bit of Earth," "Lily's Eyes," "Wick," "Hold On," "Where in the World," "How Could I Ever Know?"	Based on the 1911 novel of the same name, this is one of the few Broadway musicals to date that featured a composer and bookwriter/lyricist who were both women. Mandy Patinkin starred on Broadway and sang most of the show's big-throated power ballads. Daisy Eagan was the youngest female performer to ever win a Tony for her performance as Mary.
Crazy for You (1992) George/Ira Gershwin	"I Can't Be Bothered Now," "Shall We Dance?," "Someone to Watch over Me," "Embraceable You," "I Got Rhythm," "What Causes That?," "Naughty Baby," "They Can't Take that Away From Me," "But Not for Me"	Another Gershwin song compilation, this time ingeniously choreographed by Susan Stroman and probably the most often produced of the "new" musicals highlighting Gershwin songs.
Kiss of the Spider Woman (1993) John Kander/Fred Ebb	"Dressing Them Up," "Dear One," "She's a Woman," "The Day after That," "Kiss of the Spider Woman"	Despite mixed reviews and a pan from the *New York Times*, the show ran more than 900 performances on Broadway and won the Best Musical Tony Award, having opened first in London the year before.

(*continued*)

Table Continued

Show, Year, and Songwriters	Notable songs	Also of note
Titanic (1997) Maury Yeston	"Barrett's Song," "The Proposal," "We'll Meet Tomorrow"	The ship stayed afloat in New York for more than 800 performances of this Best Musical Tony Award winner.
Jekyll and Hyde (1997) Frank Wildhorn/Steve Cuden/Leslie Bricusse	"Take Me as I Am," "This Is the Moment," "Someone Like You," "Once Upon a Dream," "In His Eyes," "A New Life"	After an exhaustive number of revisions lasting nearly seven years, numerous out-of-town productions, and a national tour, this show at last opened on Broadway and ran more than 1,500 performances. The ballad-heavy show has enjoyed a wealth of regional and worldwide productions (including U.K. tours) in the years since its Broadway run, and that number continues to grow.
The Scarlet Pimpernel (1997) Frank Wildhorn/Nan Knighton	"Madame Guillotine," "Into the Fire," "Falcon in the Dive," "When I Look at You," "Where's the Girl?," "Only Love," "She Was There," "Storybook," "You Are My Home"	This musical version of the book of the same name underwent several revisions even after the show opened, with the final version being dubbed "3.0." The score is probably Wildhorn's most engaging.
Ragtime (1998) Stephen Flaherty/Lynn Ahrens	"Journey On," "The Crime of the Century," "Your Daddy's Son," "Wheels of a Dream," "Till We Reach that Day," "Back to Before," "Make Them Hear You"	A beautifully crafted musical based on the novel of the same name by E.L. Doctorow that won the Tony Award for Best Score and Best Book, but not for Best Musical (which went to *The Lion King*).

If *Beauty and the Beast* was visually stunning, and with a huge heart at that, then *The Lion King* (which reopened at the refurbished New Amsterdam Theatre on the newly cleaned-up and spit-shined 42nd Street, officially putting an end to the former antics on the thoroughfare in 1997) at least doubled its efforts. Director Julie Taymor's concoction was not only visually splendid with a heart of gold that championed multiculturalism and universal understanding, it also boasted the songwriting of the new kid in town, Broadway's latest British import Elton John. John's score, in collaboration with Tim Rice and a host of others (most admirably, Lebo M.), was "pop" influenced to be sure, but also frequently felt and played like more "traditional" theatre music. It deftly included "Circle of Life," "I Just Can't Wait to Be King," and "Can You Feel the Love Tonight?." Disney felt the love for John, recruiting him to compose the score for *Aida* along with Disney mainstay Tim Rice. *Aida* had evolved from a storybook version of the Verdi opera written by opera world's great Leontyne Price. The show endured a rocky transition to Broadway from developmental and pre-Broadway engagements in Atlanta and Chicago, replacing its director, choreographer, and set designer, and restructuring much of its score, and arrived on Broadway in 2000 featuring pop/rock-styled songs, some miles apart from those in *The Lion King*, but quintessential Elton John. It included "Fortune Favors the Brave," "My Strongest Suit," "Easy as Life," "Like Father Like Son," and "I Know the Truth." Both shows ran productions in theatres worldwide—*The Lion King* with the lion's share (for other notable shows and songs from this time period see chart on p. 59).

2000 onward

The Full Monty, about a group of pink-slipped workers in upstate New York who concoct a one-night-only money-making ploy to "take it all off" at a strip club, hustled into town, G-strings and all, on October 26, 2000, and was a hit at 770 performances, but a mild one on Broadway in comparison to the following season's *The Producers'* total of 2,502. These numbers were not surprising; despite a zippy, winning score by Broadway newcomer David Yazbek (including "It's a Woman's World," "Big-Ass Rock," "Big Black Man," "You Walk with Me," and "Let It Go"), *The Full*

Monty was eclipsed by *The Producers* in nearly every conceivable way. This held true in the number of performances in the West End as well; *Monty* ran only a few months, with British audiences seemingly unwilling to fully invest in the blue-collar Americanized version of what had been set in England on film. *The Producers* was, as expected, more well received, but nevertheless only ran a little more than two years.

American audiences, however, couldn't resist, and April 19, 2001, was a celebratory day on Broadway. After years of behemoth-sized musicals, some with grave, shadowy themes and (some said) heavy-handed, ear-assaulting ballads that had all but usurped the musical theatre of previous generations, a musical was penned that was in the spirit, and to some extent the letter, of the "old school." And it was very, very funny. Mel Brooks's stage adaptation of his cult-followed 1968 film *The Producers* ruled the roost for a time, and had one foot grounded in equal opportunity ribbing and satire of any number of topics, ethnicities, and social groups. Yet the other foot was plainly implanted in old-fashioned theatrical custom and conventional expectations such as splashy production numbers, appealing hum-able songs, and broad comedy. Susan Stroman's direction and choreography spiked the punch, highlighting dancing Nazis, caricature homosexuals, and toe-tapping grannies with barbed-up libidos. The show revolved around a third-rate theatrical producer and his nebbish cohort who planned to get rich by raising far more capital than needed to mount the worst Broadway musical ever written, and when the show flopped, absconding with the dough.

Brooks, who handily wrote the score himself (Jerry Herman had reportedly passed on it), delivered with songs such as "I Wanna Be a Producer," "When You've Got It, Flaunt It," and the show's piece-de-resistance—"Springtime for Hitler." Although the show won an unprecedented twelve Tony Awards and was the hottest ticket in town (prompting the show's producers to shamelessly hike "VIP" dress circle tickets upward of 480 bucks and get away with it, despite the verbal tar-and-feathering from the theatre community), *The Producers* ultimately lost steam after its original stars, Nathan Lane and Matthew Broderick, departed. This suggested that perhaps more relevant than *The Producers* the *show* was *The Producers* the *idea* in that American musical comedy, while feeble and declining as a popular art form (and considered by some to be extinct), could still pack a mighty wallop on 44th Street in Manhattan. It also pointed out that star power was key, and even more or less indispensable, on modern Broadway. Shows starring movie and television celebrities had been a steadily rising trend in London since the 1990s, and now it appeared that Broadway might need to step up the celebrity recruits as well, which of course, it did.

Mamma Mia, whose ABBA-written score was inclusive of the group's hits such as "Dancing Queen," "S.O.S.," "The Winner Takes It All," and "Take a Chance on Me," opened on Broadway only weeks after the terrorist attacks of September 11, 2001, which shuttered Broadway for two days, and the show's arrival was a mixed blessing. Broadway and New York needed a spunky escapist vehicle to lighten its heavy heart and fill the vacant seats when no one was coming to the city. However, *Mamma Mia* was also an indication that there would be no let-up from the European barrage of tourist-driven fluff shows, which in less lean eras might have ruffled many of the old guard's feathers, but under the circumstances threw a near-drowning Broadway a lifeline. The show also set a precedent—vapid storylines loosely hinging together assemblies of pop songs and standing up as musicals. It even, along with its like-minded cohorts past and present, closed the deal on the use of the term "jukebox" or "catalog" musical, indicating the repurposing of old song material not intended to share the same genetic code of being written for the purpose of musical theatre storytelling. And this was, on both sides of the Atlantic, a conundrum. It seemed that while this new formulation went over well with the under-40 demographic and got them into the theatres, the mainstay older demographic was feeling overlooked.

The music of Billy Joel, with its urban themes and street-savvy characters, leapt from concert stage to Broadway stage in late 2002 (2006 in the West End and only running a very short time) with *Movin' Out* and made use of many Joel hits such as "It's Still Rock and Roll to Me," "Movin' Out," "She's Got a Way," "Big Shot," and "New York State of Mind" through Twyla Tharp's inspired collage of dances. None of the dancers sang, but instead wove tales through choreography as representations of characters in Joel's music; vocals and verbal narrative were provided by an onstage singing "piano man." The show received a 2003 Best Musical Tony nomination as did *Jersey Boys* (which won), a telling of the rise of Frankie Valli and The Four Seasons, a few seasons later. The show staged oldies radio station hit songs such as "Sherry," "Walk Like a Man," and "Can't Take My Eyes Off of You" under Des McAnuff's direction and played to sold-out, mostly tourist-occupied houses on Broadway and the West End for seasons to come. Far less successful in New York were *All Shook Up* in 2005, although it celebrated the music of Elvis Presley, and *The Times They Are A-Changin'*, which showcased the music of Bob Dylan, in 2006. Both received unrestrained tongue-lashings from the critics, struggled, and had the hammer dropped on them, with *All Shook Up* faring slightly better at 203 performances to the latter's meager 28.

It was becoming increasingly apparent that a Broadway musical in New York, in order to generate enough revenue to reimburse a litany of backers, required stunning, unprecedented physical production elements and goods contained therein that sold themselves in pre-recognizable packaging (such as star power previously mentioned here and already-proven successful creative teams). This, in circles of reasonable thought, had now become fait accompli in commercial theatre. Corporate sponsorship became commonplace on Broadway in order to handle the ever-increasing costs to mount a musical, and occasionally, there was gold at the end of the rainbow—and then some. Universal Pictures was a lead producer of *Wicked*, which opened in 2003 to mixed notices, but hardened the long-held belief of many that the relevance of critical approval was evaporating. With songs by Stephen Schwartz and based upon Gregory Maguire's well-liked novel that imagined the back-story to *The Wizard of Oz*, but also ran concurrently with Dorothy's odyssey, the show had teenage girls blasting the strains of "Popular," "The Wizard and I," and "Defying Gravity" until relenting parents forked out the 120 bucks on Broadway for the live experience. Despite the show's infamous and much-remembered loss of the Best Musical and Best Score Tony Awards to *Avenue Q*, the little-engine-that-could musical about thirty-somethings in New York's outer boroughs on a quest to find their purpose, *Wicked* had far more Broadway staying power and box office heft in both New York City and London than its rival, which was small, fresh, funny and offbeat, and had a concept that to some extent resembled more of a cheeky grown-up *Sesame Street* than a musical typically found on 45th Street. It was an experience all its own with songs by Robert Lopez and Jeff Marx, such as "It Sucks to Be Me," "The Internet Is for Porn," and "If You Were Gay." As if some of the song titles weren't unexpected enough, the show pulled another unexpected move when it closed on Broadway after 2,534 performances, packed its bags, and shortly thereafter unpacked them again at an off-Broadway space, continuing its New York run at a lower overhead cost. Other shows did the same. *Rent* reopened off-Broadway after being closed for years. *Million Dollar Quartet* nearly doubled what likely would have been its Broadway life by moving to an off-Broadway space, and why not?

There were other beacons of vitality and refreshing originality from 2002 onward. *Hairspray*, in 2002, about a Baltimore girl finding romance and racial equality on a local television program in the 1960s, fired on all cylinders with a catchy, bubbly score by Marc Shaiman and Scott Wittman and ran more than 2,600 performances in New York, more than two years in London (starring British top dog Michael Ball and amassing a record eleven Olivier Award nominations), and notable productions across the globe. The show remains all the rage in regional, summer stock, casino, and cruise ship productions, likely because of its cheery accessibility and its inherent feels-like-a-day-of-sunshine likeability. The Shaiman/Wittman score includes many a gemstone tuner such as "Good Morning, Baltimore," "I Can Hear the Bells," "The Nicest Kids in Town," "It Takes Two," and "You Can't Stop the Beat," and is remarkable beyond the fact that you can't seem to stop the songs from continuously be-bopping about in your head. Wittman's lyrics are sharp enough to hold their own, but Shaiman managed to call to mind the sounds of 1950s and 1960s hitmakers such as Jerry Leiber, Mike Stoller, and Ellie Greenwich, doing so with not a hint of hope-they-won't-mind imitation, but rather through his own original compositional vitality. How refreshing.

The dye was cast for Sutton Foster's superstardom in *Thoroughly Modern Millie*, arriving by way of her rendition of the girl from the one-horse town hell-bent on making good on New York dreams. The show was a terrific good time, summoning the highest order of pure entertainment with heart, and no one dared argue Foster's "it girl" factor. Heightening the appeal for nostalgia junkies, the musical saw the round-trip return of the flapper tapper of the cheeky nose-thumbing kind (and weren't they all?). Not surprisingly, *Millie* has also been a darling of the stock and regional circuit on several continents. The delicious score by Jeanine Tesori and Dick Scanlan is hard to beat with songs such as "Not for the Life of Me," "What Do I Need with Love?," "Forget about the Boy," and "Gimme Gimme."

If Adam Guettel's score for *The Light in the Piazza* had grown men holding back the tears (and it did), it may or may not have been because of what was happening onstage. The show itself was ravishing to be sure, but for many it also affirmed the philosophical hope-against-hope that the unabashedly romantic score still had a place in musical theatre. Guettel, the grandchild of Richard Rodgers, wrote a remarkably complex, harmonically sophisticated score with an abundance of effusive romanticism. The show, with all of this in tow, was at once coarse and evocative, telling a nearly cautionary tale of how life can swerve in unexpected directions. Guettel won the Tony Award that year, but the show lost the best musical top prize to *Spamalot*, a Mike Nichols-staged version of a Monty Python film (*Monty Python and the Holy Grail*) replete with lyrics and music (with others) of Eric Idle. The Monty Python party lasted just under four years in New York, less in London, but tours carried on. Regional productions in the United States are sparse, with the United Kingdom and other foreign venues faring better.

Spring Awakening took a century-old relic of a controversial German play, handily mixed mediums within its storytelling and visual properties, and had an imaginative theatre-pop-alternative-indie mash-up of a score by Duncan Sheik. Sheik, an American recording artist and songwriter with relative inexperience in the musical theatre, succeeded admirably as one of the first in the latest trendy wave of popular music writers fashioning musicals. This would hit a status that could nearly be called the norm a few seasons later with Bono and The Edge, Cindy Lauper, Sheryl Crow, Sting, and others all composing scores for the theatre within a few seasons' time. Some were enthusiastic, some worried about it, and others winced, but most shrugged it off as a requisite move for a musical theatre whose determined efforts to "pop-ify" and later "idol"-ize itself made sense in bottom-line fiscal reality. *Spring Awakening* got too many things right for the pundits to register their complaints too harshly. In score terms, this was evident in the first half hour of the show with songs such as "Mama Who Bore Me," "The Bitch of Living," and "My Junk," and later with "The Song of Purple Summer," as theatrical and lovely an imagining as you could want. The show itself remains a sweetheart in regional, and particularly, college and university theatres, and has, or certainly did for a time, invigorated a new generation of theatre-goers.

Another show that titillated both teenagers and grown-ups was 2008's *In the Heights,* which transplanted the denizens of the Washington Heights neighborhood in New York City southward to midtown Manhattan. With a thermostat-raising Latin and rap-infused near bilingual score by Lin-Manuel Miranda, songs such as "Breathe" and "Everything I Know" were launch pads to musical theatre for many new to it. And if, as one argument goes, the parts themselves were greater than the whole, hardly anyone balks at acknowledging that the show magnetized a new and more multicultural audience to the musical theatre along the same lines as *The Color Purple* had done a few seasons earlier.

It is noteworthy to point out the number of shows down the middle years of this particular decade that bet largely on the alchemy of prior mega-hits and the writers and producers of them, yet ultimately failed to reach their predecessors' achievements or saleability. To many, this offered some evidence that audiences couldn't "be fooled," were discerning, and still required, in New York and London, at any rate, either a substance-over-form outing or a powza-knockout physical production to fill the seats. Many of the shows nonetheless held fragments of greatness and shouldn't be dismissed out of hand as "unworthy." (This is discussed at some length in the forthcoming section on choosing song material as a singing actor.) Disney's *Tarzan*, despite an energetic, requisite power ballad-doused score by Phil Collins, fell far short of expectations in New York, but fared better in other markets, as did Mel Brooks's *Young Frankenstein* that nevertheless had more than an evening's share of naughty lyrics and agreeable melodies. Despite its respectable run in London, Andrew Lloyd Webber's *The Woman in White* failed to take hold on Broadway even with what might be Sir Andrew's most ambitious score yet and one that perhaps elevated his work in earnest to "composer-ly." Claude-Michel Schönberg and Alain Boublil, who penned *Les Misérables* and *Miss Saigon*, could not find a means to make *The Pirate Queen* generate the same appeal in New York as those earlier shows, although the score was penetrated with those power ballad episodes that we have come to expect from the two and dazzling *Riverdance*-like moments. It took three attempts, starting with *Dance of the Vampires* in 2002 and then Frank Wildhorn's *Dracula* in 2004, for it to become evident that musicals about vampires were a hard sell in New York, even if some European theatre-goers felt altogether different. The third, Elton John's *Lestat*, closed in New York after torrential scoffing from critics and eschewing by audiences. But the abysmal failure of the show, gigantic budget and all, was vindicated for John fans a couple of years later with his next arrival.

Billy Elliot was on the lips of theatre people nearly straight away after the release of the 2000 film as an obvious choice for screen-to-stage transport. Elton John and Lee Hall created the score to the story about a dancing-phenomenon U.K. kid against the backdrop of the blighted lives of miners and a labor strike with violent clashes. After the London bow in 2005, the show made the trip to Australia in 2007, and then on to Broadway and beyond in the following years. Along the way, it picked up practically every Best New Musical award, but John and Hall's score, although inclusive of likeable songs such as "Shine" and "Born to Boogie," was a disappointment to many who struggled to acknowledge it as being at the same level of excellence as the rest of the production.

Memphis took the long road to Broadway, zigzagging its way through the regional theatre circuit to get it right, and many critics said it didn't, dismissing it as formulaic. But even so, it was a hit that opened in 2009 (West End in 2014). The show was about a southern disc jockey circa 1950 who was one of the first radio personas to champion black music at a time when a jockey's yays or nays steered many to overnight stardom. The David Bryan/Joe DiPietro score encompassed everything from a wall-shaking-can't-sit-still-juke-joint sound to gospel to rhythm and blues feel that featured self-explanatory songs such as "The Rhythm of My Soul," "Colored Woman," and "Tear the House Down."

Another show that exploited the workshop and U.S. regional theatre circuit, both of which by this time had nearly replaced the out-of-town tryout to develop and refine the show before bringing it in, was *Next to Normal*. And if the production had a slicked-up-for-Broadway regional theatre vibe, the content was certainly compelling even if it wasn't the show you'd have taken your in-laws to for a rollicking fun time. Shows had long dabbled in matters of the mind gone askew, particularly in urban locales, but mental disorder of the kind that fractures and debilitates a suburban "could-be-you-or-me" family was fresh (and delicate) subject matter. Tom Kitt, who had been a part of the frustrating (but not uncommon) let-down of a not-so-good show with a very good score with *High Fidelity* a couple of seasons earlier, supplied the music to Brian Yorkey's lyrics. The score had many a hand-wringing ballad and up-tempo (surely this explains the teenage singers' near obsession with it), including the excruciatingly appealing "I Miss the Mountains," "Superboy and the Invisible Girl," "Alive," and other gulp-inducers.

While some of the songs are sung by angsty teens, the troubled mom is the main event, a role for which Alice Ripley won a 2009 Tony Award. The show is, and should be for the foreseeable future, a favorite regional theatre venture.

American Idiot opened in New York in 2010 to eardrum-penetrating applause from Green Day fans and many critics, bringing the punk-ish sounds of the band to a Broadway house. It was loud, but it was fresh with staged versions of trendy and crowd-pleasing Green Day songs such as "Boulevard of Broken Dreams," "Basket Case," "Last Night on Earth," and "21 Guns." That particular season in New York also told two Broadway tales in polar opposition to one another: The first was one of Broadway gold, but the beleaguered second was Broadway blunder that eventually redeemed itself—sort of. *The Book of Mormon*, with songs by Robert Lopez, Trey Parker, and Matt Stone (the latter two theatre converts by way of television's *South Park*), satirized both religion and the musical theatre, inducing belly laughs heard rolling clear down 49th Street. The show was the darling of critics who lavished it with every existing superlative, creating the kind of buzz that musical theatre hadn't heard since *The Producers*, but this one didn't go weak in the knees after its stars left the Broadway version. *Spider Man: Turn Off the Dark*, with songs by rockers Bono and The Edge, became fodder for a mountain of ridicule and outright bashing as news of bodily injury to members of the cast became a near-daily occurrence in the early days of previews and beyond. The most expensive production in Broadway history, the show repeatedly postponed its opening and remained in previews in New York until critics finally grew impatient and reviewed it anyway, punishing the show with a nearly undivided trouncing. Before what producers designated as the official opening, the show halted performances, replaced its lauded director as well as other key members of the production team, regrouped, and returned to rehearsals. When the show finally opened on Broadway in June 2011, critical response was warmer, but lukewarm at best. West End audiences got *The Book of Mormon* a couple of years after the New York opening, and *Spider Man* stopped spinning in New York in early 2014, blaming low ticket sales and, it was rumored, positioning itself for a U.S. arena tour, which is perhaps where it had belonged all the while.

The next season in New York was nearly dominated by the arrival of *Once*, another diminutive (by present-day mainstream musical standards) show with the kind of earthy sentimentality that stopped short of sap. *Once* might be well remembered as the show that reminded the musical theatre, in an amped-up "star"-frenzied era of technological accomplishment, what could happen when a few simple folks sit on stage with some guitars and fiddles and entertain us with an interesting tale. The score was composed by Glen Hansard and Markéta Irglová, retaining songs from the film of the same name on which the show is based, but this was hardly the first time for that. It included the thrilling first act finale "Gold," and of course, "Falling Slowly," which got into your mind and happily just wouldn't get out.

Newsies brought songs such as "Santa Fe" from the movie it was based on with music by Disney favorite Alan Menken and lyrics by Jack Feldman, and the show thrilled the Disney crowd and others. *Nice Work If You Can Get It* opened in New York after a rocky period of creative team and star changes as well as a postponement from a couple of seasons back. It brought the great hits of the Gershwin songbook back to the big boards as well as a few forgotten sparklers such as "Delishious," "Treat Me Rough," and "Will You Remember Me?."

Perhaps like no season before it had done as tellingly, the period between late 2011 and late 2014 seemed to declare not just the state of the times, but also how they appeared to be changing. The "mega show" carried on along with the obligatory Broadway and West End exchanges, but by now other major cities worldwide were getting their own companies of the shows nearly as readily. Moreover, U.S. writers and producers continued their obsession with musicals first seen as films, although London appeared more discerning in both the creation and the transfers.

Shows in the grand traditions of the Golden Age had now all but been felled (many complained) by the assassin's bullet known as the rock-suffused shows, notable exceptions being the high-profile *From Here to Eternity* (music and lyrics by Stuart Brayson and Tim Rice) and *Charlie and the Chocolate Factory* (music and lyrics mostly by Marc Shaiman and Scott Wittman) in London, and *The Bridges of Madison County* in New York. Two of the three folded rather hastily due to weak ticket sales, and the third (*Charlie*) survived due to its family-friendliness and eye-candy stagecraft.

Most revealing as to the state of the times was a glance at the theatre listings in both New York and London, the majority of which were rock, jukebox, and/or movie adaptations (*Hedwig and the Angry Inch*, *Beautiful* [in the spirit of *Jersey Boys*], *Aladdin*, and revivals [in the case of *Cabaret* in New York, a revival of a revival]).

Indeed, the era of the known entity was holding steadfast with an ever-tightening grip. Even proven creatives such as William Finn were hard pressed to have their work produced on the Big Boards (*Little Miss Sunshine* received an off-Broadway bow), let alone most of the up-and-coming writers. Two of Andrew Lloyd Webber's shows generated so little interest that an over-the-pond transfer (once a shoo-in) was unthinkable.

Other revealing events were occurring, however, that not only epitomized the requisite slog along the road of modern-age musical financing, but also hinted at new trends that could be construed as a swerve in the more traditional trajectory of traveling a show to the main stem.

Like a saga that would normally play out in far different confines, the age of American corporate financial misrepresentation and malpractice penetrated Broadway when a major transfer from Europe was befouled and run ashore by investor misbehavior. *Rebecca* (by Michael Kunze and Sylvester Levay) was to have been at front and center of the 2012 Broadway season after setting Vienna ablaze for three years. Just days before rehearsal was to begin in New York the show was scrapped when it was revealed that much of the promised financing wasn't to materialize, and in fact, had never existed. Also significant about *Rebecca*, however, was that a show developed in Austria, an opera and concert music hub, was deemed Broadway ready and tapped for a New York production, an occurrence that foretold a novel trend.

The announced Broadway transfer of *Rocky* (music and lyrics by Stephen Flaherty and Lynn Ahrens) from a developmental process and run in Germany with an American creative team at the helm definitely stated that new musical theatre no longer required trying out on U.S. or English soil prior to a commercial run in those places. (Other shows of European origins outside London had transferred before, but mostly with Europeans at the helm.) Working it out elsewhere was more cost-effective, but it was also a more cloistered event, removed from those pariahs who thrive on rumblings of how badly it's all going.

Rocky made an impressive entrance on Broadway in the spring of 2014 (but didn't last long), and that season and the seasons just

Other notable shows and songs from 2001 to 2013

Show, Year, and Songwriters	Notable songs	Also of note
Urinetown (2001) Mark Hollman/Greg Kotis	"It's a Privilege to Pee," "Follow Your Heart," "Run, Freedom Run"	The satirical 2002 Best Score Tony winner and unexpected Broadway hit by way of the New York International Fringe Festival.
Dirty Rotten Scoundrels (2005) David Yazbek	"Chimp in a Suit," "Oklahoma?," "Here I Am," "Love Is My Legs"	In New York, Norbert Leo Butz won a much-deserved Tony Award for his uproarious portrayal of Freddy Benson in Yazbek's first outing since *The Full Monty*.
The 25th Annual Putnam County Spelling Bee (2005) William Finn	"My Friend the Dictionary," "I'm Not that Smart," "My Unfortunate Erection," "I Speak Six Languages," "The I Love You Song"	Witty and charming, this audience-interactive show charmed tourists and locals alike for nearly three years at New York's Circle in the Square.
Mary Poppins (2006) Richard Sherman/Robert Sherman/George Stiles/ Anthony Drewe	"Chim Chim Cher-ee," "Practically Perfect," "A Spoonful of Sugar"	The Broadway production more than doubled the length of the run in London that closed after just over three years.
The Drowsy Chaperone (2006) Lisa Lambert/Greg Morrison	"Show Off," "As We Stumble Along," "Bride's Lament"	A one-act-er that starred Sutton Foster and bookwriter Bob Martin as "the Man in Chair" who seeks a remedy for his "nonspecific sadness."

Show (Year) / Composer	Songs	Notes
Legally Blonde (2007) Laurence O'Keefe/Nell Benjamin	"Omigod You Guys," "Serious," "So Much Better," "Legally Blonde"	This stage version of the Reese Witherspoon film did for young girl theatre-goers what *Annie* had done for them thirty years earlier, minus orphan moppets and an exceptionally long run. It is another favorite of the regional theatre and school troupe circuit because of an appealing pop score and light-on-its-feet sensibility with a strong message of empowerment.
Xanadu (2007) Jeff Lynne/John Farrar	"Magic," "Suddenly," "Xanadu"	An example of a musical that parodies the film on which it is based, chortling at itself along the way. Terrific fun.
Curtains (2007) John Kander/Fred Ebb/Rupert Holmes	"Show People," "I Miss the Music"	Two of the original creators died before completion of the writing of the show; Rupert Holmes provided a completed and revised book and some lyrics for the departed Peter Stone and Fred Ebb.
The Little Mermaid (2007) Alan Menken/Howard Ashman/ Glenn Slater	"Part of Your World," "Her Voice," "Beyond My Wildest Dreams," "Les Poissons"	The overhauled 2012 European version added aerial effects to simulate the underwater sequences and tightened the storytelling, thereby ensuring that audiences were plentiful after a stunted New York run.
9 to 5 (2009) Dolly Parton	"9 to 5," "Backwoods Barbie," "Shine Like the Sun," "Get Out and Stay Out"	After the icy reception in New York, the show toured anyway, revamped and with a new director, Jeff Calhoun, who also directed the U.K. tour. Regional theatres, perhaps because of the recognizable title, have clamored to produce it after Broadway and the road shows.

(continued)

Table Continued

Show, Year, and Songwriters	Notable songs	Also of note
Motown (2013) Berry Gordy/Various	"Ain't No Mountain High Enough," "Dancing in the Street," "I Can't Help Myself," "I Heard It through the Grapevine"	A cavalcade of songs drawn from the great catalog of the record label strung together with biographical material from Gordy's personal timeline.
Cinderella (2013) Richard Rodgers/Oscar Hammerstein II/Douglas Carter Beane	"In My Own Little Corner," "Impossible," "Ten Minutes Ago," "A Lovely Night," "Do I Love You Because You're Beautiful?"	The old girl as Rodgers and Hammerstein imagined her (well, more or less) finally set slippered foot onto a Broadway stage some fifty-six years after the original written-for-television version. Here, Douglas Carter Beane wrote a more fleshed-out book for a show that seemed to have played onstage everywhere (including tours in the United States and Asia) except Broadway. Even newly minted versions of old Rodgers and Hammerstein songs made their way in.

prior also held a good number of other pleasures. *A Gentleman's Guide to Love and Murder*, the epitome of theatrical stylized ingenuity, had been struggling to fill seats until winning the Tony Award for Best Musical 2014, becoming the theatre's little-engine-that-could that year.

A season prior, *Matilda* was a Dennis Kelly/Tim Minchin musical adaptation of a children's novel that sounded choruses of youthful empowerment and kept plenty of show-biz kiddos employed. The show boasted a career-making performance by Bertie Carvel and a handful of tunes that resonated with both children and grown-ups, songs such as "Pathetic," "Revolting Children," and "When I Grow Up." The show was an immense hit in London, winning the most Olivier Awards for a musical in the award's history, but in New York it was kicked upstage that year by *Kinky Boots*, the Harvey Fierstein/Cyndi Lauper tuner and another show with liberation themes moving through its veins. *Kinky Boots* was based on the 2005 film about an English shoemaker who hatches a plan to save his factory by manufacturing the particular flavor of shoe that appeals to the drag queen and then enlisting an authentic one for first-hand (foot?) consult. Later, the two discover that they have a great deal more in common than first met the eye, and most importantly, a more informed sense of how it feels to walk a mile in another man's, well, boots (for other notable shows and songs from this time period see chart on p. 74).

Get it done

Throughout the remainder of this book, "Get it done" sections will be presented. These are designed to facilitate your putting into action the concepts and strategies discussed in the pages that precede them.

Already discussed at length is the importance of placing historical context on your song material. Consider the songs that you are currently singing and answer the following questions, referring back to previous pages as needed.

1   What are the musical theatre historical time frames that each of your songs falls under (e.g., 2001 to present, the 1940s, etc.)? Use the publication date, often located at the bottom of the first page of your sheet music if purchased as

an individual song, to determine this or run an Internet search to do so.

2   What musicals are your songs from, and what are examples of other shows from the same period? Since not all shows are mentioned here, a little additional digging may be necessary.

3   What significant world events were occurring/had occurred around the time frame when these songs were written?

4   Did the shows that your songs are from set any precedent, or were they significant in musical theatre history for any reason? Why?

5   Do many or all of the songs in your repertoire book fall within roughly the same time frames of musical theatre history, or are they far enough apart to allow diversity in your book of songs?

CHAPTER TWO

Song Selection for Singing Actors Part I:

What to Sing and Where to Find It—the Philosophical

"A song should never reveal the singer's inability to sing it."

—DAVID CRAIG

It's possible that no other step toward delivering a song to performance-level readiness can be as puzzling and clouded with conjecture and subjectivity as the initial step, that of choosing it to begin with. This is true particularly for auditions where song selection emphasis is placed within these pages for practical purposes.[3] It can be at best daunting, and at worst, flat-out bewildering to try to locate and select those bravura songs that get the job done right in getting you seen and heard most favorably. The question of which songs to be included in your repertoire may incessantly preoccupy you on your quest of matching your vocal self to the song ("What are my greatest vocal strengths and how do I show them off in such a limited duration of time?") and your physical realities to the song ("What 'type' am I?").

The problem is compounded in the modern musical theatre (unlike the theatre of yesteryear) where you have the option of auditioning for shows with such a variety of formats and widely varied stylistic requirements. In fact, it wouldn't be at all unusual in modern musical theatre to attend an audition for a show that is written in the "pop," the "traditional," or the '50s style and beyond, all within a few days' time. You, as a modern musical theatre performer, should expect to encounter this scenario and prepare a diverse, well-chosen, and well-rehearsed arsenal of representative songs for your audition rep "book."

Adding further to this complex equation, it seems that there is never a shortage of opinions from teachers, coaches, and others as to what makes a "good" or "great" song, especially for audition purposes. If you polled a panel of well-informed showtune-a-philes as to what the elusive "magical" ingredients are, you might well get a perplexing variety of answers, thereby muddying the waters all the more. This would be understandable. Most who are qualified to answer this question have probably already taken the time to answer it for themselves and may have set feelings about the matter. Some would say that the crafty singing actor should prowl the archives of musical theatre libraries for lesser-known show songs not performed all that often (obscure songs), and others might say that it's better to sing something that has at least a passing familiarity. It's also in vogue to have an opinion as to which songs are overused and overperformed, and many seem to have (often conflicting) opinions about this.

Adding to the pile-on, some would say that, as a general rule of thumb, it's always best to give an indication of the singer's highest notes in his singing range when auditioning, and others would say that it isn't all that important to do so. Some declare that song choices should be entirely text and dramatically driven and/or derived from the singer's personal life experience, while others might assign little merit to that point. Most confusing of all, some will say that you're an apple when you've always been told that you're an orange but really think of yourself as a plum. What the eye and ear behold is often a curious thing, especially in show business.

Personal taste toward song styles, content, and presentation is nearly always a component in these purportedly objective answers as well. Some individuals believe that stormy, brooding, torchy songs that dig deeply under the skin of the singer and into his aching psyche tend to make for enticing song performance experiences.

Others might feel that peppy up-tempos cast the most favorable light. Some prefer to keep company with Richard Rodgers and Oscar Hammerstein II or Alan Jay Lerner and Frederick Loewe songs over those of Jerry Herman, while some would rather go to Michael John LaChiusa's *Wild Party* than Andrew Lippa's.

What is clear amid the array of questions and opinions is that, unlike the classroom in which material may be assigned to the student for the purpose of living outside of his own skin (or perceived "type") for a while, audition material should decidedly be reflective of the performer's "real" self and his sensibilities in *this* specific moment for *him alone*. It should function within the realm of the performer's own reality and bear his own indelible thumbprint.

What's more, there is a staggering amount of show music in practically every conceivable musical style to choose from, and an astonishing amount of pop and rock music that once inhabited the radio airwaves has been repurposed for the modern musical theatre. More pointedly, in the last sixty years, the diversity of song styles utilized in musical theatre has evolved from some relative uniformity to be so wide-ranging that an actor making song choices could understandably feel paralyzed by the options. The music of virtually every decade of popular song and style holds an essential place in today's musical theatre, and the modern musical theatre performer must deliver it with facility, proficiency, and bravura. In bygone days, it may have been sufficient for an actor to have in his song catalog an up-tempo or two, a ballad, and, just to change things up a little, a "standard," such as one from the 1930s or the 1940s popular music era. No longer. Because the musical theatre now encapsulates every musical style imaginable, the modern actor must be well versed in as many styles as he is able to excel at.

When speaking of song "styles," I don't refer only to the brand of the song itself by classifying it with such names as "legit ballad" or "contemporary up-tempo" (more discussion about the meanings of these designations lies ahead), but also to the *material within the material* that has decidedly matured. Today's singing actor has choices of material at his disposal that range from relatively lightweight old-fashioned songs to songs that probe and exploit the innermost, deeply personal, and revealing elements of character. Stephen Sondheim, one of musical theatre's most treasured assets, remarked that audiences attending his shows that had previously attended the theatre for "escapist" entertainment were bewildered to now be seeing their own lives onstage in an art-imitates-life interchange. Perhaps the second half of the twentieth century was to the musical theatre what verismo was to opera a century earlier—a decided and calculated movement toward the execution of realism in content terms.

With all of this wooziness twirling around, it's natural that a singing actor might find comfort and refuge in definitive answers about what and where the great song choices are. I don't believe anyone can answer that with surgical precision or with any universal or collective answers, but I do have a very clear idea of where to look for them based on both the criteria of the song style and the type of actor who will be singing them. I also have keen notions about how to proceed once those songs have been found. Everything in between is as individual as the individual himself. Moreover, I don't believe that any one variety of song makes for better choices than another as some would espouse, but I do believe that what makes a great presentation of a song lies within the person who sings it. I have seen great songs bomb and mediocre songs land winningly as the result of an unfocused or compelling performance. Song choices should be made based entirely upon the actor who is singing them and what that actor does exceedingly well in tandem with what he is singing them for.

A good rule of thumb when selecting songs is to always choose and play *toward* your strengths and *away from* your weaknesses. In order to do that, an actor must have an ironclad idea of what *both* are for him personally. Or, stated another way, never let them see what you can't do.

Further, perhaps not as important as who some others tell you that you are ("You'll always play the femme fatale!") is who you believe yourself to be and aspire to keeping your options open and never limiting yourself. You should also keep in mind that whatever any of the naysayers or dosayers proclaim, *you are entitled to filter, edit, dispose of, or use their opinions. If it doesn't "feel" right to do it, don't.* After all, you're an actor, and above all, the actor must know himself and his current strengths and limitations well. Having said all of that, my belief is that, in the casting game, an actor should nevertheless garner particular ideas about and embrace who he likely is in others' eyes and thereby obtain a sense of what roles he is likely to be cast in. To that extent, he should choose audition material accordingly.

To that end, I offer a caveat: The lines in the "type" sandbox have blurred in recent years, and active efforts are repeatedly being made to cast contrary to convention, or formulaic "type," both much to the credit of visionary directors and producers. Casting minorities, for example, in roles that were formerly reserved for "like" types is growing more commonplace in the theatre, and the traditional brands of "type" no longer exist as a hard-and-fast, time-honored formula. Nevertheless, the assignment of type is still very much present within a majority of contexts, and for this reason, the actor is again advised under such circumstances to understand his overall "brand," all the while keeping an open mind and focusing his efforts upon his message (more discussion of these points lies ahead).

In elaborating on the earlier point as to the advice that some have received regarding searching for rare, unfamiliar songs to use, particularly for auditions, I maintain that if nobody knows them, there may be a good reason for that. I encourage you to judge a song on its own merits rather than taking the leap only because it isn't performed with great frequency or few have heard of it. Additionally, while I believe that digging beneath the surface to search out songs is an excellent idea, I don't believe the process needs to be obsessive and extreme the way that I have seen some approach it. I also know that there is no shortage of candidate songs and that there is an abundance of songs that make interesting and compelling audition pieces that aren't over heard. These can be found everywhere, from well-known to lesser-known shows to shows that have outright bombed. Finding them is only a matter of ferreting them out through researching, listening, and determining if they are the right song vehicle *for you*. These songs, in every style and era, are more readily accessible than ever before by viewing and listening to them on the Internet and by purchasing recordings and sheet music online. Why is it important to make song choices outside of the obvious and well-known selections? In part, because doing this supports your individuality and originality and shelters you from a surplus of comparison to others' renditions of the song. There are a few useful strategies to assist you in knowing where and how to look for new music to complement your individual attributes, and they are outlined as follows:

1. If you know what you are seeking for your book of songs or a particular audition/presentation with regard to the style of song (a contemporary ballad, for example), a smart bet is to explore the work of a composer who writes or wrote in that style (in this case, Andrew Lloyd Webber, Benj Pasek and Justin Paul, Andrew Lippa, Adam Guettel, Frank Wildhorn et al.); but don't explore only those entries that appear first when doing an online search as those will invariably be the composer's best-known works. The same can be said for searching through recordings. There are plenty of excellent songs to be discovered if you'll just dig deeper.

As another example, if you're seeking a "traditional" musical theatre song, the logical place to look for material is in the worlds and works of writers such as Richard Rodgers and Oscar Hammerstein II, Harold Arlen, Jerome Kern, and more recently, Charles Strouse and Jerry Herman. From writers of this ilk, there will be no dearth of songs or shows to choose from. As you mull over choices and keep landing in their hit shows, keep in mind that even Babe Ruth didn't hit a home run each time at bat, and that with all of these luminary composers' many enduring creations, a few (and in some cases, *most*) of their shows didn't run. This fact, however, certainly doesn't disqualify the songs from those shows, many of which will have merit all their own as stand-alone entities, independent of the ill-fated vessels from which they are drawn. In fact, I know of very few shows that have closed because of a "bad" score, although having one certainly didn't help. The problems the show suffered were usually related to libretto, direction, concept, and structure. For example, in the case of Richard Rodgers and Oscar Hammerstein II, the maverick hit-makers of the Golden Age, the natural instinct might be to look for songs in *Carousel, South Pacific*, or *Oklahoma!*, but the trouble is that these shows contain extremely well-known songs that are often performed, especially in audition rooms. A more rewarding strategy may be to look closely at these composers' shows that aren't as intimately known. *Allegro*, one such example, ran only 315 performances during 1947 and 1948, but contained many first-rate songs such as "So Far," "The Gentleman Is a Dope," and the beautiful "Come Home." *Me and Juliet*, another Rodgers and Hammerstein misfire, left us with "We Deserve Each Other," "It's Me," "No Other Love," "A Very Special Day," and "That's the Way It Happens." *Pipe Dream*, reportedly Hammerstein II's most insufferable offspring, also provided a fair amount of outstanding remnants such as "Sweet Thursday," among others, all of which might serve as sensible alternatives to songs that many singers will favor. It should not be overlooked that Richard Rodgers, following Oscar Hammerstein II's death, continued to spread musical prosperity through shows such as *I Remember Mama* and *Two by Two* (both with lyrics via Martin Charnin), *Do I Hear a Waltz?* (lyrics by Stephen Sondheim), *Rex* (Sheldon Harnick), and *No Strings* (for which Richard Rodgers himself provided lyrics). Even if these shows were less than stellar theatrical excursions, the scores provided memorable and vibrant song material in rich numbers.

Similarly, Jerry Herman, who is best known as the songwriter for *Hello, Dolly!*, *Mame*, and *La Cage aux Folles*, wrote a number of shows that were not well received by critics or audiences, and therefore did not have a lengthy run, yet had a score inclusive of many wonderful songs. One such show, *Dear World*, which had the boundless talent of Angela Lansbury onboard but still couldn't be saved, originally ran only 132 performances in New York. Despite its abbreviated run, the score held rich offerings such as "Kiss Her Now," "I Don't Want to Know," and "I've Never Said I Love You." Other Herman outings supplied lingering song impressions. *Milk and Honey*, *The Grand Tour*, and *Mack and Mabel* may be unfamiliar to all but the most astute musical theatre fanatics, but were also musically prosperous. A number of Herman's off-Broadway revues of the late 1950s and 1960s may also be appetizing song material to explore.

Other traditional song or traditional-sounding songwriters deserve attention: Let it not be forgotten that Alan Jay Lerner and Frederick Loewe together wrote *The Day before Spring*, *Paint Your Wagon*, and *Gigi*; Sheldon Harnick and Jerry Bock collaborated on the wonderful *Fiorello!* and *The Apple Tree* as well as *Tenderloin* and *Baker Street*; and Charles Strouse, known mostly for *Annie* and *Bye Bye Birdie*, wrote terrific scores to (among others) *All American*, *Golden Boy*, *Dance a Little Closer*, and *Rags*. Finally, it should be remembered that *Gypsy* and *Funny Girl* star vehicle song impresario Jule Styne also wrote fabulous scores to *Gentlemen Prefer Blondes*, *Bells Are Ringing*, *Do-Re-Mi*, and *Hallelujah Baby!*, among others. All of these, along with a host of others, contain songs that deserve serious consideration as possible additions to your repertoire.

2. Look for shows whose content and/or style matches, however roughly, the type of content and song styles that you perform well and want to use as a general audition song, or whose content resembles the type of show you are auditioning for. For example, if you excel at "pop" theatre "power ballads" or are auditioning for a show that engages this style (like *Les Misérables*, Andrew Lloyd Webber shows, Disney/Alan Menken shows, and so many others), you may have noticed that there aren't many songs out there to choose from that aren't done to death, and you'd probably be right. It seems like every guy who excels at singing in this style has, or has had, songs such as "Out There" (from the Disney film *The Hunchback of Notre Dame*) or "Lost in the Wilderness" (from *Children of Eden*) in his repertoire book at one time or another, and it's perhaps best to avoid the often-heard, obvious choices. Women are no exception and immediate "go-to" examples might include songs such as "I Dreamed a Dream" or "On My Own" (from *Les Misérables*), songs from *Wicked*, and Andrew Lloyd Webber creations such as "Unexpected Song" (*Song and Dance*). But the fact is that there are many viable options to replace these songs. Frank Wildhorn has written some of them for shows that aren't as popular as his *Jekyll and Hyde* (which contains several songs you'll want to avoid, such as "This Is the Moment" and "Someone Like You" for men and women, respectively), and these shows are suitable places to look for new material in this style. Despite a respectable run and cast recordings, surprisingly few people know the music of *The Scarlet Pimpernel* with its several plum "power-ballad" songs. Other Wildhorn offerings, such as the short-lived *The Civil War* and the more recent blink-and-you-missed-them *Wonderland*, *Dracula*, and *Bonnie and Clyde* (not to mention scant-produced works such as *Camille Claudel*), are also quite worthy of exploring. These shows hold a few polished pearls (although I am convinced that *Pimpernel* remains the bonanza of the lot) as do a number of recordings that Wildhorn muse Linda Eder has turned out as well.

Still other shows that didn't run or even make it to the mainstream count as probable places to explore. With a score by the creators of *Les Misérables* and *Miss Saigon*, *The Pirate Queen*, for example, which had a distressed and stunted run in New York in 2007, delivered several wonderful songs for both sexes as did the same team's *Martin Guerre*. When it comes to more big-throated song ideas, you might also explore as starting points the likes of shows such as *Sideshow*, *9 to 5*, *Jane Eyre*, *Lestat*, *Triumph of Love*, *Taboo*, *Brooklyn*, *A New Brain*, *A Tale of Two Cities*, *Heathers*, and so many others, like the newer shows of the up-and-coming writers listed below. Another savvy place to peruse are the not-sung-to-death animated film scores of Stephen Schwartz and Alan Menken and their collaborators. Menken's lesser-known stage creations such as *Weird Romance* and *King David* or *Leap of Faith* also hold prosperous offerings. Even the late Marvin Hamlisch had several pop-styled, big-ballad shows that fell to the critics' pen (or simply couldn't find an audience), but had memorable contemporary scores very worthy of consideration, *Smile, The Goodbye Girl*, and *Sweet Smell of Success* among them.

3. Don't make the mistake of relying solely on shows that have been on Broadway and/or played the West End for your resources. Shows that have played off-Broadway, in workshops, at fringe theatres, and off the beaten paths of New York, London, and elsewhere are all fair game. In this current era, shows finding their way to the Big Boards have become the exception rather than the rule, leaving a great worthy quantity of shows with first-class material by established household name writers and the not-so-recognizable ones, too. Shows such as *Ordinary Days* (Adam Gwon), *A Man of No Importance* (Stephen Flaherty/Lynn Ahrens), *A New Brain, Romance in Hard Times, In Trousers* (William Finn), *The Spitfire Grill* (James Valcq/Fred Alley), *Summer of '42* (David Kirshenbaum), *Dogfight* (Benj Pasek/Justin Paul), *Whoop-dee-doo* (Dick Gallagher/Peter Morris/Mark Waldrop), *Hedwig and the Angry Inch* (Stephen Trask), *The Toxic Avenger* (Joe DiPietro/David Bryan), *Tick . . . Tick . . . BOOM* (Jonathan Larson), *Bat Boy* (Laurence O'Keefe), and even lesser-knowns such as *See Rock City and Other Destinations* (Brad Alexander/Adam Mathias), *Homemade Fusion* (Michael Kooman/Christopher Dimond), *Here Lies Love* (David Byrne/Fatboy Slim), and *The Other Josh Cohen* (David Rossmer/Steve Rosen) are a small sampling.

4. Explore up-and-coming theatre songwriters' websites and browse audios and videos of their songs being performed. Most all have demos of their work, and often sheet music to the songs can be purchased directly on the site. In addition, YouTube and other sharing sites frequently provide ample clips of a writer's work. Websites such as New Musical Theatre.com and Contemporary Musical Theatre.com are also invaluable to this end. Be sure to explore writers like those listed here (and this is an ever-growing

collection), keeping in mind that some of these writers[4] collaborate with others and/or sometimes go it alone.

5. Listen to and explore the readily available song collections of established contemporary writers such as John Buccino, Marcy Heisler and Zina Goldrich, Fred Silver, Ricky Ian Gordon, and Tom Lehrer and those of previous generations such as Noël Coward, Kurt Weill, and Noel Gay. These writers are widely recognized for their compelling musical composition and inspired storytelling skill. While not all of their songs make appropriate audition material whether by reason of complexity, content, and/or length, many do and deserve your interest. Additionally, many of the more recognizable theatre writers (Cole Porter, Jule Styne, Frank Loesser, Charles Strouse et al.) also have song compilations available, usually assembled by the publishers or an independent party; and most of these collections contain lesser-known gems of songs, many of which were cut from shows.

6. It's always helpful to explore the recordings of singers who sing in the styles that you also excel at. Bernadette Peters, for example, has recorded many a worthy song within her solo recordings independent of cast recordings as has Audra McDonald (for both "legit" singers as well as "belters"). When it comes to material from eras past, you might want to poke about the recordings of any number of memorable performers such as Michael Feinstein, Bobby Short, and Mary Claire Herran, all of whom have extraordinary performances of these songs on disc and some on video.

7. Choosing "pop" songs: Again, avoid the "greatest hits" of any singer/songwriter for reasons already discussed. You might wish to explore the artist's yesteryear recordings/songs before he "made it" or songs on the CD that aren't well known. Another good strategy is to explore songs similar in nature to the singer/songwriter who appeals to you. Apps such as Pandora are incredibly helpful here as are those suggestions that sometimes include demos that often appear on music purchasing sites ("You might also like. . .").

8. Finally, you'll remember from a previous section that a great number of musical theatre songwriters, particularly from the early 1930s through the mid-1940s, endowed Hollywood with its movie

musical song wares. I think most would agree that film songs are, by and large, acceptable as inclusions in your book of songs.

In general, the key to answering the questions of which songs "make the cut" for you individually and are worthy of pursuit should ideally be the result of what has been derived from your own personal experience and research, work done in the studio, and after a frank, objective, and reasonable assessment of just "who" you are. If, at this juncture, you feel bewildered as to what any of those answers precisely are, then don't worry. The following pages are designed to aid you in the navigation of the journey.

Song choosing aside, a successful song performance and audition are defined by many factors (and in the case of auditions, not always by getting the job), but the real key is getting—and keeping—your audience's and audition panel's attention. This is done not by magic tricks that you bring with you into the room (as some actors wrongfully assume), but instead by your ability to sustain an invigorated energy with your viewers, one in which the message you bring and put before them evokes specific, genuine, and truthful responses. In the case of auditions, if an auditor endures 300 auditions in one day (this is indeed possible), he may remember only a handful of them because so few have reached him in this way. If you, through the work that you do, have the auditor's undivided attention, you must then entitle yourself not to the job per se, as that will be determined by the auditors, but rather entitle yourself to *credibility*. When you assume absolute ownership of your song material, your entitlement to the job and getting the job will take care of itself through the work that you do in the room. The message that commitment and ownership of your material sends is, "Hey! It's not okay not to be paying attention to me right now, and I am showing you why." At the end of the day, if there is entitlement to be earned, then you should strive for entitlement to be paid attention to and remembered favorably because of the work that you turn out in the room. Making such an impression for auditions and in song performance in general is the subject of the following pages.

In making additional overtures to the next chapters of this book, and as a conclusion to this chapter, I restate that there is no one-size-fits-all prescription to song selection. Whatever songs you choose, do them with total authority, commit to them completely, and personalize them with the singular and distinctive "you," being highly attentive to the story being told. You will read these mantras time and again in different forms within these pages. This is all that anyone, including yourself, can ask of you, and one of the few things within your control in the audition room and in your performances. When done in this way, the returns can be exhilarating, and sometimes, even life-changing.

Get it done

1   For now, make some objective, sweeping generalizations about yourself (specifics and caveats will come later) and the kinds of roles you're likely to play, such as "I'm the offbeat 'character' man" or "I can play the girl roles that are brash and feisty." Couple those with broad assessments of your vocal capabilities such as "I have a high belt" or "My singing is very 'classical' sounding."

2   Contemplate the songs that are currently in your repertoire book. Do these specifically highlight the attributes you've described or are they more general and applicable to everyone? If the latter, consider refining your rep selections to more selectively highlight and support the traits you've determined so far.

3   If you feel that the songs you presently sing represent you well, ask yourself whether these are songs that many other singing actors might also have in their rep books. This could be because they are very well known, were provided by teachers who only know the basic musical theatre rep, and/or because the sheet music is readily and easily available. If you feel that the answer is "yes," utilize the strategies outlined here to provide you with more original choices.

4   Is there enough diversity in your repertoire book? Are all of your songs from smash hit musicals or are there selections from lesser-known shows, off-Broadway and fringe shows, and songs by writers who are up-and-coming? What about the "pop" songs in your book? Are they the "greatest hits" of those who sang them?

5   Do the selections included in your book allow for a fresh
    and unexpected approach in your delivery? Or is the text
    predictable, old news, or too limiting for crafty and
    attention-grabbing acting choices?

CHAPTER THREE

Song Selection for Singing Actors Part II:

The Song Is You—the Practical

The feeling's the thing

With all the hoopla that goes with song selection, it seems that at times the most fundamental and elementary questions are not given much thought. Sometimes, when we're choosing song material, particularly for auditions, we are so hung up on the kind of material that we think we *should* be choosing that we overlook the very reason that we sing in the first place—that we feel the urge to express ourselves through music and text to our listeners with a mission of summoning reciprocal feelings from them in return. But all too often only the latter half of this delicate tango is taken into account and we risk losing the "me" in the songs we choose, our real "selves" becoming eclipsed and upstaged by our own efforts to "wow" them. Preoccupied with "How does it make *them* feel?," we pay little or no heed to "How does it make *me* feel?" (to sing this song). The paradox is that if we don't feel an emotional connectivity to the songs we choose, then how can we possibly expect our audience to? It's a zero gain for all.

When choosing your song material, listen to it carefully and then sing it through. As you do, test the waters as to whether or not the content of the song passes the "I connect" test for you. Additionally, be certain that it is a song that you can fully grasp given your maturity both as an actor and as an individual. Even as you do this, ask yourself if a listener/viewer would "buy it" coming from you. A very young singer or someone who has never experienced the shredded nerve-ending longing for the touch of another couldn't credibly deliver Stephen Sondheim's "Losing My Mind" (from *Follies*) let alone a song such as "The Man that Got Away" (from the film *A Star Is Born*) in a convincing fashion, although I've seen some make the attempt in vain. Furthermore, theatre people have very acute antennae and can spot an imposter at twenty paces.

Another word on feeling: There is the matter of what you feel emotionally as a result of the singing of these particular words "from the inside" and the feelings generated from the visceral responses to the music, and there is also the matter of how you feel *when you are singing them.* Singing your songs should make you feel akin to when you wear a certain dress, suit, or shirt that you know you look attractive in and that turns all eyes in your direction. As you're exploring this, don't worry about a song being currently set in a certain key that is too high or too low for you to sing well or comfortably or a musical arrangement that isn't just-so. Keys can (and should when necessary) be changed for theatre music (although this remains a no-no in the opera world) to suit the singer's comfortable vocal range. A savvy vocal coach will help you tailor an arrangement to your needs and key specifications.

To summarize, of fundamental importance to your singing performance is the song's ability to generate from you an honest emotional response as well as that feeling that you look and sound at your best when singing it. Anything short of these just won't fly. If these aren't happening, move on to other exciting prospects.

It should also be taken under advisement that an audition panel should never have to bear witness to your "trying something on." Never take into the room a song that you haven't given yourself over to completely, comprehended at the deepest levels, had tailored to suit you in key and cuts, and haven't thoroughly well rehearsed. That work is reserved for and is to be done within the walls of the voice studio and your living room, not in an audition (or performance) setting.

Forget "type": Sing who you *are*

That indispensable actor's mantra "know thyself" doesn't only pertain to how you do, or perhaps, do not excel in your acting and singing disciplines, but also to factual and objective information about your physical aesthetic (or look).

Already discussed here, the traditional manner of casting, one that remains ever-present (but not exclusive) states that your body type, skin type, and age, in conjunction with your skill attributes, combine to reveal your perceived "type." These are perhaps governing factors in determining what roles and which shows are an appropriate fit for you. Or, to state it another way, within a customary casting template the roles you are *most likely* to play. Therefore, this wisdom implies that these combined attributes should inform the making of song selections ahead of auditioning for these brands of shows. I assert that, superficially, people see and hear what they see and hear, and that they tend to clump individuals into generalities (e.g., "He's a character actor." Or, "She's the leading lady type.") and support preparing material that frames, to a certain extent, what or who you are perceived as.

However, to elaborate on the earlier point, a dynamic force continues to rapidly evolve and is in play in current musical theatre as well as theatre in general. Contemporary writers rarely write archetypal roles or those known to fit a particular "type" or "mold." What is more, creative personnel, in conjunction with producers and casting authorities, are often actively and assiduously casting *contrary* to these traditional "norms," a practice frequently referred to as colorblind casting.[5] These facts can be as confusing as they are exhilarating, especially to the young singing actor as he strives to distinguish himself as one type or another in order to discern where he "fits" and how to market himself.

As a sweeping generalization, my belief is that you, the savvy modern-day singing actor, should honor both schools of thought. You will understand for practical purposes what your traditional type is[6] and how this categorization fits into a conventional casting scheme. Simultaneously, you will keep an open mind as to where you might fit in a more innovative less conventional format that is engineered by writers and casting authorities. As one casting director put it, allow your type to find you, all the while singing material chosen not merely because you *should* sing it ("This song is my type."), but rather because it coincides with personalized messages about your individuality, likeability, and personality that you wish to share with your listeners.

With all that has been elaborated on in this section, keep the following points in mind:

- Don't get hung up on what your type is. Understand the traditional standard molds of character types in old-school musical theatre and then let them go as absolutes. Shed the notion that you fit only into one or two categories. Embrace your own diversity, even if you are awaiting full realization of it, and allow creative types and casting persons to see you for who you might not think you are and decide for themselves such things.

- Make no assumptions. You don't know what the audition panel is looking for. Even when audition notices are exceptionally specific, circumstances change. Often this is because an actor has come along with the magic "it" and turns the direction that the casting was heading on its ear. Taking the best of yourself (the most affable, interesting, and honest version) into the room will carry you much further than fashioning an alternate version of yourself to suit what you *think* the auditors are looking for. Sometimes they don't know either. Additionally, if it turns out that they are not shopping for your product on this day, don't worry. I assure you that the creative team and casting associates have many more projects down the road, and they will remember you if you have made a strong and committed impression.

- Associate type with skill set. This is where you can peg yourself as one thing or the other. If you're a contralto voice type, then you are one. If you can shatter windows with your brassy tenor, then that is a fact. If you can turn a triple pirouette without batting an eyelash, then you should use this skill as a reason to attend auditions where this will be a selling point for you. Skill requirements for roles and shows are what they are, although they can sometimes be adjusted if the right performer comes along; and these will be more reliable identifying traits of who you are than superficial ones alone.

● Let others see you for who you are by singing selections that reveal you. Choose material that speaks to you and allows you to communicate a personal message about yourself. Music and text that resonate most resoundingly with you will foster honesty in the delivery that other material will not.

In the final analysis, the songs that are most worthy and useful to you must satisfy the criterion of having been selected because they are *of consequence to you personally*. They must serve as a vehicle for you to express and reveal yourself and your skills to the listener. *No song should be chosen solely on the basis of only framing type without these accompanying characteristics.*

Two final thoughts on choosing song material based on who you are: Whatever traits render you exceptional and especially memorable should be highlighted front and center for all to see and hear. If you're a female with an exceptionally high belt, then you should "sparingly" advertise that fact.[7] Similarly, if you are a male with a profundo basso, then show it off when and where appropriate. If you play broad comedy well, then let it be played, and if your quirky vulnerability frames who you are, then choose material that allows you the freedom to express the same. Be mindful that you are the CEO and marketing director of your unique product and that the objective is to attract buyers (in the form of interest and having been memorable from and to the audition panel).

Get it done

1 Do the songs you are currently singing or are contemplating singing make you feel, look, and sound at the top of your game in a competitive way? Why or why not?

2 Are there songs in your repertoire primarily because they suit what you believe to be your type and less because they reveal something of interest about you and/or your set of skills? If so, consider using the latter criterion to ferret out new songs by using the tools you have been given here that can perhaps accomplish both. Once this is done, key cuts and arrangements that fully support your work can be established and created.

What are the styles of songs that you need to prepare and include in your repertoire "book," how many, and why?

As you know by now, the modern musical theatre makes use of musical styles and strands of styles from virtually every common manner of musical expression. Rock and pop, jazz and blues, classical and operetta, country and folk (to all-out hoedown), Latin, rap, gospel, and "world" music are all heard on the musical theatre stage. This is in addition to the standard show-tune fare, which in common practice spans more than 100 years of musical and stylistic diversity and evolution.

In a performer's audition repertoire "book," or personal folio of prepared songs, it's usually unnecessary to include examples of all of these many musical styles and better to place emphasis on several commonplace styles and then on any additional singing styles through which you truly shine. For example, I know an actor who possesses a heaven-sent mellifluous baritone and also boasts an astonishing facility in the rock-a-billy style. In that type of situation, the inclusion of a song or two in the latter style in his book is advisable because his ability to impress in that style is a take-it-to-the-bank asset to him (see number 10 below). And, yes, there are shows that require that particular expertise. Additionally, when an actor is native to the style (such as Latin or what is known as "world" music), I advise him to prepare several selections in that style or styles.

Notwithstanding the above, for the majority of modern musical theatre performers, your book should contain at least one song (and in some cases, two songs) in each of the following styles. This is in order to meet the varied song style requirements that must be met when auditioning in today's musical theatre.

This course of action (to prepare one or more of each) is, of course, based on your individuality and your capacity to sing in the style winningly. If it's an unreasonable stretch, move on and focus your labors on those styles in which you do excel. Additionally, with regard in particular to the "pop" and "rock" singers and songwriters mentioned below, you should align your own sensibilities and vocal capacity to the songs and song style of a particular artist. Of course, older, more mature singing actors whose brand is a more appropriate fit in less youth-driven shows should prepare accordingly and may avoid, for obvious reasons, many of the categorizations below.

1. Two contrasting up-tempos (those with an energy that is bouncy and lively) from a Golden Age-era show,[8] such as those by Richard Rodgers and Oscar Hammerstein II, Richard Adler and Jerry Ross, Alan Jay Lerner and Frederick Loewe, Leonard Bernstein, Jule Styne, Sheldon Harnick and Jerry Bock, Frank Loesser, John Kander and Fred Ebb, Charles Strouse, and Jerry Herman.[9] (This is hardly an all-inclusive list of Golden Age composers, but rather a representative cross-section.)

The songs of these composers and their distinctive hallmarks, all markedly individual and exceptional, represent well the songs of the Golden Age and are consistent with audition song requirements of Golden Age-era Broadway musicals.

In choosing from the songs of this category, you must make selections congruent with the compositional aesthetic, vocal style and roles (whether "legit" or "belt"—see below), and demands of the show(s) you are auditioning for (e.g., a more typically "operatically" and dramatically sung selection from *West Side Story* is obviously an ill fit for the "show-bizzy," belty-razzmatazz song aesthetic found in many of the songs in a show such as *Chicago*). Perhaps, most importantly, you must choose in accordance with your individual vocal and/or dramatic prowess. There is no situation more unpleasant for the singer or for the auditor than witnessing a singer struggle through a song that is out of the range of his capabilities and/or sensibilities or that he otherwise fails to grasp.

A cross-section of commonly performed shows that the songs of the above-mentioned songwriters may be appropriate for include:[10]

- *South Pacific*; *The Sound of Music*; *The King and I*; *Carousel*; *Cinderella*; *Oklahoma!*

- *Damn Yankees*; *The Pajama Game*

- *My Fair Lady*; *Camelot*; *Brigadoon*

- *West Side Story*; *Wonderful Town*; *Candide*; *On the Town*

- *Gypsy*; *Funny Girl*; *Peter Pan*

- *Fiddler on the Roof; She Loves Me*

- *Guys and Dolls; The Most Happy Fella; Where's Charley?;
  How to Succeed in Business without Really Trying*

- *Cabaret; Curtains*

- *Annie; Bye Bye Birdie*

- *Hello, Dolly!; Mame; La Cage aux Folles*

- Stephen Sondheim shows (see Item 9)

- And shows such as *The Music Man; Oliver!; Kiss Me, Kate;
  The Fantasticks; Annie Get Your Gun; The Light in the
  Piazza; Once upon a Mattress; Babes in Arms; Finian's
  Rainbow; Show Boat; The Pirates of Penzance; Seven Brides
  for Seven Brothers; Sweet Charity; She Loves Me; Carnival;
  I Do, I Do; Man of La Mancha*; and possibly some modern
  "singer-ly" shows.

2. A "down-tempo" ballad or two from a Golden Age show, such
as from and sung for those listed above. These songs are indispensable
for the reasons cited below, and also as antidotes for those moments
when the "Do you have anything contrasting?" request is lobbed
across the casting table onto your side of the court.[11]

The inclusion of this make and model of song is most useful
under the following circumstances in order to illustrate the following
to the panel that you:

- the singing actor, possess the resources to be personally
  "revealing" and show a willingness to openly expose
  innermost private moments through song, particularly if
  your first offering has not revealed as much.

- are endowed with a vocal technique able to sustain and
  carry off the "singer-ly" musical phrases of a ballad.

- can "pull it in" and/or work from the "inside out" in a less
  presentational fashion.

3. *Two* (or possibly more, if this variety of show is where you earn
your bread-and-butter) contrasting Great American Songbook class
of songs, such as those written by Cole Porter, Irving Berlin, Richard

Rodgers and Lorenz Hart, George and Ira Gershwin, Harold Arlen, Nacio Herb Brown and Arthur Freed, Hoagy Carmichael, Vernon Duke, Duke Ellington, Sammy Fain, Jerome Kern, Thomas "Fats" Waller, Jimmy McHugh, Johnny Mercer, Arthur Schwartz and Howard Dietz, Jimmy Van Heusen, Louis Jordan, Harry Warren, Vincent Youmans, the writers mentioned above, if applicable, and many others.

The broadly defined Great American Songbook is a collection of songs by American (although some were American immigrants, they were unconditionally American at heart) composers roughly written between the early years of the twentieth century and the late 1950s (overlapping with the encroaching rock-and-roll revolution). Criteria for inclusion on this list are, to some extent, uncertain and nonquantifiable as to term any musical entity "great" is largely subjective. In the end, perhaps the public song buyers were the arbiters who determined the inclusions. Nevertheless, the Great American Songbook is an expedient term placed upon a group of perhaps thousands of songs written by a relatively small number of composers who consistently, through the craft of their songwriting, made an indelible impression on the American and world popular song landscape. You need barely scratch the surface of the musical theatre past and present to find these songs in shows written for the musical theatre stage within "original" storylines, offshoots, and shows derived from and/or structured around a song or group of songs and never-ending varieties of revues.

The singing actor will certainly find these songs useful when auditioning for many shows that predate the 1950s (and often beyond) that were written in the spirit and style of what is sometimes labeled as the "musical comedy." These songs (and in some cases, the shows they were written for and/or included in) are often of the highest old-fashioned order, having achieved that mantle of greatness by their persistent longevity and/or from their pure entertainment value.

Utilizing these songs and also a sizeable number of Golden Age-proper shows that contain songs that "play" as musical comedy numbers (e.g., *Damn Yankees*, *Babes in Arms*, *Where's Charley?*, etc.) in auditioning for shows such as the following is a sensible strategy:

- *42nd Street*
- *Ain't Misbehavin'*
- *Anything Goes*
- *Crazy for You*
- *Five Guys Named Moe*
- *George M!*
- *Me and My Girl*
- *Meet Me in St. Louis*
- *My One and Only*
- *Nice Work If You Can Get It*
- *No, No, Nannette*
- *On Your Toes*
- *Singin' in the Rain*
- *Sugar Babies*
- *The Boyfriend*
- *The Producers*
- *Thoroughly Modern Millie*
- Revues that compile the above composers' works (there are dozens of them, mainstays of stock, regional, and community theatre)

4. Two contrasting modern (again, the choosing of which depends on the vocal distinctiveness of the singer, and of course, the show you are auditioning for) contemporary up-tempo theatre songs such as those of Andrew Lloyd Webber, Alan Menken, Marvin Hamlisch, Stephen Schwartz, Robert Lopez, Frank Wildhorn, Jeanine Tesori, William Finn, Marc Shaiman, Stephen Flaherty, and Maury Yeston. Also not to be overlooked is the newer generation of up-and-coming theatre writers.

These songs are most useful when auditioning for a show such as:

- *A Chorus Line*
- *Aspects of Love*
- *Avenue Q*
- *Baby*
- *Blood Brothers*
- *Cats*
- *Dreamgirls*
- *Evita*
- *Falsettos*
- *Godspell*
- *Jekyll and Hyde*
- *Joseph and the Amazing Technicolor Dreamcoat*
- *Nine*
- *Once on this Island*
- *Pippin*
- *Ragtime*
- *Starlight Express*
- *Sunset Boulevard*
- *The Full Monty*
- *The Secret Garden*
- *The Wild Party* (Andrew Lippa)
- *Wicked*

5. Two contrasting songs written by and/or recorded by contemporary "pop" singers from the mid- to early 1970s and more recently. Singers and songwriters worthy of consideration for women include Pink, Sara Bareilles, Carrie Underwood, Michelle Branch, Fiona Apple, Avril Lavigne, Madonna, Cyndi Lauper, Deborah Harry, Mary J. Blige, Shawn Colvin, Britney Spears, Olivia

Newton-John, ABBA, and Carole King. Men should consider Duncan Sheik, Bruno Mars, U2, Elton John, Luther Vandross, Boy George, Kenny Loggins, Stevie Wonder, Paul Simon, Bob Dylan, and Simon and Garfunkel. Additionally, a song written and/or performed by one of the superstars of disco also isn't a bad idea, if you are appropriate for this.

These songs are useful to have on hand when auditioning for an exceedingly wide variety of contemporary shows as long as you have characteristically matched pop singer/songwriter to the show you are auditioning for (i.e., a Luther Vandross song at a *Spring Awakening* audition would seem an inappropriate choice):

- *Spring Awakening*
- *Beautiful*
- *Priscilla Queen of the Desert*
- *Kinky Boots*
- *Xanadu*
- *Next to Normal*
- *Footloose*
- *Mamma Mia*
- Certain "Jukebox" shows ("book" musical or revue)
- Contemporary musicals that ask auditioners to prepare a "pop" song
- Cruise ship and theme park shows

6. A 1950s–1960s-era song or contrasting songs, such as those written and/or recorded pop rock by The Beatles, Ellie Greenwich, Elvis Presley, The Everly Brothers, early Simon and Garfunkel, Jerry Leiber and Mike Stoller, Paul Anka, Diana Ross, and any number of girl groups so ubiquitous in this era. Also to be considered and included in this category are the songs of the clean-cut, tight harmony guy groups of the 1950s and onward that for a time ran concurrently with the onslaught of rock and roll. Many songs, most of which had a gentle beat in contrast with the more aggressive beat style of Elvis and The Beatles, are useful for shows set in this time frame.

In many respects, the songs of this particular era are in a stylistic category all their own, and seem pervasive in the modern musical theatre owing to the fondness for nostalgia-based book musicals set in or out of the era, and revues. Songs of this category are useful when auditioning for shows such as:

- *Grease*
- *The Rocky Horror Show*
- *Little Shop of Horrors*
- *Smokey Joe's Café*
- *Hair*
- *All Shook Up*
- *Jersey Boys*
- *Motown*
- *Memphis*
- *Forever Plaid*
- *Hairspray*
- *Beehive, Shout!, Leader of the Pack*, and similar revues

7. A "rock" or "hard"' contemporary-era song such as those written and recorded by Bon Jovi, Aerosmith, Billy Joel, Journey, Guns N' Roses, Queen, Meat Loaf, Elton John, The Who, Pink Floyd, and The Rolling Stones for guys, and, for women, Alanis Morissette, Joan Jett, Blondie, Aretha Franklin, and Janis Joplin.

The writers of the scores to some shows have made conscious decisions to present the score in its entirety in a rock format, whereas others include an occasional well-placed hard rock number driven by the situation and the character singing it. Dozens of contemporary musicals utilize this as a gadget of dramaturgy, and I make no attempt to supply an all-inclusive list here. The singing actor is advised to know his shows and roles well, and when appropriate, prepare one of these types of songs for shows such as:

- *Tommy*
- *Aida*

- *Rent*

- *Jesus Christ Superstar*

- *Rock of Ages*

- *We Will Rock You*

- *Hedwig and the Angry Inch*

- Many more, including revues and shows for cruise ships and theme parks

8. A Disney show song or song from a similar brand of film such as *Enchanted*, *The Hunchback of Notre Dame*, *The Prince of Egypt*, and *Tangled*. At one time, these songs might have fallen to the margins in theatre rationale. However, because of the ever-increasing popularity of Broadway musical-izing, these types of films, and the increasing number of prolific shows being penned by the composer/lyricist gurus of this genre (notably Alan Menken and Tim Rice), a separate category is integrated here.

Songs of this type are useful when preparing material to audition for shows such as those listed below, bearing in mind again that some shows use this style exclusively and some selectively:

- *Newsies*

- *The Little Mermaid*

- *Beauty and the Beast*

- *Mary Poppins*

- *The Lion King*

- *Sister Act*

- *Aladdin*

- Any number of other shows with music and/or lyrics by Andrew Lloyd Webber, Stephen Schwartz, and Tim Rice, to name a few (see Item 4).

9. Unfortunately, auditions for Stephen Sondheim shows crop up all too infrequently, and musical theatre ethos would be an all-the-more sanctified place if more theatres produced his work.

Nevertheless, these auditions do occur, and it's worthwhile to include one or more of these songs in your collection. When you consider the extent to which the songs can be so extraordinarily syllabic and word dense, so inescapably tethered to character that they edge toward sung dialog, and yet other times, so soaringly lyrical that they are approaching the operatic, you swiftly realize that the Sondheim style is difficult to match trait for trait, merit for merit with any other theatre composer. Even if your auditions rarely require musical selections that are as sophisticated as the Sondheim collection is, if you exert yourself assiduously to realize its many virtues, you'll become a better singing actor. I've not seen it fail.

Expect to see auditions with some regularity for at least four shows for which Sondheim supplied both the music and the lyrics (*A Funny Thing Happened on the Way to the Forum, Into the Woods, Sweeney Todd, Company*), others occasionally (*Assassins, A Little Night Music*), and others almost never, although the shows contain riches of mesmerizing material worthy of any well-planned repertoire songbook, including yours.

10. Song styles that boast any extraordinary skill, like the ability to play any or all brands of comedy particularly well, sing extraordinarily in a particular style (country, operetta, jazz, Latin, rap et al.) or styles not on this list, or any other remarkable vocal or performance facility that you believe should be showcased.

Belt and legit

The song types listed here, of whatever the compositional style, are (with exceptions) generally fashioned to be sung (and to some extent, classified in a vocal style known generically) as either "belt" or "legit," terms that will be broadened and refined in the section to follow.

These words, especially for females, are tossed about in the musical theatre with terrific frequency and should be clarified (if not satisfactorily defined as absolute) here. Like so much else, you're likely to accumulate a collection of diverse answers while on a quest toward having these terms made clear, as voice pedagogues and theatrical creative and casting types might well disagree as to the semantics. Before moving forward to the assortment of song and vocal styles used in the modern musical theatre that are, in essence, offshoots of these, I will attempt to make clear how these terms apply to you in practical terms, whatever the opinion as to true definition.

For women, casting notices may instruct you to prepare a "belt" song or "sixteen bars of a belt song" or to bring something to "show off your 'belt,'" or even indicate a specific note to "belt" to, such as "belt to an F." Broadly speaking, the vocal timbre characteristics of this style of singing vary from singer to singer and song to song, but may consist of a singing tone that is:

- "heavy"
- "twangy"
- "punchy"
- "chesty"
- "strident"
- "weighty"
- "thick"
- "piercing"
- "forward" in the "mask"
- "robust" or "loud"
- more "bright" than "warm"
- "nasally"

Some of musical theatre's most famous belters include Idina Menzel, Bernadette Peters, Eden Espinosa, Stephanie J. Block, Alice Ripley, Elaine Paige, Andrea McArdle, Liza Minnelli, Patti LuPone, and of course, belting icon Ethel Merman.

The "legit" sound and style is to some extent more instinctive to characterize as it is closely related to what most singers (male and female) understand as a singing tone that is:

- "warm"
- "beautiful"

- "lofty" or "vertical"
- "Bel canto" or Western "classical"
- "fluid" and "even"
- "pure"

Some of musical theatre's most familiar "legit" singers include Barbara Cook, Julie Andrews, Rebecca Luker, Audra McDonald, Brian Stokes Mitchell, John Raitt, and Norm Lewis.

It may illuminate the discussion to point out that the "belt" songs are, by some, often associated with the "chest" register of the voice (this is far too narrow a distinction in reality as we will see), and that some have described it, quite subjectively, as "yelling on pitch." "Legit" singing and "legit" songs, on the other hand, are most often associated with the more supple elasticity of the "head" register and the still "bright" but more tempered and "mix" (or middle) register of the female voice.

It is not my intention to exclude or minimize the men's vocal styles in this discussion, but the fact is that the situation for them is far less complex and is more intuitive. Argument aside as to whether or not the male voice contains a true "belt," you'll rarely encounter a casting notice requesting male singers to prepare a "belt" (although this phraseology seems to be gaining traction). More likely, the male singer will be requested to "show range" or to sing a selection that highlights his falsetto.

Get it done

1   Make a frank assessment of your repertoire book. Have you included enough songs in the varied styles listed above to represent any era and musical style that you may be auditioning for? What's missing?

2   Are there any musical styles included on the list in this chapter that are outside of your comfort zone and that you are purposefully avoiding? Would it behoove you to make some inroads into singing winningly in that style because there could be gainful employment for you therein?

3   Are there any musical styles that you excel in that are not included on this list? If so, contemplate highlighting and

representing those styles prominently in your repertoire book.

4   Particularly for women, make some generalizations about your voice pertaining to "belt" and "legit." Do you sing both? Equally well? Where are the holes in your facility for either? Use this assessment and have a forthright discussion with your voice teacher (if you have one) as to where you need to grow.

Beyond belt and legit: Understanding and performing the diverse song and vocal styles used in modern musical theatre

Our broadly drawn definitions of *belt* and *legit*, having to some extent been clarified here, are now in need of further streamlined categorization as they pertain to theatre singing today. The pages that follow constitute an effort to succinctly clarify and categorize (with these two vocal modes as foundation) the wide-ranging stylistic vocal ethos of today's musical theatre. More directly, the nail-biting melee of varieties of theatre songs coming at us these days begs a left-brained organization of the character and qualities of each of the musical styles used in musical theatre today. These extend several generations beyond the straightforward classifications of "belt" and "legit" without qualification.

What follows is an extended elucidation, relative but not all-inclusive, of the types of songs and vocal attributes of each heard in today's musical theatre. Its usefulness should not be underestimated as a tool of delineation helpful to theatre singers, creatives, and pedagogues on nearly a daily basis. I became aware of the usefulness of this list soon after articulating the distinctions; the adoption of these in my own studio greatly enhanced my concise communication with singers, directors, musical directors, other teachers and coaches, and creative types.

For purposes of the discussion, the song types most prevalent in the modern musical theatre include:

- The traditional mix-y[12] legit song
- The traditional heavy legit song

- The traditional mix-y belt song
- The traditional heavy belt song
- The contemporary legit song
- The contemporary mix-y belt song
- The contemporary heavy belt song

The traditional mix-y legit song

This type of song's easy and natural lyricism recalls music of the earliest days of the musical theatre. With its antecedents in light opera, the presence of this type of song on the stage extended well beyond the primeval stages of musical theatre through the integrated era and is still frequently utilized in today's theatre writing.

This variety of song may sound luxuriant, with somewhat elaborate musical lines and phrasing, or may be chipper and jovial. It may, and in many cases does, have an underlying gentle (or more substantial) toe-tapping beat. These songs often, but far from always, appear in comparatively light-hearted musicals or situations within them but do not necessarily indicate that the situation itself is lightweight, only that the character, via the songwriter(s), has chosen to express it in such a way.

Songs of this class occur throughout musical theatre from the old-fashioned "boy-meets-girl" harebrained musical comedies to the more multifaceted "tired businessman" musical "drama-dies" of the early 1950s to present day. The vocal style has been described as "trained" and even classical, but not leaning too heavily toward the operatic.

The terms "belt" and "legit" were coined especially to differentiate the heavier chest dominant singing style and the more "classical" head register dominant sound. As this distinction proved to be far too general and limiting, the term "mix" (literally a mix between the two, resulting in a sound neither too "classical" nor too "chesty")[13] came into fashion with a vocal tessitura in the middle range (neither too high nor too low).

Familiar songs that fall into the traditional mix-y legit category include:

- "Almost Like Being in Love" (*Brigadoon*)
- "I Could Have Danced All Night" (*My Fair Lady*)
- "The Simple Joys of Maidenhood" (*Camelot*)
- "De Lovely" (*Anything Goes*)
- "Mister Snow" (*Carousel*)
- "I Really Like Him" (*Man of La Mancha*)
- "Oh What a Beautiful Morning" (*Oklahoma!*)
- "Mira" (*Carnival*)
- "With Anne on My Arm" (*La Cage aux Folles*)
- "The Beauty Is" (*The Light in the Piazza*)

and multitudes more.

Vocal style/sound descriptors that often occur in the traditional mix-y legit song style

- a "warm," but not "dark" or unduly "heavy" sound (the distinction lies within a bright-ish "ring" in the tone and in the "chest weight" (thickness of the vocal cords) that is present but not dominant.

- a "vertical" (lofty) but nevertheless still rather "forward" sound that makes use of natural (not "pressed," for it is too charactery sounding) nasality.

- clean and purely formulated vowels, but not so much that the resulting sound is indulgent or overtly rounded (a too "classical" sounding aesthetic for this type).

- a "not too sung," conversational quality (The distinction here lies in the fact that the more "sung" it sounds the more attention the singer has given to precisely, seamlessly connecting one word to the next. On the other hand, the "conversational" approach is rather "choppier" and tends more toward the liberal usage of glottal stops and articulator interruptions, the moments that the column of breath, and therefore, the flow of the sung line are momentarily interrupted by stopping the outflow of breath).

- crisp consonant formations with particular weight often granted to final consonants (those that close or terminate a word).

It is important to note that all of the above can and will vary contingent upon dramatic intent and general disposition, and social factors within and around the character singing.

The traditional heavy legit song

While perhaps not as frequent a visitor to musicals as its mix-ier counterpart, this closer-to-"classical"-style brand of song does hold a prominent place in the musical theatre song repertoire. The dramatic tone and gravity of these "big-voiced" songs are informed by the often hefty dramatic topical matter that frames them. Often, they can be discovered well placed in musical dramas in moments of fever pitch.

These songs often require a more refined, perhaps profound and even near-operatic (another arguable point) vocal approach and beg to be sung by singers who are able to pull this off well as a matter of course. As in every brand of song, the variables of these points change, bend, and recalibrate in accordance with the variables of the character, situation, style of dramatic presentation, and of course, he who sings them.[14]

Examples of songs that fall into this category include:

- "I Have a Love" (*West Side Story*)
- "One More Kiss" (*Follies*)
- "The Impossible Dream" (*Man of La Mancha*)
- "Lonely Room" (*Oklahoma!*)
- "You Are Love" (*Show Boat*)
- "Climb Ev'ry Mountain" (*The Sound of Music*)
- "You'll Never Walk Alone" (*Carousel*)

- "If Ever I Would Leave You" (*Camelot*)
- "My Lord and Master" (*The King and I*)

Vocal style/sound descriptors that often occur in the traditional heavy legit style

- A "warmer" or "darker" and probably more "vertical" or "lofty" sound than mix-y legit.

- Vowel formulations that often are entities of uninterrupted clarity and more "classical" or "round" sounding in nature than those of mix-y legit.

- A "formality" of sound that no other musical theatre vocal style encapsulates so fully.

The traditional mix-y belt song

Again, the distinction of "mix-y" exists to clearly distinguish this type of song from its "heavy" alter ego. For example, a full-throttle delivery of a heavy belt number such as "Blow, Gabriel, Blow" (*Anything Goes*) is an altogether different affair than a still "brassy" but not as brash delivery of a song such as the more "mix-y" "I Cain't Say No" (*Oklahoma!*). The former inherently implores a fatter, more robust "belt" sound while the latter seeks a "chesty" sound that nevertheless doesn't carry as much punchy heft.

A distinction should also be drawn between "belting" and "twanging" (a "mask-y," "forward" sound that engages overt nasal tone) in this vocal style. Although it's erroneously thought by many that "belting" is the descriptor used to indicate a song to be sung only (or nearly only) in the "chest" vocal range (or that which is not the customarily "legit" soprano vocal range), the truest distinction of this style ("belting") lies within the aesthetic of the sound itself. Moreover, "belt" songs, those in a general sense often thought to be "chest" dominant, rarely (unless placed in a key that creates a low range vocal line) contain only the notes of the "pure chest" region (the exact specifications of which are slightly variable and arguable, but for ladies roughly F3 [below "middle" C] to F#4 or G4 [above "middle" C]). Most "belt" songs, in fact, venture in pitch upward beyond these notes, often as high as Es or Fs (an octave higher). When faced with this, is the singer truly being asked to "push" her pure chest register as much as an octave higher? Certainly not. And to do so would be detrimental to the singer's voice and agonizing to the listeners' ears. Occasionally, she might, when the sentiment of the song lyric supports the choice, "pop" a heavy chest note or two above and beyond the typical chest range, but the remainder of the time when singing above she is often "twanging" (see below) and navigating in and out of "belt" and "twang."

Some songs, however, require more vocal chest weight than others, contingent upon the traits of the character singing them and the dramatic situation within the song lyric. Those that require less weight and vocal beefiness (or perhaps more twanging than chest) can be called "mix-y" belt.

Examples of traditional mix-y belt include:

- "I'm Not at All in Love" (*The Pajama Game*)
- "A Little Brains, A Little Talent" (*Damn Yankees*)
- "It's a Perfect Relationship" (*Bells Are Ringing*)
- "This Can't Be Love" (*The Boys from Syracuse*)
- "The Lady Is a Tramp" (*Babes in Arms*)
- "I'm in Love with a Wonderful Guy" (*South Pacific*)
- "Always True to You (in my fashion)" (*Kiss Me, Kate*)
- "If I Were a Bell" (*Guys and Dolls*)

Vocal styles/sound descriptors and what the singer feels that often occur in the traditional mix-y belt style

- A "forward" placement (in contrast to the often more "vertical" or "lofty" sound of "legit") that lunges slightly into the facial mask. Nasality is engaged without being overtly nasal. Too much nasality is neither pleasant nor easy on the listener, although many musical theatre singers claim it as a trademark of their singing style.

- A "brassy," "twangy" tone that is brighter and shriller than its "warmer," "beautiful" legit counterpart. These characteristics, including the "forward" position discussed above, occur in part because of vocal tract positioning, particularly an often elevated laryngeal position and arched, elevated tongue position.

- A conversational, "talkish" quality that is perhaps embedded in "telling" mode more so than "singing" mode. The idea here is that the former sounds in a less "lyrical" place than the latter and has a natural delivery in the manner of "I have to tell you."

- A tone that has elasticity, pliability, and a naturally occurring vibrato that is anchored in a forward placement and that "mixes" the head and chest registers into one. Chest weight is present and more dominant than mix-y legit, but not as dominant as in heavy belt.

- The singer feels that "vocal reserves" are present, not singing at "full throttle."

The traditional heavy belt song

The heavy belt song will often come about when the character singing it is in an elevated state of mind or in crisis. This is likely the reason that such a great number of singing actors favor this song type, especially for auditions, but doing so creates a small assortment of risky scenarios discussed below and throughout this book.

In sound terms, this state may induce a full-bodied, nearly forceful output vocally, an unmistakable indication that the character is in a state of extreme. This type of song may also be paralleled in temperament of character terms. "Heavy" character roles are those that are, situational elements aside, often in keyed-up states of mind and/or are bigger than life as a matter of their daily activities. A cluster of women's roles of this ilk instantly come to mind: Mama Rose (*Gypsy*), Reno Sweeney (*Anything Goes*), Mama Morton (*Chicago*), Sally Bowles (*Cabaret*), Anita (*West Side Story*), and Aldonza (*Man of La Mancha*) among them. In the traditional era of musical theatre, as a vocal style there is ever-widening discussion of the "male belt," although men singers have been singing in such a punchy and aggressive approach probably since the companion song style of "legit" began. This fact requires discussion concerning the female belt where it is customarily heard and talked about in this song style. Male belting does, however, become a topic all its own in contemporary belt terms.

The heavy-handed situations and brash personality that these kinds of characters have or find themselves in naturally engender, in vocal style terms, a heavy and brash sound profile from the characters.

Representative traditional heavy character belt song titles include:

- "A Boy Like That" (*West Side Story*)
- "Maybe This Time" (*Cabaret*)
- "Aldonza" (*Man of La Mancha*)
- "Everything's Coming Up Roses" (*Gypsy*)
- "Blow, Gabriel, Blow" (*Anything Goes*)

Vocal style/sound descriptors and what the singer feels that often occur in the traditional heavy belt song style

The characteristics of this singing style share many similarities with the mix-y belt style, with notable additions:

- A vocal sound that is heard as consistently stout and heavy (in part, due to the increased thickness and density of the vocal folds [cords] in this style of singing) and is aggressive and seems to anchor itself in and engage the entirety of the upper torso and chest cavity, neck, and head, with high activity in the neck muscles.

- The singer may feel no sense of vocal reserves.

- A hard "punchy" quality at certain times, often when singing lower tones to upper tones.

- The singer may feel that the sound is often more yelled than sung.

- A sound that is sometimes shrill and strident in addition to robust and dense that comes about, in part, because of occurrences within the vocal tract (e.g., a high larynx position rendering a shorter vocal tract, a narrow pharynx, tongue positioning, etc.).

- There may be an absence of naturally occurring vibrato.

The contemporary legit song

To some, this division will seem a contradiction of terms. "Legit," sometimes pigeonholed both in compositional style and vocal aesthetic as the "old-school" musical theatre sound sung closer to the western "classical" style, seems not to share much in common with what some typically think of as "contemporary" music for the theatre. If pressed to assign descriptors to the latter, we might aptly answer that contemporary musical theatre music is a derivative intermingling of the many beat-driven styles of popular "radio" mixed with the sound indigenous to those who write it and dominated perhaps by "chesty" and "belty" singing.

A brief backward glance[16] reveals the writing of an abundance of theatre music that contains trademark characteristics of contemporary sounding music in tandem with vocal trademarks of the legit style. The present category has intermingled both mix-y and heavy as the hallmarks of the two should by now be evident. This music is immediately discernible not as the belty and beaty style of the modern radio era, but rather more akin to the easier, graceful, and often elegant musical sound of yesteryear and motivated by the same fundamentals. What is more, there is a considerable amount of theatre music written within the last few decades (and often by the same group of composers) that purposefully engages the legit vocal style with or without contemporary modifications, but also perhaps sounds as if it could have been written several decades prior. Therefore, a division is fitting, foggy as the lines may sometimes be. (Is song X contemporary or legit in light of the fact that it was written recently but sounds as if it could well have been written in the Golden Age?)

With all this as fodder for what to call this brand, perhaps it is most appropriate to intermingle the terms and declare that the style is, in fact, "contemporary legit." This style is especially deserving of an individual categorization here because, for auditions, when told to prepare a "contemporary" song, a singer handy in the legit style (and perhaps not quite comfortable singing in an aggressive contemporary vocal style) might turn to this kind for appropriate material.

Representative contemporary legit song titles/shows and composers include:

- "If I Can't Love Her" (*Beauty and the Beast*)
- "Children of the Wind" (*Rags*)
- "All I Ask of You" (*The Phantom of the Opera*)
  - and a fair amount of Andrew Lloyd Webber's scores for *The Phantom of the Opera*, *The Woman in White*, *Sunset Boulevard*, and others
- "On the Steps of the Palace" (*Into the Woods*)
  - and a great deal of Stephen Sondheim's output in general, but with some notable exceptions
- "Awaiting You" (*Myths and Hymns*)
  - and a large amount of Adam Guettel's music for *Myths and Hymns*, *The Light in the Piazza*, and *Floyd Collins*
- Other songs, such as "How Could I Ever Know" (*The Secret Garden*), "Empty Chairs at Empty Tables" (*Les Misérables*), and "The View from Here" (*Darling*)

Vocal style/sound descriptors that often occur in the contemporary legit song style

- may share much in common with both mix-y legit and heavy legit. However, modifications in phrasing and/or articulation may be present in order to contemporize the musical result. These may include more relaxed or conversational diction, phrasing that is more grounded within the character's innate thought processes and less within traditional musicality resulting in a more "natural" delivery.

- may engage a vocal quality far exceeding that of the "traditional" musical theatre sound that is derived from, and is a consequence of, disposition and status of character (how you sound is "who" you are).

- may depart from sung tones that sound "singer-ly" with a great deal of "loft" and overtly "heightened" or "vertical" tones or opt for a "warmer," more "classical" sound analogous to the "heavy" legit style. The inclusion or exclusion of these traits is contingent upon character, song, tessitura, and composer.

The contemporary "mix-y" belt song and the contemporary "heavy" belt song style

It would be convenient, as it was with "mix-y" and "heavy" legit as they pertain to the contemporary legit category, to conjoin the next two categories as one, having previously discussed the "belt" sound characteristics and descriptors in the old-fashioned style. However, in the last approximately forty-five years of popular music and musical theatre transformations, "pop" and musical theatre singing styles have undergone sweeping transformation, at least in part because the topical matter of musical theatre and the complexity of its characters have become much more far-reaching. "Belting" has evolved from a vocal aesthetic generally used by a performer of the "character" type and/or one who is in a state of extreme to a full-bodied and realized *dramatic device* all its own and spun out with its own merits.

The tried and true vocal characteristics of the belting style of yesteryear still boomerang off theatre walls worldwide, but have expanded to include ostentatious terms such as "power belt." Terms like this have evolved to describe the vocal representation and response of and to higher extreme dramatic situations and/or characters' emotional responses to them. Maybe this is because a great many volatile musical theatre characters and situations now inhabit an era in which it is hardly necessary to temper or filter raw emotional content. Instead, they often opt, sometimes fittingly and sometimes not, for the "hell hath no fury" route of "blood on the floor" delivery.

On the one hand, this seems as natural an evolution as Gioacchino Rossini to Giacomo Puccini or Oscar Hammerstein II to Stephen Sondheim. On the other hand, it means that vocal subtlety in song execution is an endangered concept if unabated heavy-throated delivery isn't used judiciously and *as entirely commanded by the text and the situation.* Failure to adhere to belting without good reason and/or because "everyone else is" is a fool's errand and one for which you might be punished with demerits in the audition room. In other words, save the big vocal guns for when they are needed the most.

The above crusade aside, and notwithstanding those that qualify as contemporary legit, contemporary musical theatre songs can generally be separated into two camps—the "mix-y" belt and the "heavy" belt. These may be delineated by the heft of the dramatic content therein, the extreme state of (s)he who sings it, and the resulting weight of the vocal sound. In general, the "mix-y" belt song is not your full-throttle vehicle, but may well have any number of full-throttle moments in which a heavy sound is appropriate. By contrast, the "heavy" belt song on the whole can easily register a ten out of ten a great deal of the time with any number of "mix-y" lighter, less hefty vocal passages.

Further clarification of what song material should qualify as "mix-y" or "heavy" belt can be found in the following guidelines: For women, the more extreme the state, character, or song (or phrase or line), the more extreme the sound, resulting perhaps in a "heavy" belt or nearly shouted vocal sound. For men, the same is largely true with an important addition of a vocal range consideration: Women rarely "belt" above or below what is essentially more than a one octave range, but for men, it is not uncommon to require them to extend that sound well over an octave.

Points of note and sound descriptors for the contemporary "mix-y belt" song

Theatre songs are conceived and constructed with a dramatic contour indigenous to scene/situation and character. This means that each phrase should be sung with the appropriate amount of vocal weight emphasis (heavy chest or a sound more mix-y "buoyant") as indicated by the text in that particular dramatic moment. This is true whatever the song era, traditional or contemporary, but the latter routinely dwells in a more vivid universe than its predecessor where the characters are often more dimensional, volatile, and revealing and their language more specific and direct. As a result, the singing (certainly the belting) tends to be more directly linked to the dramatic, and is often more extreme and even brasher than in bygone times. In addition, certain "rules" of "good" singing tend to be subverted in favor of a more "casual," "real," or "lifelike" approach (or some other effect). These facts must all be taken under advisement when studying the traits of the style.

A rule of thumb (in whatever the era, but perhaps especially, in the contemporary style) is to determine the amount of vocal weight to apply to your sound as if being directed by explicit punctuation markings (your own, and mostly exclamation points).[17]

If you think that a word, musical phrase, or entire section requires emphasis with one, two, or even three exclamation points, then most likely it requires the same equivalent in vocal weight; and "belting" plays its role in "mix-y" belt (the degree of heaviness depends on the number of exclamation points present in your version). For the other musical phrases, perhaps the points in the song that aren't so overtly emphatic, the mix-y, lighter dynamic blend of chest and head is most appropriate.

Of course, the musical accompaniment will give you highly explicit cues and should serve as your guide as well. The more intense the musical goings-on underneath the vocal the more is typically (with exceptions) expected from your vocal weight by the situation and the composer, who is always steering your delivery by what he chooses to write underneath. This is especially true of contemporary theatre music composers who more than ever tend to write accompaniment that echoes the unique psychology of the character and the moment. If, after exploring all of these indicators, you find that you aren't able to supply the necessary amount of vocal expertise to fulfill the composer's wishes, perhaps it is best to move on to another song more becoming of you with your present attributes.

Vocal style/sound descriptors and what the singer "feels" within the contemporary "mix-y" belt song

The sounds of this style and the sensations that the singer feels share much in common with those of the traditional "mix-y" belt. In rock- and pop-styled songs, there are several notable additions that sometimes occur:

- Diphthongs (see Chapter 6) are often present, although these should be utilized with discretion.

- More "swallow" or "pull/cover" may be present in the sound as though it is "sitting" on the back of the tongue rather than "high" and "in the mask," and/or a slight "yodel/pop" may be heard at the onset of the tone.

- For effect, rather than "spinning air" outward or "staying on air," those steadfast rules of "proper" singing, the singer may hold his air subglottally for the duration of long or held notes and release the air eventually or even not at all.

Examples of songs that fall into this category

The Rock/Pop Style	The Conventional Style
"The Bitch of Living" (*Spring Awakening*)	"Unexpected Song" (*Song and Dance*)
"Santa Fe" (*Newsies*)	"What I Did for Love" (*A Chorus Line*)
"Easy as Life" (*Aida*)	"Not for the Life of Me" (*Thoroughly Modern Millie*)
"21 Guns" (*American Idiot*)	

Points of note and sound descriptors for the contemporary "heavy" belt song

These songs are designed to make a no-mistaking-it impression that the singer is in an extreme state of mind (or perhaps is simply an intense personality type; some characters just "belt" because that's the bigger-than-life manifestation of who they are). They occur inevitably after spoken words and song can no longer ably do the job. They happen when a character needs to emphatically say to an audience that something HUGE is happening (or is about to happen) to/for them right now.

Sometimes they are called "power ballads," and there's a good reason for that: They hold a powerful place in the arc, or progression, of character and show by marking turning points and points of no return and/or musicalize the apex of the character's experiences. They may also frame what he is most longing for. Because of their naturally heightened presence, they require a vocal vivacity and weight that extends beyond the "mix-y" belt style.

These types of songs present equal part opportunity and problem for singers. As an opportunist, you'll enjoy the fact that you can express a wide range of vigor and vim with these songs. They provide opportunity for an impressive vocal turnout and dramatically supply a lot to chew on. However, you must be exceedingly cautious that these songs don't chew you—as they easily can. This isn't necessarily because you don't sing the song well enough to have pulled it off; in fact, this is rarely the reason. I have found that most singers innately know what is vocally not within their ability to pull off well and what is. In reality, it may or may not be because of my (our) own narrow mindedness that I expect a tour de force delivery that would at least equal and preferably surpass any that I have heard before of the song. This happens by not only singing the bejesus out of it, but also by having taken the time to do the dramatic homework and delivering a compelling story that moves me. In fact, I feel let down if those needs aren't met. Perhaps this is due to this type of song's now lofty importance within the dramatic contexts of the modern musical theatre.

As mentioned above, "heavy" belt songs often seek to inject a kind of kick in the journey by providing revelatory signposts in the character's (and the show's) arc; therefore, I have higher expectations of their delivery both dramatically and vocally, so approach with caution. Mind the storytelling more than the decibel levels, and do them only when the situation, audition, or performance warrants them.

Vocal style/sound descriptors and what the singer feels in the contemporary "heavy" belt song

The sounds of this style and the physical sensations that the singer feels share traits in common with the "heavy" belt traditional style as well as with the contemporary "mix-y" belt, with some notable additions:

- The singer may need to engage yet know how to harness the most intense possible emotional and dramatic fever pitch and translate this to vocal power.

- A vocal wherewithal is required to sing at extremely high amplitudes, doing so with attention given to vocal health and well-being.

- The singer may not feel that there are vocal "reserves" left over when singing at this level, and may feel a much higher than normal level of muscular activity in the neck and sternum.

Examples of songs that fall into this category include:

- "The Confrontation" (*Jekyll and Hyde*)

- "Holding Out for a Hero" (*Footloose*)

- "Gethsemane" (*Jesus Christ Superstar*)

- "Smash the Mirror" (*Tommy*)

- "What Is It about Her?" (*The Wild Party*)

- "And I Am Telling You I'm Not Going" (*Dreamgirls*)

- "Defying Gravity" (*Wicked*)

- "Get Out and Stay Out" (*9 to 5*)

- "Goodbye" (*Catch Me If You Can*)

- "Maybe I Like It This Way" (*The Wild Party*)

There are a great number of song styles used in the contemporary musical theatre. The above cover a lot of that territory as you would as likely use a "mix-y" belt vocal approach, for example, in certain 1950s songs as you would in certain 1990s songs (with attention granted to the vocal idiosyncrasies that held sway in that particular time period). There are still other styles used today, although some not widely, which may depart radically from the indicators and sound descriptions above and warrant mentioning. The Noël Coward-type "patter" song appears from time to time, "character" songs in which the singer "speaks" the notes more than sings them are everywhere, certain ethnic music (like that heard in *The Lion King*) is present, country and folk, rhythm and blues, jazz, rap, and virtually every other variety is present somewhere, sometime. To list the vocal inclusions of each in detail goes beyond this writing's scope, but the contemporary singing actor should have familiarity as needed, applying the above vocal traits when and where appropriate.

Get it done

1   From the list above, what song categories do the songs in your repertoire book fall under? Do these accurately represent your greatest strengths as a singer? Are you singing them when auditioning for the kinds of show associated with each? If you're book "building," be certain that you recognize what song type "matches" with each show type and what kind of song represents your singing skills.

2   Are the vocal qualities you engage when singing in these styles congruent with the sound descriptors listed here? In which of these do you excel? Where are you lacking?

3   Do you cognitively understand and are more or less able to "feel" and hear the sound qualities described above? If not, ask your voice teacher to clarify any of the descriptors you are unclear about. Trust (and trust your instincts) that he or she is guiding you in a way that fosters vocal health. If you feel vocally jeopardized in any way, stop. If you wish to continue learning to sing in that particular style or styles, research voice teachers in your area or school who have a track record of teaching singers in that style, and don't be afraid to make a change. It's your voice and your career. Health and safety come first.

Mutual plausibility between you and the song: Getting closer than "one-and-the-other"

Some time ago, I had a number of coaching sessions with a young actress preparing for her first audition in New York City, and some of the content of the first session is of value here, particularly for readers in the age range that she was at that time. This is despite the fact that most song-choice misfires are not nearly as cut and dried as the one that follows. Nevertheless, the parable is a useful one and serves to double down within the discussion of "singing who you are." Straightaway, I noticed her fiery, but cheery, personality type and that she was, I presupposed, no shrinking violet. Temperament aside, I noted that the actress who stood before me was more homespun than glamorous, and that she was not of modest frame. The brand of song choices suitable for her seemed very clear to me (sweeping generalizations are a fact of life as previously discussed), considering all of her specificities and definable elements. These seemed, to my way of thinking, far clearer than the more broadly based set of song choices we face with a more average personality type.

What came as a surprise was the song she wished to coach on that day. Curiously, she had chosen a slice of Stephen Sondheim's "The Ladies Who Lunch." This, of course, struck me as an ill fit.

Theoretically, an actor with any maturity can decidedly perform a selection like this *from* and *with* a point of view, and you'll get no argument from me that informed perspective is an indispensable ingredient to a compelling performance. But there was a fact much greater in play here: This song (certainly under the present circumstances) had nothing to do with *who* this actress was. There was little to convince me that this young woman would have *any* reason to sing a song like this, launch into this rant with such unstinting fervor, or to have become, in her limited number of years, as cynical or as embittered as the singer of this song is. Why would this young woman concern herself with the variety of women that the lyrics of this song illustrate with such venom?

Eager to glean an understanding of the choice after a sing-through of her cutting and an affirmation by her that she had sung it well (she had), I asked, "How does the song speak to *you*? How do you relate?" After looking momentarily blank, she thought for a moment and replied, "It's that the song goes a little berserk. I can act it, and that's not like 'me' at all."

"So, the fact that you find it *active* is good," I said, "and useful as an exercise, but you're not acting in a classroom. In this case, you're acting in an audition room. Let's deal with class work in the classroom, which is probably the *only* place you should be singing this song," I said with a smile, "except for kicks. The fact that you *like* the song is a huge plus; it means that it 'rang your bell,' but you became enamored with it without practicality coming to mind. If

I'm understanding you, you enjoy performing it in part because the song lets you 'act' someone other than *you*, and the real you thinks that the auditors in an audition somehow inexplicably want to see another 'you.'"

Now on tenterhooks, "So what do I do about this?" she asked. I replied, "We find another song that expresses what an eighteen-year-old girl would express with subject matter that is within her immediate realm of consciousness. What it comes down to is that you have to dispense with any hiding of 'you' behind 'her.' This woman character in the song is probably experiencing a mid-life crisis and has had just enough to drink to go on and on about how these foolish lunching ladies behave as though their lives are completely fulfilled and meaningful, when, in fact, she herself is probably one of these varieties of women. When I'm an audition room auditor or even an audience member looking to get to know you and your work, you telling me this kind of information is useless to me, the auditors, and most of all, to you because, at the end of the day, it has nothing to do *with* you. When light is held up to the lyrics, it's counterfeit currency. It shows me little about you except that you can hide in back of a character who couldn't be further from the reality of *you*. In an audition, it gets us nowhere. It's a dead-end road. You have a terrific vocal facility and are quite commanding to watch, but I am hard-pressed to imagine that a girl your age would have such a burning desire to express to me her feelings about such a thing."

The material you should be playing should capture the immediacy of you in the moment, in the here-and-now. It shouldn't be out of the question, based on your sensibilities, age, wherewithal, and range as an actor *in this moment*, that you could play the role from the show you are singing from *right now*. My belief is that it should be more or less plausible that you could, notwithstanding making the deliberate choice to perform the song in order to "spin it" or for the purposes of deliberate irony.[18] When choosing your song material, be candid with yourself when you ask the following:

- Do you personally have feelings and are passionate about telling me your feelings about this subject matter in the song?

- More importantly, do the types of characters that you'll typically be auditioning for need me to know this particular kind of information?

- Is it critical to your state of well-being that you express these kinds of feelings in your here-and-now so emphatically and in such an impassioned way?

This is not to say, however, that you will not be asked to prepare additional material. This will happen sometimes because an audition panel occasionally will want to see how imaginative you are, how well you improvise, or to what giddy heights your creative thinking can carry the embodiment of a piece of dancing fruit for a television commercial.

Does the song cut well?

Finding a song that speaks to you in a personal way and that fits the profile of a role or type of show you are auditioning for only to later discover that the song is difficult to cut into a shorter, audition-length version or doesn't "play" well when cut can be discouraging and frustrating. It's best to know these answers before you extend your heart to a song.

Notwithstanding songs for standard length presentation, the universally requested song length for a great number and variety of auditions in the United States (certainly professional auditions, and a good number of amateur and school auditions, use this practice as well) is sixteen to thirty-two bars (or measures) of music. The United Kingdom is known for a more liberal policy of length, but nevertheless you must not wear out your welcome. When auditioning in the United Kingdom, it is best to prepare your standard short length and sixteen- and thirty-two-bar cuts as contingencies. This is a sticky matter in the United States. The dilemma that this irritating doctrine presents is that sixteen bars of an up-tempo song in "cut" time in which the beat or pulses are counted as two pulses per measure can sometimes only "feel" like one or two phrases of music. This is in stark contrast to sixteen bars of a slow, dirge-like tempo in which the four pulses to a bar can often feel never-ending and too long, especially for audition purposes (and most especially, if the song is not being sung well). The singer in either case has obediently sung the cut as requested, but one singer (the one who has sung the up-tempo song) has gotten less (sometimes far less) stage time than the singer who sang the ballad (slower song). There is a simple solution to this confounding situation. Rather than set a *bar* limit for the singer at auditions, a more equitable option might be to set a time limit, say thirty to forty-five seconds.[19] When the singer has reached his time limit, he could be politely cut off by a timekeeper as is the case with most combined auditions[20] and certain auditions for admission to college and university programs. But the sixteen- to thirty-two-bar practice persists and remains the standard in America, and sometimes, the United Kingdom. This is much to the disappointment of the eager-to-show-off-their-goods-but-time-strapped-and-bar-constrained auditioners.

If your songs don't cut well to thirty-two, sixteen, or even eight bars (it's not unheard of for the panel to request an eight-bar cut at the last minute, especially if they are attempting to see as many people trot across the floor and give it a go as possible in the audition day or if they are running behind on time—another frequent reality), you will have a frustrating time in the audition world. If your audition songs don't cut seamlessly to one of these configurations, it may be best not to plan to use them for your auditions. Ascertaining the number of bars in a piece of sheet music is easy even if you don't read music—simply count the divisions of notes between the vertical lines (bar lines). The notes that lie between these lines equal one bar. Not as easy sometimes is finding songs that cut logically to the right number of bars *and* register the impression that you require them to make in order to give the casting eyes and ears the information that they need to see and hear from you.

As previously stated, audition notices will often request that you show range in your song choice and request a sixteen-bar cutting to carry that out. There are multitudes of songs that can accomplish this. Often, but not always, the grandest, most striking notes of a song lie at the end. Try looking there first. A couple of examples come to mind in the contemporary variety of songs, both by Andrew Lloyd Webber: The last sixteen bars of "Seeing Is Believing" (*Aspects of Love*) and "Too Much in Love to Care" (*Sunset Boulevard*) are excellent samples. Both songs contain impressive high notes within wildly romantic musical gestures, which give the singer a good deal of "height" both emotionally and within the range of the notes. In the traditional song world, the last sixteen to thirty-two bars of songs such as "I Have Dreamed" or "My Lord and Master" (*The King and I*) or the reprise of "When Did I Fall in Love?" (*Fiorello!*) accomplish that same goal.

Other songs don't cut as easily. Songs with phrases not written in a relatively short, tapered manner are more difficult to find a fluid cut in. Some writers such as Jason Robert Brown, Stephen Sondheim, and many contemporary songwriters often write in very extended musical phrases that don't all conform to being "square." Another bugaboo that sometimes occurs is that much of the information delivered in any one portion of the song is, to some degree, contingent upon information that has been delivered in *another* portion of the song. This may mean that, by picking up the story somewhere in the middle or at the end, a cut is clumsy and difficult to play (as an actor) because the text in isolation is confusing and cryptic to listeners. This may render it exceedingly difficult to execute sensibly.

It should also be emphatically stated and adopted by you as policy that the cutting you use should contain a clear, intuitive musical finish as you would hear at the end of a phrase, section, or conclusion of a song. In other words, a distinct and discernible cadence should be present. Too often, actors will choose a cut that dutifully satisfies the required number of bars, whether exact or approximate, but will end in the middle of a phrase of music or in mid-thought. Your ear (and your common sense) will let you know if this is happening, and it's never a good idea to leave either hanging as it makes both you and the panel feel as though there has not been the sense of completion that is desired.

Musical key consistency within the proposed cut

Another precarious situation to be mindful of in the cuts in the music that you choose are internal key changes within the song. When this occurs, the song begins in one key and then either passes through multiple keys or changes key once, ending in a different key than it began in. This is problematic only if you choose a cut that is in one musical key to start and the back half, or conclusion of the cut, is in another key with no transition to connect the two. The standard published version of the well-known "Unexpected Song" (*Song and Dance*) contains such an example. A plausible cut of this song would be to begin the cut at the second verse and then cut to the last seven bars of the song for the conclusion. This is a fluid, logical cut both in textual terms and with brevity in mind. This choosing allows the singer to reveal some of the trappings in the song through the chosen text and then sport her singing wares through the inclusion of the held high note in the last few bars. The foil in the plan occurs because there is a change of musical key that occurs in between. In this case, the selected cut begins in one key and ends in another with no key transition within the bars chosen for the cutting. What this precarious situation renders is a musical scheme that isn't functional for the singer, the pianist, or the listener. The lesson here in choosing song cuts is to cover all of your bases. If you aren't certain that there is key consistency in your cut, check with a teacher or coach or musical director who can provide you with the "all clear."

Playing the song out of context

Some songs just don't make a great deal of sense when removed from the show and the context for which they were written. These are songs that serve the storyline of that particular musical, but can often come off as confusing if you, the actor, invent your own "take" on the song. Not a great deal needs to be relayed here about these types of songs except that in choosing them you should be aware that you may not be able to tell a fluid and entirely accessible story to your audience, although you may find usefulness in the songs in other regards (such as vocal range, comedy, etc.). Some examples of this song type may include "And the Money Kept Rolling In" (*Evita*), a production-style number whose point within the musical is to deliver the narrative to the audience that the Eva Peron brand was raking big bucks into her "charitable" foundation (of some questionable ethics) and to denote the passage of time over which this occurred. The song is a spark plug, but might be perplexing if played out of the context for which it was intended.

Another example of a terrific number within the show itself, but one that doesn't translate well out of context and in isolation, is "Love Is My Legs" (*Dirty Rotten Scoundrels*). Here, the singer, who has been feigning paralysis of the lower extremities that rendered him "unable" to walk, makes attempts to garner sympathy from the girl by convincing her that he could be "cured" and made to walk again if she and her "love" could inspire him to do so. (He really has other things in mind.) The number is a showstopper, but without the setup of the back-story, it fails to land and be of much use when going unframed by its intended dramatic setup. It is always a good idea to choose songs not *entirely* contingent upon context and that are perhaps more universal.

Choosing songs with, and understanding, a playable "arc" (and "cutting" them accordingly)

Songs, like the larger unit scripts that contain them and that, all together, create a unified, playable whole (the show), should include mini-playable scripts of their own. Ideally, these contain, like any piece of reliable drama, distinct traits of character, conflict (with another, the self, or a situation), and obstacles to surmount encapsulated within a beginning, middle, and end. Some are more densely packed with these components than others. If the songs in a musical can be thought of as smaller units within the entire script that, when functioning together, create the overall, then these units (the songs) can be broken down even further into smaller units, or "beats," in the same fashion that nonmusical scene work is.

Most songs have many such beats, transitioning from one to the next when something changes, like the character's progression of thought, his reaction to another's actions and words, a realization, or by a thought process related to what he wants. As we explore in great detail in the next section, in the musical theatre, as in all drama, *everyone wants something* and everyone has a problem that begs, internally and/or externally, to be solved.

These moments within a song, when strung and tied together, create a series (or arc) of moments, just as when entire songs are strung together throughout a script, they help create the arc of the entire musical. The arc is the journey of the piece, its storyline, and its beating heart; it is what happens moment to moment in order to establish and define the overall. It is conflict presented, dealt with in one fashion or another, and possibly resolved. Songs with evident, comprehensible, and playable arcs make for the most useful, playable songs. They contain stimuli with and through which the actor can respond (react) and that translate into action.

In "Some People" from *Gypsy*, Mama Rose implores her stubborn and fed-up-with-her-antics father to lend her the money to fund her daughters' vaudeville act. Rose states emphatically over and over again that she and her daughters are bound for a fate bigger and brighter than "playing bingo and sitting still," and if she can only raise the money for the act, she's certain that outcome can be realized.

Over the course of the number, it becomes clear to the audience that (a) Rose is desirous of a more meaningful life for herself and her children (the "want"), and (b) she desperately needs money to finance the whole ordeal. When, after a great deal of elaborate pleading, her unrelenting father still refuses, she remains unfettered and vows to go it alone, and the arc of the song is clear and has played out. She asks for the money (stating the reasons why she needs it), doesn't get it, reacts to her father's actions, and regroups to initiate plan B over the course of a series of beats.

In *Rent*, Maureen reacts to her lover Joanne's jealousy and mistrust of her (the "problem") in "Take Me or Leave Me." Within the number, there exists a clear statement of the issue at hand, argument as to how to resolve it, and finally, a resolution of the situation (if not the problem as there exists an impasse between them) and they break off their entanglement ("I'm Gone"). This, then, is the arc of "Take Me or Leave Me," and Maureen, like Rose, having had someone onstage to "push against," resist, or defy, and whose actions have motivated their reactions, has helped give the singer of the song a great deal to "act." They have been given specific tools to keep their stories active and actionable.

But what happens when there is no scene partner present (a monologue set to song) or if the singer is singing about something that has happened either offstage or in the previous scene or scenes? In the penultimate scene of *My Fair Lady*, Henry Higgins has just been told (and told off) by Eliza, his "pupil" (although she believes that she has been egocentrically manipulated as his "puppet"), that she is leaving and is never to return. He storms tempestuously from his mother's house ("Damn! Damn! Damn! Damn!") and is suddenly, in the next beat, thunderstruck by the realization that "I've Grown Accustomed to Her Face." In the subsequent beats, he entertains ideas about what will happen to Eliza without him, that she will become destitute and alone ("not a penny in the till and a bill collector beating at the door!"), and then in the next beat, evokes sympathy for her ("Poor Eliza, how simply frightful . . . how humiliating"), but in the subsequent beat, thinks better of it and finds a giddy satisfaction in the prospect ("How delightful!"). Several beats later, Higgins finally comes back around to a confession that he'll miss "her joys, her woes, her highs, her lows."

The arc of the song is very transparent and playable, and has presented itself across a series of individual beats. Even as no scene partner exists onstage during the number, Higgins is both reacting to the powerful statement from Eliza in the previous scene that "I will do very well without you" and also reacting to the fantasies he is concocting *inside his own head* about her eventual fate.

In choosing your song material, the clearer the arc of the song, whatever the length it must be pared to for presentational (particularly audition) purposes, the more focused and more playable your reactions to it can become. The stronger the actions of your scene partner (who you will often invent in your creative mind), the stronger your reactions to his actions will be. Although most audition songs must fall within a very short duration, playability can still exist in abundance if the actor chooses a cut-down version of a song that presents a succinct and clear arc (constituting contrasting beats) in order to plant the seeds and if the songs he chooses have fertile soil.

Get it done

1   What is the subject matter of the songs you are presently singing or are contemplating singing? Are any of the songs' subject matter so linked to the context of the show for which they were written that in isolation they don't "play" well or make sense? Would the average listener get the general gist of the song if he wasn't familiar with the musical for which the song was written?

2   Is there an unmistakable journey, however long or short, within the songs? Chart the series of beats in your songs one to the next.

3   Do your songs contain the kind of discernible beats that an interesting cutting could be construed in the form of

contrasting beats? Or is there so much repetition of thought and/or words and actions that your cuts are repetitive and don't give or provide you with a lot of ground to cover? Chart the beats of your cuttings and ask yourself if there exists enough of a beginning and end to give you "playing room."

Often-heard[21] and iconic songs

Nearly always a spirited debate, the questions surrounding whether or not to use a certain song because it is too often heard, especially in the audition room, endlessly rankles singing actors. As for having firsthand accounts of the goings-on in any audition room, the singing actor is at a severe disadvantage because he generally doesn't have the opportunity to audit audition rounds. Therefore, he couldn't possibly know from experience the exact content of a typical day of singing auditions and must rely on others who do to pass along reliable information about what songs may be "overdone." Even when the source of that guidance makes the information available, his or her opinion is often slanted and always subjective and may not reveal the sacred answer, if there is one to be revealed, hence, the frustration.

I will attempt to clarify a few myths, reinforce a truth or two, and generally make an effort to further steer you toward how to choose your material with discretion. (A lengthy discussion has previously transpired, providing and generating leads about where and how to find material that perhaps is not overused.)

The real truth is that there aren't as many songs that are done to death as you might imagine, but the ones that are virtually define the concept of cliché, and it is these "greatest hits of the musical theatre" set that you may wish to avoid. Singing actors choose these songs again and again for several solid reasons. The songs are great vehicles for doing what audition/performance songs are supposed to do, which is to show off a singing actor to his best advantage. They may also choose them because they studied these songs with their teachers and coaches or even out of convenience because the sheet music is readily available. We discuss all of these reasons (and the possible pitfalls), but before we do, I address the first point: choosing the song because you feel that it represents you well. This is a good reason. The paradox, though, is that even though you may rightfully feel that you're being presented to your best advantage by performing that often-used song, the song choice may very well be working against you (specifically in auditions). The reason for this is simple: It is heard so often in the audition room that the panel:

- may view the song as iconic or hold an iconic performer's version of it as sacrosanct, and therefore, your version is held to extremely high standards.

- will sometimes feel conscious or unconscious resentment toward the actor for not making a more original song choice, especially an experienced, interesting actor.

- has heard the song performed blandly (or badly) so often that it might not have the disposition toward the song to be fully cognizant of your performance of it.

- may have heard the song so often, well sung or not, that it is just plain bored by hearing it again. Imagine listening to a radio station that plays the same song several times per hour all day long.

To cement at least one of the above points, I offer the following example: I once had an actor in my studio who told me that before I met him someone on the panel of an audition he had attended breached protocol after the actor had finished singing "On the Street Where You Live," and as a means of constructive criticism, pointed out to the actor that singing that particular song didn't do anyone any favors—especially that actor. The auditor pointed out that the panel was bored to death (I paraphrase) hearing this song for the umpteenth time that day. I would add that certain songs simply tend to render themselves flaccid in the audition room to begin with, and I would count this as one. While lovely and lilting, and a song that serves its purpose amiably on the stage in *My Fair Lady*, "On the Street Where You Live" tends to flat-line in the audition room as many songs do, which is not to demerit them whatsoever, but rather to point out their impact in an audition setting. *There is possibly nothing more frustrating or time-wasting in an audition room than an interesting actor singing a boring song.*
Other songs, while inherently more stirring, suffer the same fate of being done endlessly. "Vanilla Ice Cream" (*She Loves Me*), for

example, is heard so often that it has been known to evoke a palpable and even audible cringe from behind the audition table. Again, the actor's choice of the song is surely because the high, held note on the final "Ice" shows off her voice. However, the song choice may be, as we have noted, working against her. There are plenty of songs that could accomplish the same goal for the actress. It's simply a matter of finding them. The last sixteen bars of "I've Been Invited to a Party" from Noël Coward's *The Girl Who Came to Supper*, for example, have a similar concluding melodic contour inclusive of an impressive high note. "What Do I Need with Love?," "Forget about the Boy," and "Not for the Life of Me" (all from *Thoroughly Modern Millie*) are terrific songs, but as one casting director pointed out, "Terrific, yes ... the first six thousand times you hear them they are terrific."

The common denominator in all of these songs is that they are fabulous numbers, and it's little wonder that actors choose to sing them. Sometimes, though, it's not even a matter of the actor having two song choices side by side—one an often-performed song and the other less performed—and willfully and consciously choosing the well-known one. Many actors own the very same sheet music anthology books (such as *The Singer's Musical Theatre Anthology* that has expanded in so many directions that it makes the head spin)[22] and choose their audition material from within those pages. The problem with choosing audition songs from these sources is that so many other people are also pulling songs from this same pool, especially the well-known songs and ones that are especially useful for learning purposes. The predictable result is often overexposure of those songs.

Finally, there is another more philosophical point to be brought up. When told to avoid certain songs because they are often heard at auditions or because the songs are iconic in one way or another, the actor may retort, "But I do the song really well, and I'd hate to lose it just because it may be done too much" or even "My version of the song is very original and personal, even though someone famous did the song" as a counter to the "often-heard iconic" discussion. I completely understand this line of reasoning. Individuality, originality, and invention are undeniably key in song presentation, and I believe that if Edith Piaf (the French chanteuse) and Barbra Streisand had *both* sung "Don't Rain on My Parade" (another song I believe to be of the greatest hits variety), both versions, while delivered in completely opposite fashion, would have been equally compelling. What's key here in moving ahead with a song choice for the above-stated reasons is to know that your version of the song had better be a home run. If you're going to audition with an often-used or a well-known song, or even a song that is associated with someone iconic, it should be your personal best, preferably stocked full of the unexpected and sung with vivacious originality.

So, it comes down to a few good rules of thumb to live by for the well-informed singing actor concerning often-used songs or songs made famous or sung famously by others:

1 When contemplating whether a song is often heard in audition rooms, trust your instincts. If you have heard it a great deal in whatever the setting, heard other singers frequently speak of it, or viewed too many versions of the song on YouTube, the song is probably heard often in audition rooms.

2 Don't necessarily use a song in an audition setting that you studied in your voice lessons; often those songs should remain in the for-learning-purposes-only category.

3 If the song has been famously sung by a celebrated performer, approach with caution; you may be inviting comparison.

4 If the song is too "out there" at the present time, having shown up on a recent television program or is currently being heard in the main stem, it is probably better to move on to other possibilities that aren't so pervasive in the collective conscience.

A subjective, arguable "Top 25" often-heard list (and runners-up)

What follows is a compilation not resulting from any casting director's list of "no-no" songs or from any source other than my own personal experience. Like so much else, it is in the eye and ear of the beholder as to what should be included here. Rather, the list that follows is predicated on patterns I have noted from perusal of countless singing actors' repertoire books (on multiple continents), sheet music that appears in song anthologies known to be owned by many, songs known to be studied by many singers, and from witnessing and accompanying thousands of auditions over more than twenty-five years.

No teacher, coach, or casting director should be granted responsibility or held liable for being judge, jury, and executioner of excising any of these songs or the runners-up from your repertoire. If you love a song or songs included here, I encourage you to understand this list not as stricture, but as an advisement to approach with caution *if you believe, as many do, that songs performed by many individuals should be avoided*. If you choose to include any of these in your book, the unbreakable rule is to bring something to the table when performing these songs that is refreshing and radiates originality.

As a final disclaimer, I'm certain that by the time the ink dries here, there will be new inclusions that have perhaps upstaged some of the present song titles.

Also, certain often-heard songs (such as any number of songs from Andrew Lippa's *Wild Party*, *Next to Normal*, or *Edges*) are not listed here because these are contained within "Shows to Avoid in General" listed below. This fact compounds the "real" number of songs to be included here into multiples.

- "Always True to You (in my fashion)" (*Kiss Me, Kate*)
- "But the World Goes 'Round" (*And the World Goes 'Round*)
- "Being Alive" (*Company*)
- "A Cockeyed Optimist" (*South Pacific*)
- "Don't Rain on My Parade" (*Funny Girl*)
- "Fly, Fly Away" (*Catch Me If You Can*)
- "Dyin' Ain't So Bad" (*Bonnie and Clyde*)
- "Goodbye" (*Catch Me If You Can*)
- "Green Finch and Linnet Bird" (*Sweeney Todd*)
- "I Could Have Danced All Night" (*My Fair Lady*)

- "If I Loved You" (*Carousel*)
- "I'm in Love with a Wonderful Guy" (*South Pacific*)
- "Johanna" (*Sweeney Todd*)
- "Larger than Life" (*My Favorite Year*)
- "Lost in the Wilderness" (*Children of Eden*)
- "Maybe This Time" (*Cabaret*)
- "Never Neverland (fly away)" (*Home*)
- "On the Street Where You Live" (*My Fair Lady*)
- "Pulled" (*The Addams Family*)
- "Run Away with Me" (*The Unauthorized Biography of Samantha Brown*)
- "Someone Else's Story" (*Chess*)
- "Someone to Watch over Me" (George and Ira Gershwin, *Oh, Kay!* et al.)
- "The Spark of Creation" (*Children of Eden*)
- "There's a Fine, Fine Line" (*Avenue Q*)
- "Vanilla Ice Cream" (*She Loves Me*)

Runners Up:

- "All Grown Up" (*Bare*)
- "As Long as He Needs Me" (*Oliver!*)
- "Back to Before" (*Ragtime*)
- "Can't Help Lovin' Dat Man" (*Show Boat*)
- "Corner of the Sky" (*Pippin*)
- "Disneyland" (*Smile*)
- "Fly into the Future" (*Vanities*)
- "I Know the Truth" (*Aida*)
- "It Might as Well Be Spring" (*State Fair* et al.)

- "Mister Snow" (*Carousel*)
- "Moonfall" (*The Mystery of Edwin Drood*)
- "My New Philosophy" (*You're a Good Man, Charlie Brown – revival*)
- "Much More" (*The Fantasticks*)
- "Nothing" (*A Chorus Line*)
- "Out There" (*The Hunchback of Notre Dame*)
- "Purpose" (*Avenue Q*)
- "Raining" (*Rocky*)
- "A Quiet Thing" (*Flora, The Red Menace*)
- "Shy" (*Once upon a Mattress*)
- "The Simple Joys of Maidenhood" (*Camelot*)
- "Till There Was You" (*The Music Man*)
- "Will He Like Me?" (*She Loves Me*)

Shows that contain many often-heard songs that you may wish to avoid include:

- *Edges*
- *Hair*
- *Jekyll and Hyde*
- *Les Misérables*
- *Little Women*
- *Next to Normal*
- *Phantom of the Opera*
- *Songs for a New World*
- *Spring Awakening*
- *The Last Five Years*
- *The Light in the Piazza*

- *The Wild Party* (Andrew Lippa)
- *Thoroughly Modern Millie*
- *Wicked*

Delivering the goods

There is the issue of performing often-heard and iconic song repertoire, and then there is perhaps a weightier issue—the *cost of ownership* of songs that often occurs with certain song materials, regardless of whether the song is often heard or associated with an individual.

We've all seen performances of songs that we've perceived as somehow falling short of out-and-out success or witnessed song performances that we feel have somehow misrepresented the song itself. This may happen in spite of the performer who, in his own way, delivers an enticing and respectable rendition. Perhaps the cause is that we naturally have preconceptions about certain songs on which we place a *standard of performance that we hold the performer to.* It's an incontrovertible fact that many songs out there *have* been pedestalized by listeners because of the high demand and/or well-remembered performances of them, especially in theatre circles (and, especially, at auditions).

Our holding of songs to such lofty standards could be due to many reasons, including perhaps hearing a singer who has impressively "belted" the song with full-throated vigor and then others who have had to compromise by "flipping" upper notes, thereby diminishing the effect and leaving us feeling unsatisfied. Or perhaps we have witnessed performers who may, in fact, "feel" invested into the span of the emotional "acting" range that many songs require, but just can't "land" outward expression of it without coming off as awkward where others have succeeded ably, providing us a cathartic experience. Remember, as important as it is to connect internally to your song and enjoy the feeling of singing, it doesn't always mean that you *should* sing it.

This is not to imply that you should shoot lower. The fact is that you can stake your ownership in and deliver inspired performance of *any* song that you fully commit to and that does not expose any weaknesses. It's far more useful to you to excel at a song that you may not feel is as exciting or lands the same punch than it is to fall short of your audience's expectations. A good litmus test is to take the performance of the song in question, whether live, on a recording, or on video, that *you admire most* and apply your own standard of admiration to yourself to meet or exceed it. If you feel that you don't or can't, then you've proven this point to be correct. And it's best to wait until you can do so and move forward wholeheartedly toward more fruitful endeavors that will yield higher returns.

In summary, if as a performer you aren't able to rise to what you should anticipate as an auditor's discriminating expectations because of the steep burden the particular song places on the performer to deliver or even surpass the audience or panel's remembrances of past performances that *did* deliver the goods, then *you may very well be working against yourself.* In this event, you should take under advisement that it is likely in your best interest to seek songs that you can perform without compromise and ones that are free of preconceived notions of how the song "should" be performed because too many others have set elevated standards for the song.

Choosing (and performing) pop and rock songs

To some, they're a nuisance, and to others, liberating. Some see performing them as a necessary evil, while others welcome doing so since it places them in their comfort zone. Pop and rock music in musicals is certainly not new; it has been on musical theatre stages since at least the 1960s.[23] What is new is that those performers who were adept at performing in the pop and rock styles, once "specialty" performers, are becoming at least as in demand in the modern musical theatre as those who sing in more conventional musical theatre styles. In other words, pop and rock music are as present in the theatre mainstream today as the more customary theatre song style and are ever-present on musical theatre stages globally. Young performers, especially, should pay careful attention to the trend, and feel confident when singing and performing in these styles in order to remain (or become) competitive.

While some voice teachers, especially the younger ones, in college, university, and other training programs are incorporating the pop and rock styles into the varieties of songs they require their students to study and include in repertoire books, this number is woefully limited. As a result, too often young singing actors are finding themselves in the unenviable position of being dangerously unprepared for the wide number of auditions that require the style, thereby severely decreasing their marketability. Most who are placed in this regrettable position have had little or no steady-handed guidance about how to prepare songs and sing them *in a theatrical* manner, let alone with care in regard to maintaining vocal health. This is to say nothing of teaching the singer how to perform these songs in *his unique* style and with a sturdy storyline. Rather, most information about performing in these styles has been gathered ad hoc via radio and recordings, often overproduced (and frequently, engaging an oversung rendition by the so-called artist) exploitive music videos and concerts, and the usual doses of well-ordered hype that go hand in glove with these types of music.

At the opposite end of the spectrum, many performers who say they *do* feel confident performing these songs haven't formally trained in either singing or theatre. They are performing on raw, gut-driven instinct that results from their exposure to music videos, concerts, and so on, and often fail to take into account theatricality, storytelling, and craft, delivering instead emotionally overcharged, vocally unnuanced performances. Competition-based television shows certainly haven't helped. The performances too frequently do little by way of delivering much else but blasted performances long in amplitude and visuals, but short in storytelling, which is *entirely antithetical* to theatrical custom (with due respect paid to those who aren't guilty of the above and the undeniable talent they demonstrate for pop and rock singing). It's no wonder then, with all of these visual and aural messages floating around in singers' heads, that they, too, often disconnect from *theatricalizing* pop and rock songs and fail to *act* them, but why should they? Too few have been shown how to do otherwise and, for the purposes of these competitions there seems little need.

In pop and rock music, there is still another problem that may explain to some extent the disconnect that is felt by those who engage the acting of a song: The song lyrics are often written in cryptic, opaque language that may require a lot of digging through to create a fluid storyline and logical delivery. In other words: a silk purse from a sow's ear. Compounding the challenge is that most pop and rock songs are not pinned to a particular character indigenous to a developed storyline, relying on what has occurred before them to be put into action. In fact, the opposite is true. They are written as stand-alone entities sung in the "voice" of the personality singing them, whatever his or her idiosyncrasies may be.

These facts alone place the burden on the singer to *assign* the song a reason to be sung by developing his own one-act play that supports the singing of it. His creative mind must be heavily engaged and relied upon to theatricalize the song with the intention of *creating theatre* out of it in theatrical terms and not of the concert stage. Additionally, it must be stamped with the singer's personal style intact, not those of the original singer. When a singer takes it upon himself to do this work, structuring and interpolating tangible, instinctive theatrical situations, the songs instantly turn into entities that give the singing actor the necessary tools he is accustomed to working with and a means to frame the *song with specificity rather than with generality*. The following chapters are dedicated to providing the actor with the techniques to do so, not only for pop and rock songs but for *all* songs theatrical as the same regimen should be applied to them all by way of placing the songs on *theatrical turf.*

Get it done

1   Take a comprehensive and honest look at the songs you are singing or are contemplating singing. Are any so well known and often heard that by doing them you are inviting comparison?

2   Looking at each of your songs, what do you do to put your thumbprint on them? How is your approach unique and original? Are you singing your songs with what others would perceive as "star power" or "it" factor? Do your song choices enable you to do that to begin with?

3   Bearing in mind that many songs have those ever-impressive "triple pirouette" moments of vocal and performance "bling," do any of your songs have one or more that you are (or might be) purposefully avoiding (like skipping the section that contains one of these magic tricks or even changing the key to avoid an anticipated

"money" note)? Remember that not doing what is sometimes expected in certain songs is like an open admission that you aren't up to the task.

4   Which "pop" songs in your book foster storytelling through the song? Who are your favorite "go-to" pop singers who tell great stories through their song work?

5   Are the "pop" songs you are singing compatible with the idea of placing flesh and blood human beings within the storyline of the song? Do they have clear, uncoded language that allows the listener an easy comprehension of the storyline without having to unscramble the lyric to make sense of it?

Song Preparation

"Put the truth of your feelings and your thoughts first and the sound of your voice will follow."

—MARIA CALLAS

CHAPTER FOUR

Introduction to Song Preparation

It's the actor's reoccurring nightmare: appearing in front of an audience and experiencing the startling realization within the dream that he has had little or (worse) no proper rehearsal whatsoever. He hardly recognizes the set or costumes in this dreamed-up milieu, and the people sharing the stage with him are a fuzzy haze, each as indiscernible as the last, all none too helpful in navigating this unenviable course. He has no idea where or when he is supposed to move onstage and is milling about without purpose. He has not taken or had the opportunity to invest himself in the overt meanings of his lines or in their subtext, or worse, he may have no idea what his lines are or when to speak them. He is plunged onto the stage in a state of woeful unpreparedness.

This scenario is terrifying to imagine and an occurrence in our lives as performers that we are hyper-vigilant to avoid. After all, in order to achieve full discovery and comprehension of the emotional, psychological, and physical life of the play or the musical, the rehearsal period (length is perhaps not as important as content) must occur. Ultimately, our offering to our audience will result from this process, and our rehearsal process is an intimate, private matter between the text, ourselves, and our collaborators.

Taking all of this into consideration, however, I often find that, apart from rehearsal for a "real" show, actors are often prone not to approach the learning of new material for the purposes of solo presentation (especially the audition) as the due process that the former is granted. The fact is that the approach to *any* new material being prepared for presentation should undergo the same rigorous rehearsal process, a search for truth and playability, as any rehearsal process for a well-crafted and fully staged production or presentation.

While rehearsing for a production, whether fully staged or not, the actor follows a particular set of guidelines over a timeline and moves toward a finished "product." For example, the first day of rehearsal might consist of a "table" reading. These sit-down and un-staged sessions allow the piece to be heard by the most unaffected means. It allows the actors to glean objective—moving steadfastly toward subjective—information about the characters and the characters' circumstances from the text itself. This rehearsal technique also allows the actor to grasp and deliver the text in its most organic form and free from a great deal of physicality. Importantly, this first step in the process enables the actor to begin the discovery process of *the message* of the piece as an article of theatre.

The second phase of the process might be learning and memorizing the notes for the songs (if the show is a musical) and the words of the dialog and lyrics, along with further thought and frank discussion about understanding and realizing the overall content of the piece and the material that links the piece together as an uninterrupted whole. At this point, the actor has begun to make informed, personalized, and more subjective choices in tandem with his collaborators in regard to his performance.

The third phase of the process may consist of staging the material after the actor has a handle on the order of the notes and text and begins to associate the physical movement in the piece with the same (which may further aid in the memorization process). The actor continues to make discoveries about the relevance of the text and his character's interactions with fellow players and develops a collective consensus with his collaborators about the overall message of the piece and what the message (or take-away) of the piece may be for the audience. The work in progress begins to emerge as a fully realized occasion, or in other words, a presentation, and over time and through repetition materializes as "the show."

The process for purposes of any presentation (and I stress *even for auditions*) shouldn't be vastly different than what is described above, although it might be more brief or even longer, depending on the rate of speed at which the actor works on his own (an individual luxury that is not as available in a more formal rehearsal process). It bears emphasizing that you, as the performer preparing songs for auditions and/or performing them outside of the shows for which they were written, should be mindful that you have license to prepare the songs (unless otherwise directed to do so, such as in the case of a callback) *out of specific context* pertinent to the musicals for which they have been created, and *to place focus rather on the circumstances of the character and the situation at hand within the song.* Going on, you may now *transport the circumstances of the song into your here-and-now and "personalize" the lyric as though being spoken (sung) directly from your own point of view and your own personal experiences. In an out-of-context presentation such as described here, the circumstances of the character singing the song are given, but the feelings are yours.*

Table Work I:
Ascertaining (and understanding)
objective information

Before projecting your own subjective and singular voice onto the material, we've established the importance of gathering the necessary information about what to use as the grounding for your performance. At this juncture, we must do some of the aforementioned "table work." This allows us, with a bird's-eye view, to amass information about the present circumstances and background of the singer and the song. "But hold it!" you say. "I'm intending to use this for auditions, and I thought this was *me* singing this song. Why do I need to ascertain all of this information about the character in the musical?" The reason is because what the writer wrote is irreversible and that defines and informs the singer, experience, and event. You'll eventually draw intersecting lines between the character's circumstances and your own subjective feelings, whether for audition purposes or in preparing to play the role. But for now, we are seeking as much factual and circumstantial information as possible. The facts of right now, including what the singer wants, can be found in a number of ways, perhaps the most obvious being all that the character says about himself. The most self-evident of these comes in the form of "I want" (or "I think I want"), which can be stated directly or indirectly and directed toward another character (as scene) or the audience itself (as monologue).

The "givens" of a character, as they are sometimes known, on the other hand, involve hard facts such as the character's age, background, social standing, socioeconomic status, physical attributes, present circumstances, and so on. Information can be had about both the right now and the "givens" not only by taking into account what the singer says about himself and the actions he takes, but also by paying attention to the things that other characters and the playwright (or lyricist) say about him.

In song work, you often need to look no further than the lyrical content itself as some lyrics are very direct with regard to facts about the singer and what the singer wants as well as the "givens":

"Mira"
(From *Carnival*)

Excerpt

> Would you believe,
> Would you believe,
> That this is the first I've traveled?
> I came from a town,
> The kind of town
> Where you live in a house
> 'Til the house fall down.
> But if it stands up
> You stay there.
> It's funny, but that's their way there.
> I came from the town of Mira
> Beyond the bridges of Saint Claire.
> I guess you've never heard of Mira,
> It's awf'ly small but still it's there.

This portion of the lyric provides us with some of the needed objective information ("givens"), while through other portions of the lyric, we can derive still objective (also taken at face value from the text) information about the singer's wants and needs:

> I'm very far from Mira now,
> And there's no turning back.
> I have to find a place,
> I've got to find a place,
> Where everything can be the same.
> A street that I can know,
> And places I can go,
> Where everyone will know my name.

The difference between performing this song playing the role of Lili in the musical *Carnival* and performing this song out of context, as in a general audition room, is that in a theatre the audience sees Lili and in an audition room the "audience" (panel) sees you.[24]

Other lyrics are equally forthcoming in expressing the wants and needs of the singer. It is important to remember that at this stage we are still seeking objective, factual information, and we are not yet placing too many *subjective* feelings onto our reading of the text.

"Much More"
(From *The Fantasticks*)

Excerpt

> I'd like to dance till two o'clock,
> Or sometimes dance till dawn,
> Or if the band could stand it,
> Just go on and on and on!
> Just once,
> Just once,
> Before the chance is gone!

Still other lyrics allow us access to "givens" (some through logical inference) and what the singer of the song wants: In "The Beauty Is," from the luminous *The Light in the Piazza*, we are introduced to Clara, a young woman teetering on a precipice in a romantic place far from her own home.

Excerpt

> Everyone's a mother here in Italy.
> Everyone's a father, or a son.
> I think if I had a child
> I would take such care of her,
> Then I wouldn't feel like one.
> I've hardly met a single soul, but I am not alone.
> I feel known!
> This is wanting something
> This is praying for it,
> This is holding breath and keeping fingers crossed.
> This is counting blessings.
> This is wondering when
> I'll see that boy again.

Via the baseline (objective) facts, we are provided certain factual information.[25] The inclusion of the word *here* reveals that Clara is in Italy and has not just returned from Italy. In the song itself, we are told nothing of the social or socioeconomic status in her life, but can conclude that, given her ability to travel, she is not of greatly limited means. We are also told nothing about her age, but as we will discover, while we could make a case for other than a young woman singing the song, it should be relatively evident that the song is sung by someone in her youth.

By identifying and considering the inclusion of choice words and phrases, the lens through which we understand the singer of the song focuses and informs our playing of the song. But we should not miss the overall: So universal is ". . . This is wondering when I'll see that boy again" that it is immediately understood to be what the singer wants and what all the talk has been about and for. "Girl wants boy" or "boy wants girl" or "boy wants boy" or "girl wants girl" is all of us at some point, and because of our internal connectivity to the notion, we become more invested in the story before us. Clara is flushed; she feels butterflies; young love is afoot.

> I've got a feeling he's just a someone, too.
> And the beauty is when you realize,

When you realize
Someone could be looking for a someone like you.

She is both directly and indirectly addressing the audience. She says, "like you" and not "like me," which of course means "like all of us."

Table Work II:
Why sing it and not just speak it?

The idea of why a song exists needs some introduction and interpretation at this point. Simply put, songs don't just appear with no reason whatsoever. Obviously, in an integrated musical, a song, in most cases, stems from the action that has preceded it. In that case, the reason for being of the song is provided for us. A song isolated from the context for which it was written, however, requires us to do that creative homework. Before we begin to merge objective, baseline facts with more subjective (personal and/or creative) data, we arrive at a juncture important to the work that we are required to do when preparing a song outside of a given context. Under these circumstances we *assign* the song a reason to be sung based on the information we are granted within the given text. When we are excising the song from the context for which it was written, the palette of possibilities widens considerably.

The answer to the following critical question becomes of utmost importance to us at this point: What has just happened in the moment or moments before the song begins to create the present situation (song), so why is it not sufficient to simply *say* these words instead of *singing* them? What is the occasion, incident, or happening that has provoked, incited, or prompted the song into action?

The answer to these questions provides the reason the song is to be sung, and all songs are sung in the present and as a direct response or reply to some impetus—an external stimulus from the immediate past or even long ago.

Because it is more concrete and logical to speak in tangibles than in intangibles when answering the above question, we'll take one song and apply the above criteria. Later, after we have a comprehensive understanding of this first building block of song presentation, we'll explore many more variables, ideas, and choices. To begin, we'll look at a song that, upon reading and hearing, seems like a straight-down-the-middle theatre ballad about love and longing.

"Make the Man Love Me"
(From *A Tree Grows in Brooklyn*)

Verse:

You kissed me once by mistake,
Thought I was somebody else.
I felt that kiss and I envied
That somebody else.
I wanted you for myself.
I guess I was shameless and bold.
But I made a plan in my heart,
I've never breathed,
I've never told.
Chorus
I must try to make the man love me,
Make the man love me now.
By and by I will make the man happy.
I know how.
He must see how badly I want him,
Want him just as he is.
May I say that should the man ask me,
I'll be his.
(Bridge)
Can I tell the man just how dearly
Blessed we could be?
All the beauty I see so clearly,
Oh, why can't he?
So, I pray to heaven above me,
Pray until day grows dim,
For a way to make the man love me
As I love him.

In the pages ahead, remain mindful that the most thrilling challenge of creating a performance of a song out of context (the context, in this case, is the largely forgotten musical version of *A Tree Grows in Brooklyn*) is that the circumstances that have inspired *your* rendition of the song, the timeline, back-story, the "you," the "they," and so on, must be entirely born from your creative imagination. Under these circumstances, *you hold the responsibility for the creation of an entity heretofore never seen or heard.*

A few basic facts have arrived ahead of our turning over any subjective information and are already clear as the text has provided them for us:

1   This is a lady with a very specific problem (and a universal one).

2   This is a lady who is experiencing the feelings brought on by unrequited, or as of yet, unreturned love.

3   This is a lady who holds a secret.

4   This a lady who doesn't yet have what she wants.

There is other significant information for us to initiate before we get on to why the song is being sung. We should ask ourselves about the history and relationship of the character singing and the individual and situation being sung about. This is evident, but not particularly specific, in the given text. We have to fill in those blanks and connect the dots of a vague lyric. Often you'll find (even if you don't perform the entire song because of time constraints) that the verse of the song contains clues as to the reason the song is being sung, and the history of the singer and situation. In this case, the first two lines of the verse emphatically state that the singer and the "other" (the "him") have some thread of an intimate history with one another:

You kissed me once by mistake,
Thought I was somebody else,

Is it plausible to surmise that this was actually an unintended kiss because of a mistaken identity? Probably not. On the other hand, did this kiss occur in a previous romantic entanglement that later resulted in the lady being jilted because the "him" discovered that he had misjudged the "her"?

The latter answer is more probable and will foster deeper and more meaningful content. Your version of the back-story could go something like this:

The lady and the "him" were romantically involved with each other at a time when she had recently been jilted by another and she was recovering from that upset. Her words and actions at that time had been cavalier and hurtful to the "him," but time has soothed her formerly confused heart and rendered her able to "show up" for this man.

This is a fairly simple "Hey, I've changed!" scenario, but the simplest answer is often the best answer, particularly when searching for the truth, and no one else's version will be exactly like your personal version. In the playing, what is key is that you establish in your mind, as a playwright would on paper, the history so that you have a foundation from which to build and *a fundamental reason to sing the song in the first place.*

As stated up front in this section, songs don't simply materialize. They generally exist in musicals as a means through which to "heighten" a scene of spoken dialog. When performing a song out of a particular context and to fully comprehend the given circumstances when playing the song in context, it is helpful to our creative process to imagine the scene that has taken place just prior to the beginning of the song.

Some dramatic event has just happened to trigger this internal response from the lady, and this event must be significant enough that *spoken dialog alone would not suffice.* The vessel through which these thoughts and feelings must be expressed is the singing of the song. I suggest that her response should be internal since this scene reads and plays more effectively when played in internal monologue fashion. This method also exposes the actor to a greater extent, requiring him to play the scene from the "inside out," quite individually.

When deciding on the specific happening that the singer is *responding to* by singing this song, ask yourself this question: How high are the stakes that are being sung about? Remember that the stakes are those which are yours to lose. If the stakes in the song are high (and we know what the stakes are by simply reading the text of the song), then there is a likelihood that the events that triggered them both in the moment before as well as in the back-story were very dramatic as well. I suspect that she has run into him by happenstance, possibly accompanied by his new love with whom he has become involved since ending his love affair with the singer of the song. *The deeper the entanglement, the more meaningful the song*. Each of these clarifies the reason for the song now being sung and antes up the "height" of the scene. When the preceding event is pitched higher, the response automatically pitches higher, which equals playing height, which all stage-worthy songs seek.

On the heels of the encounter, the lady expresses that she wants the man exclusively, and she has a plan:

> I must try to make the man love me,
> Make the man love me now.
> By and by I will make the man happy,
> I know how.

But she has a problem, and it's a tactical one. (Tactics that characters use to get what they want are discussed at length in the coming pages.) How does she convince the man to requite her love?

> Can I tell the man just how dearly
> Blessed we could be?[26]
> All the beauty I see so clearly,
> Oh, why can't he?

Until finally she expresses the problem to God and asks for concrete answers:

> So, I pray to heaven above me,
> Pray until day grows dim,
> For a way to make the man love me
> As I love him.

The rationale of the thinking and behavioral psychology of the character should also be taken into account when singing the song.

Even though she has been shaken by the encounter with the man, how rational is the character's state of mind when singing the song? Is the character running at a fevered pitch or settled, calm, and methodical? Is there a combination of these at different intervals in the song?

How would *you* react to this event internally? Bear in mind that external and internal behavior may often be completely different. Since the lady clearly hasn't put this love affair behind her (and doesn't intend to as we are to find out), the first lines of the song might well be sung by a lady who is rattled and disturbed and who hasn't yet reminded herself of her resolve. She might be visibly shaken, or she might be cool on the outside but breaking on the inside. This will affect the lady's (your) body language, and these are fundamental choices to make.

The *actual* outcome of the song isn't clear because the stated problem hasn't yet been solved (lady gets man back), but her resolve to get him to return to her couldn't be more clear and emphatic. It is our empathy with her situation and our perception of her sincerity, her likeability, and her unflappable will to succeed that engages us as an audience, causing us to root for her to get what she wants. Moreover, even though the lady is singing about him, we are much more interested in and compelled by *her*.

Table Work III:
Theatre song "brands" and traits that inform style and lead to playability

"Make the Man Love Me" might be thought of and described as an "I Will Get/Have" song, an "I Want" song. Songs of this powerful sentiment are pervasive in theatre songwriting. They provide transparency into the singer's frame of mind and agenda and can easily sum up in one or two verses (sometimes less) what drives the character to do this or that and what he hopes to get out of doing it. Other well-known Get/Have/I Want songs are exemplified by those such as "Matchmaker" (from *Fiddler on the Roof*) where the sisters sing about their want for the perfect match/husband, "Before the Parade Passes By" (from *Hello, Dolly!*), where Dolly looks to the skies and asks her deceased husband for his permission and his blessing to let her love again, and "I Want to Go to Hollywood" (from *Grand Hotel*), where the title says it all. These types of songs are frequently written as "internal monologue" numbers (as is the case with "Before the Parade Passes By" and as we have appointed in "Make the Man Love Me"). Full awareness of the "mission" of a song, even by categorizing it broadly as such, gives us clarity and trajectory of thought as we chart our way forward.

Accordingly, it is useful to discern which "brand" of song you are singing from the multiple varieties of them in order to understand the overarching message that the text is communicating. Song types include the following (in no particular order and bearing in mind that many songs incorporate two or even three of these traits):

The "Precipice" Song—These types of songs usually occur as the singer appears to be on the verge of an extremely high-stakes, life-changing event, and/or is convinced that there is no turning away from the inevitable. Examples of this type of song include "At the Fountain" (from *Sweet Smell of Success*), "Lonely Room" (from *Oklahoma!*), "Something's Comin'" (from *West Side Story*), "Yes, My Heart" (from *Carnival*), "I Can See It" (from *The Fantasticks*), "The Wizard and I" (from *Wicked*), and "Goodbye" (from *Catch Me If You Can*). The playing energy of these songs is usually extremely heightened and can even go as far as controlled musicalized mania.

The "Comes the Dawn" Song—These songs will usually come about as a result of a character having passed through one or a series of life lessons/realizations, or upon the conscious comprehension of what he really wants, thinks, knows, or believes after all is said and done. These songs are often delivered directly to the audience (as inner monologue or even directly) or to one other actor onstage (possibly his beloved whom he has forsaken in some fashion). Examples of this brand of song include "I Know the Truth" (from *Aida*), "There But for You Go I" (from *Brigadoon*), and "On the Steps of the Palace" (from *Into the Woods*).

The "Ode to You" Song—These songs occur when a character is singing to or about another character and offers superlatives relative to how character A (the singer of the song) appreciates character B (for whatever the reason). The important performance quality that character A should bring to the proceedings is that he should allow us (the audience or panel) to completely feel, see, and understand the effect that character B has on him. Examples include "Mama, A Rainbow" (from *Minnie's Boys*), "You Do Something to Me" (from Cole Porter's *Fifty Million Frenchmen*), "She Wasn't You" (from *On a Clear Day You Can See Forever*), and "You're the Top" (from *Anything Goes*).

The "Narrative" Song—Through this type of song, the singer generally delivers either back-story pertaining to his life or sometimes illustrates some whimsical, often exaggerated, or extravagant description of events yet to come that now exist only in his mind. Examples of this kind of song include "Nothing" (or any number of songs from *A Chorus Line*), "The Miller's Son" (from *A Little Night Music*), "The Best in the World" (from *A Day in Hollywood/A Night in the Ukraine*), and "That's the Way It Happens" (from *Me and Juliet*).

The **"End of the Line" Song**—This song type usually signals some mode of moving forward past the current state. Important to note is that these songs are not always gloom and doom, but instead may actually be upbeat and optimistic in nature. In addition, there's sometimes a fine line between this kind of song and the "comes the dawn" sort. Examples of this variety include "Back to Before" (from *Ragtime*), "Defying Gravity" (from *Wicked*), "Moments in the Woods" (from *Into the Woods*), and "Serious" (from *Legally Blonde*).

The **"Existential" Song**—This type of song may exist where the singer asks questions about himself (who am I and where do I fit in?) or with the singer acting on the cusp of the emergence of fresh self-realization. Examples include "Who Are You Now?" (from *Funny Girl*), "Where Do I Go?" (from *Hair*), "Alone in the Universe" (from *Seussical*), and "Is It Really Me?" (from *110 in the Shade*).

The **"I Am What I Am" Song**—These songs state what the character believes is factual information about himself and may exist as a means of working through what he believes is some obstacle related to that self-truth. Sometimes these songs will occur at the beginning of the musical, and serve as songs that frame the character and profess specific traits for the audience. Examples include "Man" (from *The Full Monty*), "Different" (from *Honk!*), "I Cain't Say No" (from *Oklahoma!*), "Aldonza" (from *The Man of La Mancha*), "Whatever Lola Wants, (Lola gets)" (from *Damn Yankees*), "Take Me or Leave Me" (from *Rent*), "Corner of the Sky" (from *Pippin*), and "I Believe" (from *The Book of Mormon*).

The **"It Is What It Is" Song**—This type of song often makes sweeping commentary about a state of life or the facts of the singer's relationship to another. "Love Changes Everything" (from *Aspects of Love*), "It's the Perfect Relationship" (from *Bells Are Ringing*), and "The Music that Makes Me Dance" (from *Funny Girl*) are examples of this song type.

The **"Hat in Hand" Song**—This type of song will often occur as the singer humbly asks someone for something related to matters of the heart, and may often occur as the singer attempts to win the heart or confidence of another. Examples include "Unworthy of Your Love" (from *Assassins*), "You Should Be Loved" (from *Side Show*), and "They Were You" (from *The Fantasticks*).

The **"Love Affair Gone Awry" Song**—These songs are often sung as a result of the singer's heartbreak, or when the singer is at the mercy of another's disinterest, insensitivity, and/or carelessness. Examples include "I Got It Bad (and that ain't good)" (from *Sophisticated Ladies* et al.), "But Not for Me" (from Gershwin's *Girl Crazy* et al.), and "Maybe I Like It This Way" (from Andrew Lippa's *The Wild Party*).

The **"I Remember" Song**—This type of song is often sung as the singer reflects on past events and is sometimes nostalgic in nature. Examples include "Those Were the Good Old Days" (from *Damn Yankees*), "Too Many Mornings" (from *Follies*), and "I Had Myself a True Love" (from *St. Louis Woman*).

The **"I Did It Because" Song**—These songs are sung as the singer is explaining himself or discussing some action taken, and often occur to describe some action or event that has taken place offstage or before the play's setting. Examples are "Cell Block Tango" (from *Chicago*), "All for You" (from *Seussical*), and "Rose's Turn" (from *Gypsy*).

The **"This Is What I (or You or We) Have to Do" Song**—This type of song is often sung as a "charge" song, wherein the singer attempts to encourage or inspire himself or another (or both) to overcome some obstacle and/or "take the plunge." Examples include "Climb Ev'ry Mountain" (from *The Sound of Music*), "You've Got Possibilities" (from *It's a Bird ... It's a Plane ... It's Superman*), "We Can Make It" (from *The Rink*), and "Say the Word" (from *The Unauthorized Autobiography of Samantha Brown*).

The **"Survivor" Song**—This type of song is sung when the character is offering narrative of past events and describing his plight therein. Examples might include "Another Suitcase in Another Hall" (from *Evita*), "I'm Still Here" (from *Follies*), and "Your Daddy's Son" (from *Ragtime*).

Get it done

1   Take a look at the lyrics of your song material. As you do, write down what the general situation is in the songs.

Phrase it simply, such as "In this song the singer wants to take someone on a date, but is afraid the person will say 'no.'" Don't place the song within any context, like the show it is from. Work only from the isolated lyric in front of you.

2   What do you learn by reading the song lyrics about the singer of the song's general disposition and frame of mind when singing the song? Also note any information the lyricist has provided about what is sometimes known as the "givens" or baseline facts. Be as specific as possible, but remember to work from a purely objective viewpoint.

3   Why is it important that the sentiment expressed in your song(s) happens through music? What impetus does the music provide that propels and influences the telling of the story of the song?

4   Using the list of theatre song "brands" provided, into which categories do your songs fall? Are there a number of them that are roughly the same in what the singer is experiencing when singing them?

CHAPTER FIVE

Off the Table and
Off the Page:

Techniques for Playability

Speaker–receiver interaction
and relationship

The speaker–receiver relationship has two important and quite different distinctions: to whom am I singing, and where do I direct my focus while singing? Songs either do or do not have scene partners (and consequently, may or may not include another player) or may be fashioned as an internal "thinking aloud" process by the singer and delivered alone onstage. In any solo performance and in the audition room unless a scene partner has been specifically dedicated (as in a callback), the scene partner (if there is one in your version) in the song is always, of course, *invisible* to the audience (panel). This leaves the singer of the song with the responsibility of crafting the audition so that viewers recognize the presence of the other, even though we cannot see him or hear him speak—those distinctions will exist and be born from the singer's creative mind. We should, however, from the singer's *responses* to the imaginary player, have specific ideas about what has been said between the singer and his "partner." These points are clarified by pointing out, as examples, two songs, both from the musical *Carousel*. In "Mister Snow," it is clear both in and out of context that the singer has important news that she is bursting to tell another (she has become engaged), and the song becomes imminently more "playable" with the invisible, silent "responses" from the scene partner (*which, again, the actress singing the song must imagine and respond to because no flesh and blood scene partner is present*).

This point is illustrated as follows:

"Mr. Snow"
(From *Carousel*)

Excerpt

Imagined Scene Partner's Response:
(Gasp) "You're engaged!?! I didn't even know you were dating anyone! Who is he!?!"
Singer:
"His name is Mister Snow and an upstanding man is he. He comes home ev'ry night in his round-bottomed boat with a net full of herring from the sea."
Response:
"Oh my God! I can't believe you've been keeping him a secret! I'm in shock! Go on . . ."
Singer:
"An almost perfect beau, as refined as a girl could wish, but he spends so much time in his round-bottomed boat, that he can't seem to lose the smell of fish!"
Response:
(Laughs) "Wow . . . I'm so happy for you both. Wonderful news! But this fish smell (making a face) . . . doesn't sound appealing."
Singer:
"The first time he kissed me, the whiff from his clothes knocked me flat on the floor of the room, but now that I love him, my heart's in my nose and fish is my favorite perfume!"
Response:

"Tell me how he proposed. I'm dying to know what happened!"
Singer:
"Last night he spoke quite low, and a fair-spoken man is he. And he said, 'Miss Pipperidge, I'd like it fine if I could be wed with a wife, and indeed, Miss Pipperidge, if you'll be mine, I'll be yours for the rest of my life!'"
Response:
"And what happened then?"
Singer:
"Next moment we were promised! And now my mind's in a maze, for all I can do is look forward to that wonderful day of days!"
Response:
"Have you set a wedding date? What kind of wedding do you want?"
Singer:
"When I marry Mister Snow the flowers'll be buzzin' with the hum of bees. The birds'll make a racket in the churchyard trees, when I marry Mister Snow."

And so on. Although the singer must perform the lyric of the song as written, the variety of imaginary responses from the scene partner is virtually unlimited as long as they are pertinent to the content being sung about.

Of course, the "cues" the singer receives from his invisible scene partner may also be nonverbal. Highly specific responses from you are easily justified by him "doing" the following while you are singing or between your lines (and you can easily understand how these quite disparate responses will elicit highly differing responses from you in return):

- Shaking his head with wide-eyed amazement

- Yawning

- Checking his texts or emails

- Nodding in agreement

- Telling the children to be quiet

- Giving you a patronizing look

- Taking off his clothes
- Rolling his eyes
- Shaking his head in disbelief
- Internally passing judgment on the situation
- Telling you to get on with your story

Since much of acting is reacting to someone else's words or actions, it's no wonder that too often solo performances, with no scene partner present, fall flat and are boring. When your creative imagination inserts specific responses such as the ones above, you are given much more to react to, making your solo performances more truthful, intuitive, and believable.

Interior monologue in song

Unlike "Mister Snow," where a scene partner is present, in the "Soliloquy," the singer is engaged in internal monologue, dreaming up scenarios of what will and won't be once his son (or daughter) is born. Whatever stimulus the singer is responding to as a matter of engagement must be crafted and imagined inside his *own* head and not in that of another.

"Soliloquy"
(From *Carousel*)

Excerpt

Singer's internal thought:
"A daughter! . . . I might be the father of a little girl! Wow . . . A father . . . me!"
Sung:
"I got to get ready before she comes! I got to make certain that she won't be dragged up in slums with a lot o' bums like me."
Singer's internal thought:
"My parents raised three boys and I've never even been a father before . . . how do I be a dad to a daughter?"

Sung:
"She's got to be sheltered and fed and dressed in the best that money can buy!"
Singer's internal thought:
"But I don't even have any damn money to buy her clothes . . ."
Sung:
"I never knew how to get money, but, I'll try, by God! I'll try! I'll go out and make it or steal it or take it or die!"

The singer's internal thought process shares a great deal in common with subtext, which we explore further later, but there is one stark difference: subtext, the unspoken (unsung) words under the actual spoken (sung) words—those that the speaker (singer) may be *really thinking*—does not necessarily prompt the next line. Internal thought process such as is described above should, however, generate for the singer *something specific to respond to*.

As to the point of focus of the eyes, singers often experience confusion and even frustration regarding where to focus their eyes when playing a song in the audition room or when playing the song "out front." A good rule when playing a song with an imaginary scene partner is to establish a "home base," usually above and over the audience's (panel's) head, from which to comfortably and predictably return eye focus when "engaging" with the "scene partner." This allows everyone in the room the silent understanding that a scene partner is present and is engaged with the singer, and vice versa. With internal thought songs, whether in the audition room or in a production, singers often find that using the right to left and above the panel's or audience members' heads technique is useful. This technique frees the singing actor to "ask, search, and find" what he is singing about with the greatest amount of flexibility. In an audition, contrary to what some would say, I don't feel that it's ever a good idea or at all advantageous to play a song directly to or make any eye contact whatsoever with the panel during the presentation, except on the rare occasion that it is appropriate based on the content of the material to do so. Outside of those times, involving the panel as any more than observers often tends to make the panel members ill-at-ease and may seem to prompt them to participate and validate in some fashion.

The lines under the lines (subtext in song)

The companion strategy to the imaginary (although, again, it should be emphasized that to the singer they are very real) lines between the lines discussed above is that of what occurs *simultaneously* with the sung line as it is being sung and that may indicate its true meaning. *Subtext* is as ever-present in the sung line as it is in the spoken one, and the use of it indicates the threshold through which the singer of the song is no longer simply delivering music and lyrics, but instead becomes a thinking, feeling human being who is singing the song.

Subtext is always present in our daily lives. For example, if you were to say to yourself or to a friend, "I just feel like being a couch potato today," what seems like a simple and innocuous statement of fact may actually mean, "*I know I should be doing laundry/calling my mother/studying for my exam/ironing my shirt for tomorrow but I really don't feel like doing any of those things.*"

Listen for the subtext in *West Side Story* when Anita sings: "A boy like that who'd kill your brother, forget that boy and find another!" What she is *really* and *also* saying is, "This boy cannot be trusted! He will lie to you, deceive you, and probably worse! Your heart will be shattered! He is not one of 'us.'" This will affect and color the delivery considerably. Conversely, when Maria responds with "I have a love, and he's all that I have. Right or wrong, what else can I do?" what she is *really* and *also* saying is "*But Anita . . . please . . . I beg of you to understand. . . . I need your support and I trust this boy. Please try to understand.*"

Subtext is that which is not *expressly* stated but rather *implicitly* stated (the difference between what we say and what we are thinking), and that the audience perhaps understands to be true either immediately or over some period of time as the scene or play unfolds.

It may help foster a better understanding by placing the idea of subtext in even more general terms: If the words of the song (or play) are the fabric of the creation, then the subtext, along with many other components, is that which stitches and weaves it together, creating an interesting, creative, and realistic union.

Using subtext in the singing of songs out of context is vital because it keeps the singer away from generalized, one-dimensional, and flat performances. (Further exercises in personalization relevant to this topic are found in the following pages.) Consider the added subtext to the following George and Ira Gershwin song as an example of this:

"I've Got a Crush on You"
(From *Strike up the Band*)

Verse

Sung line:
"How glad the many millions of Annabelles and Lillians would be to capture me!"
My added subtext:
I'm kidding, but in truth I have always thought of myself as an eternal bachelor.
"But you had such persistence, you wore down my resistance."
And to be honest . . . it was way over the top sometimes . . .
"I fell, and it was swell."
It made a nice change from the last time when I had my heart broken.
"I'm your (lyric changed from "You're my" to accommodate a male singer) big and brave and handsome Romeo."
That's what all women want, isn't it?
"How I won you I shall never, never know."
All joking aside . . . I feel like I've won the lottery here.
"It's not that you're attractive."
That was a stupid thing to say . . . I'm just nervous . . . I should probably get to the point, shouldn't I?
"But, oh, my heart grew active when you came into view."
Well . . . to tell the truth, it threw me for a loop . . . but . . .
Chorus
"I've got a crush on you, Sweetie Pie."
I can't believe I'm coming clean and this is me talking . . .
"All the day and night-time hear me sigh."
I used to roll my eyes at all this corny love stuff, but now it's happening to me.
"I never had the least notion that I could fall with so much emotion."
Especially the first time we met when you were wearing that hideous hat.

"Could you coo, could you care for a cunning cottage we could
share?"
Well, what about you? Do you share my feelings?
"The world will pardon my mush,"
Exactly the stuff I used to make fun of and scoff at.
"'Cause I've got a crush, my baby, on you."
*So there it is ... that's my whole story ... it's all out in the open
now.*

Music as subtext

The above example is evidence that even simple language and
expression of feeling can easily have the kind of undertext that
propels the story along, fills out the story with interesting choices to
play, and then notches up the performance content considerably.
Those who sing in the theatre also have an added advantage: Music
can be, in and of itself and by its nature, both affirmative of the text
and sometimes contradictory of it. In other words, unlike a character
onstage who may be saying something, thinking something entirely
different, and even behaving contrary to both, *the music most often
tells the truth about what the singer of the song is actually feeling.*

Consider several examples: In "Where in the World," Archie's
emotional song deep into Act II of *The Secret Garden*, the fiery
stampede-like musical accompaniment mirrors precisely the internal
tempest that the character is experiencing and singing about.
Conversely, in disposition, in *Oklahoma!*'s "Many a New Day,"
Laurey sings about things such as "many a light lad may kiss and fly
... a kiss gone by is bygone ..." in a flippant, *c'est la vie* fashion,
and the airy and flitting musical accompaniment supports the
sentiment quite literally. By contrast, the musical accompaniment in
"Colored Lights," the Act I opening song in *The Rink*, often
contradicts the singer's text. The music answers a song lyric filled
with pleasant, grounded, and earthy images like "sitting on a sand
dune in Santa Cruz" and "sailing out of Long Beach on a catamaran"
with restless and deliberately ungrounded accompaniment reflective
of the singer's true inner restlessness and conflict, and sometimes
utilizes musical dissonances to further substantiate those interior
quarrels.

Perhaps one of the most salient and easily recognizable moments of musical "truth telling" in theatre occurs in the magnum opus "Rose's Turn" late into the second act of *Gypsy*. As Rose instructs her imaginary audience to "hold your hats and hallelujah. Mama's gonna show it to you," the music turns sour underneath and then quickly transforms a moment of consonant unadulterated show-biz-manship into a moment of poisonous self-doubt and dissonant self-hatred. As the music turns momentarily agreeable again, Rose sings "Mama's doin' fine" and "Mama's gettin' hot" into "Mama's all alone" as the music disintegrates yet again, and Rose spirals into an unmitigated breakdown. As Rose sings the final "Everything's coming up roses this time for me," outwardly convinced that it is indeed "her turn," fragments of the music appear once again inharmonious, signaling perhaps the truth that Rose is deeply aware of her own fate: The possibility of her "moment" has long passed. The scene is seminal, and an exemplary example of how music can support and confirm the character's inner dialog, and at times, contradict it, sometimes only moments apart.

Get it done

1   To whom are you speaking (singing) in each of your songs? Another person? Yourself? A group? The audience? If you are addressing another person in your song, write down just who that person is and the imaginary lines he or she is speaking between your lines that may motivate your next line. If you are working from interior monologue, what thoughts are going through the singer's (your) head that you respond to and that may prompt the next line?

2   Look at your song lyric very carefully. What is the subtext? What lies beneath the sung line that lives only in the singer's (your) mind that is not explicitly stated? In other words, what are (or might be) you *also* saying, just not aloud through these chosen words? What is in the back-story and how does it affect your choice of words? Why have you chosen to use these particular words instead of just saying (singing) what you're really thinking?

3   How are the musical melody and accompaniment related
to what you are singing? Do they support the sentiment
and expressions of each of the lines and phrases?
Contradict it? How and why? Pay attention to musical
texture and energy and the contour of accompaniment
figures and melodic phrases. Also, pay close attention
to dissonances (a "clashing" note or chord) at moments
within the song and ask yourself why they exist. Could
any or all of these be providing you with glimpses
into the singer's true mindset, perhaps especially
that which may be lurking underneath what is
explicitly said (sung)?

Objectives: What's the problem?
(the *want* is always stronger)

Often, the most artistically and creatively profitable songs for both
the singer and the audience are those in which the singer is, before
our eyes, confronted with some problematic situation and is in the
midst of actively determining how to fix it. Sometimes the singer is
even sorting through a variety of large or small crises that are often
more situational than existential.

If it's true that everyone *wants something* in the theatre, then it's
also true that in all likelihood they have a problem (or multiple
problems) in *getting it*. In other words, there are issues to sort out
or overcome before the "have" as a result of the "want" can occur.
These stumbling blocks, or obstacles, can be in or of the moment,
or may occur as a larger problem or problems over the course of the
entire play (musical). There is no quantifiable percentage of which
happens more in songs as the singer will as often state what he
wants in life as what he wants right now. The obstacles blocking
the way of his getting what he wants may be a person or persons
or a situation or circumstance that create conflict, and conflict is,
of course, the basis of all drama. Songs will often begin with a state
of being (the now or the past) that indicates how things are/
were without having "it" (what he wants) and move on to a
description of how he plans on attaining it and possibly what

his life will be like once he gets it. Additionally, the songs will often include details about the obstacles that prevent him from immediately having it.

Consider the following lyric fragments from *Shrek* (the Broadway musical) that sums up the above perfectly:

"Who I'd Be"
(From *Shrek the Musical*)

Excerpt

An ogre always hides
An ogre's fate is known
An ogre always stays
In the dark and all alone
(Cut)
Of course, I'd be a hero,
And I would scale a tower
To save a hot house flower,
And carry her away
But standing guard would be a beast
I'd somehow overwhelm it,
I'd get the girl, I'd take a breath,
And I'd remove my helmet.
We'd stand and stare we'd speak of love
We'd feel the stars ascending
We'd share a kiss, I'd find my destiny
I'd have a hero's ending
A perfect happy ending.

The lyric reveals exactly what the singer wants (the girl) and the result(s) of getting it (true love and a happy ending). While most song lyrics may not paint the picture in such a storybook fashion (one perfectly appropriate for this particular story), this lyric provides an overview of how singers will make statements about what they want and the results of having it.

Other lyrics are more conventional:

"Sweet Liberty"
(From *Jane Eyre*)

Excerpt

It's twelve o'clock in the pitch-black night,
I can't contain my wanderlust.
I seek a new adventure,
And search the skies because I must,
I hunger for new faces,
To find a better destiny.
And fly among the swallows,
Far above the troubled sea.
Over mountains,
Over oceans
Heaven take me away.
For I long for my liberty,
For sweet liberty I pray.

Witnessing the singer (the "wanter"), who in this case is a young woman who aches for liberation from her present circumstances, "push against" the obstacle (the thing that resoundingly says "you can't have it!") is what keeps us in our seats and paying attention as audience members. The obstacle is the limited means that she has and the customary role of women in the time period in which the musical occurs. In the theatre, the *want* is *always* stronger and more compelling than the *have*, and it seems that all of the characters in the theatre (certainly the leading characters) have a "big brass ring" that they actively endeavor to acquire.

Tactics: How do I solve the problem?

As in "real" life, the singers of the songs use a variety of ways and means, or *tactics*, to get what they want. If the boy wants the girl, but the girl doesn't want him, then the boy must conjure up tactics in order to win her heart, or vice versa. In the musical *Legally Blonde*, Elle Woods devises a strategy to get her former boyfriend back: She will smarten up and make him realize that she isn't as superficial and one-dimensional as he thinks she is. In short, she will become more "serious." Tactically speaking, Elle studies for the LSATs, applies to Harvard Law School, and even decides to change her hair color in order to win his affections anew.

Of utmost importance to the singer during the process of getting what he wants is to work out *vivid ideas and images of what "having it" means, looks, and feels like. After all, if I have it, then my problems are solved.* These pictures will remain with you throughout the building and performing of the song, and are the fire in the eyes of the singer. Without specific images and internal responses to specify how it would feel to "have it," the singer is likely to be "acting" in a far too general way because the payoff of "getting it" is fuzzy and unclear to him. Retaining these images and responses and keeping his eyes on the prize in every moment of the song work will act as the singer's compass, keeping him on message.

Finally, where or what is the *danger* of the situation? "Danger" is powerful and can be present in many forms, including the danger of:

- fighting for something
- getting "it"
- not getting "it"
- lying
- the unknown
- time not being on your side
- wanting something that is forbidden
- being found out
- hurting someone else emotionally or physically
- walking away from someone or something

Placing emphasis on and playing the danger of the "want" and associating these with the tactics of getting what you want stirs up compelling, vivid deliveries of text. If you stop to consider it, if the "want" is potent and powerful enough to evoke the singing of a song (which again, can and should *only* occur if speech won't get the job done), then there is probably at least a fair amount of "danger" that accompanies it.

All of the above from this section and the one prior can be summarized in four methodical steps, and writing down answers and responses to these is always a good idea when approaching a song:

1   Have a clear statement of the state of the situation and the players and/or of the objective or problem to be solved (if there is one) along with a succinct declaration of the "want" of the singer.

2   Have a clear statement of what the obstacle is that is standing in the way of having it and the resulting conflict (internal or external) as well as a clear idea and understanding of what having it feels like, looks like, and means. What, then, if you don't get it?

3   Identify the tactics that the singer of the song is using to get what he wants to solve the problem (when and if these are present in the song).

4   Have a clear statement of how the matter is resolved (when applicable).

Get it done

1   In the songs you are singing, what do you want (your objectives)? What are you fighting for? What are you asking for from others or from yourself? Why? What does it look and feel like to get it? How do you benefit from getting it? What happens if you don't? Perhaps most importantly, what does it look and feel like to not get it? Keep in mind, especially as you explore the next question, that "fighting" for something does not necessarily involve anger or being angry.

2   How do you plan on getting what you want? What are your means of getting that thing that means everything to you in the song and you are therefore singing about? What are the steps you will take or are taking to execute this plan? Be exact and specific. Perhaps you plan to do nothing. What then? What does that look and feel like? Why is it "dangerous"?

Charting it out: Hitting objectives and tactical points and identifying obstacles

As mentioned earlier, it's useful to create a written account (a worksheet is included to assist you with this process) of what you need to accomplish over the course of the song (objectives); the means through which those objectives could be met (tactical measures); and the thing, things, person, or persons preventing you getting it or providing resistance to the course of you getting it. In other words, which obstacles need to be removed in order to get what you want? As has been pointed out previously, it's also extremely important to know what has occurred leading up to the present song being sung, as has also been pointed out previously.

Begin large with the most overarching of all the points: "This song exists in order to _____" and "By the time the song ends, _____ needs to be accomplished." If your objective in the song is to get someone to do something, take an action, or behave a certain way (as in a "This is what I/you/we have to do" song or "I want" song), then the statement might read, "This song exists in order to get the recipient to listen to me and understand and empathize with what I need and why I need it" (through the tactics that I use to do so) and "By the time the song ends I need for him to agree to loan me fifty dollars" (as in the aforementioned "Some People" where the sum was actually eighty-eight bucks).

In "Everybody Says Don't," a song from Stephen Sondheim's *Anyone Can Whistle*, the singer has a very particular task to complete by song's end and highly specific modus operandi.

"Everybody Says Don't"
(From *Anyone Can Whistle*)

Partial lyric for illustrative purposes:

Section I
Everybody says don't,
Everybody says don't,
Everybody says don't,
It isn't right.

Don't! It isn't nice!
Everybody says don't,
Everybody says don't,
Everybody says: don't walk on the grass,
Don't disturb the peace,
Don't skate on the ice.
Well,
I
Say
Do!
I say
Walk on the grass, it was meant to feel!
I
Say
Sail!
Tilt at the windmill,
And if you fail, you fail!
Section II
Make just a ripple.
Come on be brave.
This time a ripple,
Next time a wave!
Sometimes you have to start small,
Climbing the tiniest wall,
Maybe you're going to fall,
But it is better than not starting at all!
Section III
Everybody says no,
Everybody says stop,
Everybody says: mustn't rock the boat!
Mustn't touch a thing!
Everybody says don't,
Everybody says wait,
Everybody says: can't fight city-hall.
Can't upset the cart,
Can't laugh at the king.
Well, I
Say
Try!
I

Say:
Laugh at the kings or they'll make you cry!
Lose
Your poise!
Fall if you have to,
But lady, make a noise!

At face value, this song serves as a vehicle for the singer to establish his disagreement with some of the boundaries that the establishment has ordered onto society at large. What the song is really about, however, is convincing the recipient (the hearer of the song) to get onboard with him, resist the rules, and probably do something in particular that would no doubt be of benefit for the singer, although in the song we aren't told just what that benefit would or could be. Therefore, by the time the song ends, the singer needs to have convinced the listener to buck the system and stand up and voice her opinions on matters that seem unreasonable, which probably means some gain to the advantage of the singer.

At the next stage of the song analysis, the song breaks into smaller and then ever-smaller elements until finally it is individual words that become the subjects of our attention. The song has been divided into three sections for the sake of illustration. In charting what needs to be accomplished in each section (which is the logical follow-up to the objectives of the entire song as a whole), the following could be stated:

Section I exists in order to establish the singer's point of view regarding obedience and conformity, whatever the outcome.

Section II serves to motivate, instigate, and cajole the listener (the scene partner) to shake things up, not resolve herself to the status quo (presumably if she feels strong injustice or inequity), and not become discouraged if the result or the outcome disappoints.

Section III uses more elevated, motivational, and exclamatory language and exists to reinforce the message in a no-uncertain-terms way, but likely also to overcome any objections that the recipient has about her comfort levels and willingness to do what the singer is asking or telling her to do.

Breaking the song into smaller components (actual lines of sung dialog or lyrics within each section) promotes understanding of the singer's objectives and thought processes as well as a better understanding of the point of singing the song as exemplified by the following:

"Everybody says don't" means what seemingly everyone who is a figure of authority or otherwise powerful person is saying to the singer in an attempt to guide or influence the singer's moral/political or social consciousness by pointing out what the rules are.

"Well, I say do. Walk on the grass, it was meant to feel" points out what is the singer's mantra in this song: The rules should be challenged and authority questioned.

"Make just a ripple. Come on be brave" indicates the singer's first appeal to the recipient (the listener) to get her to do what he wants her to do and adopt the same credo.

"Lose your poise. Fall if you have to, but lady, make a noise" is the singer's impassioned plea for the singer to have no fear of consequence and become irate and even enraged over or about whichever rule or idea she challenges.

Further, there exist within these lines "power" words and phrases that reveal and describe what is most relevant in the lyric with respect to the overall point(s) of the song:

"Everybody says don't," "I say do," "feel," "sail," "fail," "make just a ripple," "be brave," "next time a wave," "it's better than not starting at all," "no," "stop," "mustn't," "fight," "upset," "laugh," "try," "they'll make you cry," "lose your poise," and "make a noise" are all powerful words that the singer will, in delivery, find very useful when making his case.

"Power" words and phrases more often than not are filled with vivid verbs that the singer will want to "punch up" when singing the song, and are the moments that sometimes beg to be "belted" (when possible and applicable). They assist the singer in putting over the most brilliant and dramatic performances, allowing the listener to comprehend his message in no uncertain terms or cloudy language.

As you know by now, general tactics are the means through which the singer gets what he wants. In the case of this song, they are used in pleading his case and include coercion, appealing to the recipient's sense of injustice, "egging on" the recipient, and describing the advantageous outcome if the recipient does what the singer asks (tells) and the nondesirable outcome or consequences if the recipient fails to do what the singer asks.

Important tactical phrases that the singer uses to get what he wants could include: "I say do," "walk on the grass, it was meant to feel," "I say sail," "if you fail you fail," "make just a ripple," "come on be brave," "next time a wave," "it's better than not starting at all," "lose your poise," and "lady, make a noise."

As was the case with powerful words and phrases, powerful tactical phrases deserve the utmost attention and investment from the singer as lynchpins of his performance.

The obstacles are what is preventing the singer from getting what he wants or having his needs met. In "Everybody Says Don't," these would include the listener's repeated objections to what she is being asked to do, her nonwillingness to conform, her sense of self-preservation, and her fear of consequence.

Song worksheet

Items 1–4 are most relevant when preparing the song within the context of the musical it appears in and requires an overview of the entire libretto.

Title of Song _____

Composer/Lyricist _____

Show (if any) _____

Year of Premier _____

Finding the "Givens" (when known as supplied by the playwright/lyricist):

1) Biographical:
   a) Name of character _____
   b) Age _____
   c) Hometown _____
   d) Now lives in _____
   e) Occupation _____
   f) Significant other or married? _____
   g) His or her name(s) _____
   h) How long? _____
   i) Children _____
   j) Ages of children _____
   k) Parents' names _____

l) Parents living or dead? _____
m) Siblings _____
n) How many? _____
o) Character's socioeconomic reality _____

2) What the character says about himself in his text (script or song lyrics):
   a) _____
   b) _____
   c) _____

3) What others in the play say about the character in their script or song(s):
   a) _____
   b) _____
   c) _____

4) Actions the character takes to support, substantiate, or contradict what he or others say about himself/him. It is important to remember that true character is revealed not only by words but also by actions. What a character says about himself and/or what others say about him may, in reality, be radically different from his "real" self:
   a) _____
   b) _____
   c) _____

The "Moment Before," Character, and Song Objectives:

In the moment(s) before the song begins, the following has/have occurred that propelled the song into action (when preparing the song out of context this may be supplied by your creative imagination):

_____

_____

1) Super objective(s) (what I the character) want(s) over the course of the play if performing in context):

The character wants to get/have/do/accomplish:
   a) _____
   b) _____
   c) _____

2) Song objective(s) (what I (the character/singer) want(s) over the course of the song when preparing the song either in context or out of context):

This song exists in order to:
a) _____
b) _____
c) _____

By the time the song ends, I need to get/have/do/accomplish:
a) _____
b) _____
c) _____

Section (or verse) objectives:
a) In section (verse) one of the song I, as the singer of the song, need to get/have/do/accomplish: _____
_____
_____

b) In section (verse) two of the song I need to get/have/do/accomplish:
_____
_____
_____

c) In section (verse) three of the song I need to get/have/do/accomplish:
_____
_____
_____

3) Line objectives: certain select key lines that reveal what the song is about and support what I need to accomplish by and through singing the song:
a) Line: _____
which means _____
b) Line: _____
which means _____
c) Line: _____
which means _____
d) Line: _____
which means _____

4)   "Power" words or phrases that reveal/describe/are important to my cause/mission/getting what I want:

a)   _____ is important because_____

b)   _____ is important because_____

c)   _____ is important because_____

d)   _____ is important because_____

e)   _____ is important because_____

f)   _____ is important because_____

g)   _____ is important because_____

h)   _____ is important because_____

i)   _____ is important because_____

j)   _____ is important because_____

TACTICAL MEASURES

1)   The general tactics I use in the show/song in order to get what I want:

a) _____

b) _____

c) _____

d) _____

e) _____

f) _____

2)   Key tactical lines: lines that are sung as tactics to get what I want in the song:

a) _____

is sung in order to get/have/do/accomplish_____

_____

b) _____

is sung in order to get/have/do/accomplish_____

_____

c) _____

is sung in order to get/have/do/accomplish_____

_____

d) _____

is sung in order to get/have/do/accomplish_____

_____

e) _____

is sung in order to get/have/do/accomplish_____

_____

OBSTACLES:
The obstacles that must be removed in order to get what I want/
my needs met are:

a) _____

b) _____

c) _____

d) _____

e) _____

THE IDEAL OUTCOME:
If all goes as planned, the following happens:

_____

_____

THE LESS THAN IDEAL OUTCOME:
If all does not go as planned, the following may happen:

_____

_____

THE ACTUAL OUTCOME (if applicable):

_____

_____

Methods and modes of song delivery

As an audience member, you're far more likely to remain attentive to a riveting story with absorbing storytelling where the stakes are high and the storyteller is committed rather than to the one with apathetic and energetic low-stakes storytelling. It's only natural.

The trouble far too often, however, comes when an audience witnesses singing actors who appear to have little or no sense of urgency or investment as to the outcome or who claim to "feel" involved but that so-called involvement isn't playing or "reading" enough or not at all. He may be working from the inside out, but what's coming out hardly registers with the viewer. Performances where the performer is merely telling us and not showing us can result in a performance that comes off as being in neutral, flat-footed, and frankly, a bore.

Because of their nature, songs seek height and exist because merely speaking about whatever is driving their sentiment and reason for being isn't enough. In other words, songs, when viewed functionally, are "elevated" naturally over spoken dialog, but the moment isn't yet at its zenith. This can only occur through the singer, who must not just match that elevation but rather must exceed it if the delivery is to be truly successful.

One technique for accomplishing this task is to begin your work from the energy levels of crisis mode downward (when needed), modifying it appropriately as you proceed to match the moment-to-moment and overall sentiment and intention of the material. The theory behind this method is simple: It will keep you, the singer, out of the apathetic and indifferent zone, and it's easier to tone down and dial back a performance than to do the reverse. It's also helpful toward this end to always be thinking and planning several steps beyond normal, real-life responses for readability in the playing. What this entails in practice might pan out as follows if the expressed sentiment of the song or portion of the song is:

Expressed Sentiment:	Try Playing:
Romantic Love	Obsessive Passion
Anger	Rage
Confusion	Bewilderment
Anticipation	Anxious

Lonely	Forgotten
Apathy	Lethargy
Overzealous	Frenzied
Hopeful	Desperate

Other practical applications that ably serve this cause are select methods or modes of delivery designed to heighten the playing of the text. These are scenarios in which the actor "places" himself when delivering the song lyrics that by their nature elicit amplified deliveries and responses. There are undoubtedly infinite variables in this exercise for the singer to contemplate and conjure, but these might include:

- The "Therapist" Delivery—This is a method or mode whereby the song lyric is delivered to an imaginary therapist as though in a psychoanalytic session in which the speaker (singer) is revealing the issue or problem at hand with elevated emotion and gesticulations, and seeking advice and counsel to a solution.

- The "Telling a Child a Story" Delivery—This encourages clear and calculated articulation of the subject of the lyric with certainty toward the child's (audience's) understanding and comprehension.

- The "Explanation to a Traffic Cop in Order to Avoid a Ticket (or otherwise making an explanation to an authority figure)" Delivery—This one is self-evident.

- The "Writing a Letter that You Never Intend to Send" Delivery—This method is executed by revealing the song lyric as though writing a no-holds-barred letter and baring your soul in order to get it off your chest. It may result in illuminating the speaker's (singer's) true uninhibited feelings and thoughts fluidly and without reservation.

- The "Lion's Den (or Shark Tank)" Delivery—Here, you deliver your text to your scene partner as though explaining where the key is to unlock the door that will get you out of this precarious predicament.

- The "First Date" Delivery—In this approach, you feel compelled to reveal personal information to someone hearing it for the first time and then navigating their responses.

- The "I Wish I Had Said It This Way" Delivery—We've all had moments, particularly after a heated and elevated confrontation with another person, in which we replay the events in our minds and edit and revise what we said in the interest of having our feelings and sentiments clearly understood. In this type of delivery, we are liberated to express ourselves succinctly and with candor.

- The "Punching Bag" Delivery—This works particularly well when singing those "I Want" songs. Rehearse the song with an imaginary punching bag in front of you and punch at it repeatedly and with fervor. You might notice the tendency to punch with all the more veracity in those key moments within the lyric in which you are revealing what you want and/or that the music itself is especially heightened with excitability, subtextual or not. This may help you physically connect body and lyric.

- The "I Only Have Two Minutes" Delivery—Imagine that the receiver is aboard a train soon to pull away from the station or is about to walk down the aisle and get married. Here, you only have two minutes to tell the recipient how you really feel.

Take a moment to contemplate your current song lyrics or those supplied in this book within the above scenarios. You'll likely find new vistas into clarity of emotional articulation and even revelation. Using these techniques goes a long way toward keeping performances out of the doldrums and enlivening the singer's responses. This is likely to create a three-dimensional performance. If the delivery is overextended and overwrought, the singer will nearly always realize it instinctively; but in my experience, using these techniques only serves to liberate and free up the singer's impulses toward vibrant and truthful deliveries of the song.

Finally, there are a few tips to remind yourself and be reminded of as you apply the concepts set in motion in this section:

- Play the moment to moment/stay in the moment (and don't project the result):

This point is perhaps best exemplified by pointing to the kind of song in which the singer is actively working through a problematic situation or conundrum, methodically or not. Allowing each beat to propel and feed the next is key. Proceed moment-by-moment and beat-to-beat, playing the process until finally there arrives an outcome (and possibly consequence).

- Leave yourself someplace to go/pace yourself appropriately:

  This goes hand-in-hand with the previous tip in that the text must always dictate your output dramatically and vocally, but also in the sense that you must continually check in with the text to be certain that what you are doing and what you are saying are in agreement. Equally important, however, is that your output must play as levels of varied energy as a mirror of the journey of the song. For example, on a 1 (rather contemplative or matter of fact) to 5 (fever pitch) scale, very few songs play as one number and stay there consistently for the duration. Know where your 1s (often at the beginning), 5s (often at the end), and each number in between are and play your output accordingly.

- Constantly ask yourself what has happened to propel the singing of this song and how that makes you feel:

  If enough powerful feelings are present in the singer of the song so that he *must* sing about whatever has just occurred, then chances are you'd have fervent feelings too if placed in that or a similar circumstance. Use your own experiences not only to deepen, but also to help make exact your personal and singular delivery.

- Don't let the train leave you behind; the song is always in motion:

  No song must ever be in neutral, and there must be an ongoing sense of discovery of the next thought, sentiment, or statement throughout the lyric. Music and lyrics must never be static or devoid of active forward movement. Always have the interest of advancing the plot through

tactics chosen to break through obstacles at the core of
your approach and your resulting delivery.

- Constantly ask yourself "What does the composer/lyricist
mean when he says _____," "What does the character mean
when he says _____," "What does the music mean when it
goes _____," and so on. Subtext may or may not be
emphatic, but is undeniably present in words and also in
music. You need only listen carefully to the music to
understand the feelings and mood the composer wishes to
evoke. The text may require more digging. When a
character says, "I like your shoes," he may or may not be
actually referring to the shoes themselves, but rather to
what the shoes represent. Other, more direct statements or
questions from the pen of the lyricist and the mouth of the
character will also transmit the causes of carrying forward
the plot, aiding the character in problem solving, getting
what he wants, or existing for any number of reasons.
Know these reasons well before singing the lines yourself.

- What does the composer/lyricist want me to feel and want
the audience to feel through me? Often, the reason we
stand before an audience in the first place is subverted by
the other goings-on in song work. Staying connected to
the song's *raison d'être* will ground your work and provide
a home base from which the experience will extend
outward.

Get it done

1   Which mode of delivery best suits each of your songs?
Which of your songs is largely confessional? Instructional?
Nervous? Excited? Is the singer desperate for a result or
needing desperately to get something off his chest?

2   For any of the above temperaments, go over the top,
kicking up the delivery several levels. Note your discoveries
through using this technique and adjust the delivery
downward as appropriate to feel more natural, while still
retaining extroverted and clear objectives and intentions.

3 Assume that no character has ever stood offstage and meditated on what he would say to the audience once he came onstage. Instead, he is discovering all that he is singing about right here and right now. What is the singer discovering as he goes along? What are the responses to these discoveries?

CHAPTER SIX

A Music and Musical Theatre Term Lexicon

This section alphabetically lists words and phrases that are used in preparatory work in music and the musical theatre. I strongly advise using this lexicon as an essential reference source for fluidity of communication and understanding here and in the rehearsal room. It's a good idea as well to commit as many of these terms to memory as possible as they are ever-present in the "process."

This is not an all-inclusive list. For example, words such as *consonant* and *downstage*, while being musically and theatrically relevant, are presupposed to be words that you can already define and need no further explanation here.

Many of these terms (especially the musical terms) have multiple or even absolute definitions as found in music dictionaries, but some have been tailored here *to apply to those singing and auditioning for the musical theatre.*

AABA form: A musical structure format indicating that the song begins (in the *truest* definition) with an *A* section (typically eight measures of music) that is followed by a second *A* section (again, typically eight measures of possibly the same melody but a different lyric) and then followed by a *B* section (typically eight measures with different melody *and* a different lyric) then returning to another *A* section (eight measures with a different lyric). This structure is somewhat antiquated in contemporary songwriting, but was prevalent in songwriting throughout much of the early and mid-twentieth century. Nowadays, an eight-bar-per-section status quo is no longer necessarily the standard[27] as the sections in modern songwriting can and will have any number of corresponding bars. Additionally, a section will frequently return in a modified format with varying numbers of bars (often elongated and sometimes wildly abbreviated from the original appearance) and musical content. Often directors, musical directors, and vocal coaches (including myself) will use phrases such as "let's go back to the *A*" as a point of reference when they are referring to an entire section of a song even when the song is not written in AABA structure. Accordingly, it's useful to think of *A* and *B*, and even *C* structures, as catch-all terms when referring to specific musical sections.

Air: The term used to describe any point within a song that the singer isn't singing. The introduction, instrumental-only sections, and any music between the end of the vocal and the end of the song itself would all be considered air.[28]

Arpeggio: A somewhat rapid succession of notes that are often, but not always, common to a particular musical chord played by the pianist either upward or downward through the musical range (up or down the keyboard). Sometimes an arpeggio will appear as the "lead-in" to the vocal entrance.

Bar: In musical structure, bars indicate the separation of groups of beats for the sake of organization and for emphasis. Beats may be grouped into bars four at a time, three at a time, two at a time, and with many other combinations. For our purposes here, we will primarily concern ourselves with these groups as they apply to a certain number of bars to be used for an audition and other routine matters such as a "sixteen-bar cut," or a "thirty-two-bar cut," or "the first eight (bars)."

Bell tone: Most often, the bell tone is the starting note of the vocal line of the song for the singer's reference. ("What's my first note?") The bell tone may be used when there is no "intro" to the song or where there is an intro and the bell tone appears at the end of it. Although the bell tone is used in musical theatre scores, it is most widely used in audition settings in which the singer does not require (or would be inhibited by) a more extended introduction before beginning to sing.

Book (the book of a musical): The "book of a musical" may be used as a slang term for the libretto of the show. However, the two are not the same. The *libretto*, in the truest definition, is the sum of all text, including the lyrics (and in many musicals, the dance may be considered a form of text) used in the work to tell the story. The book of a musical is the script or the text in the piece that is not sung (the dialog).

Widely regarded to be the patriarch of the modern musical theatre libretto, Oscar Hammerstein II (who wrote both the dialog and the lyrics for his shows) laid groundwork for and realized what was called the "completely integrated" musical. Although other true librettists (those who write both the dialog and the lyrics) have been and are plentiful, musicals will often have three different writing collaborators—the book (script) writer, the lyricist, and the composer.

Book (the singer's songbook): This book is the collection of songs (most often placed in a notebook or binder) tailored for and used by the singer for auditions and on other performance occasions.

Caesura (railroad tracks): Any point within a musical entity in which the music (and possibly the singer) comes to a halt and there is silence. The caesura may be used for pragmatic (i.e., stage business) purposes, dramatic effect (i.e., the character is having a realization), or for other means if desired. The term "railroad tracks" is slang and is often used in musical theatre parlance and designated by two parallel lines slanting upward from left to right.

Catch breath: A quick breath taken by the singer within a relatively brief amount of time. Sometimes known as "top off" breaths, these are taken by the singer needing supplemental air to complete the vocal line if it is a particularly long one. Catch breaths should always be approached with discretion so as to not have the effect of adding punctuation to the musical sentence.

Chord symbol: An indication on sheet music of the musical "progression" of the song. The presence of the chord symbol in sheet music is primarily designated for guitar players' ease of reading (as they see chord symbols and often improvise accompaniment patterns around these) and very often appears in theatre and other music above or within the piano accompaniment. This is because of the often improvisatory nature of theatre music, or possibly, as a musical shorthand. Chord symbols being present on the singer's sheet music, particularly in auditions, can be very helpful for the singer in two ways: If the singer's offering is a song that the audition pianist is not familiar with or if the written accompaniment is particularly dense, the audition pianist may refer to the chord symbols to get an overview as he plays and improvises an accompaniment. Second, if the song is transposed, chord symbols in the transposed key (rather than the entire accompaniment being written out) may be utilized for the audition pianist. Audition pianists generally assume that if the sheet music is presented to them with transposed chord symbols (but nontransposed written accompaniment), then it is that transposed key that the singer desires to be played. Whatever the case, the singer should always state which key (the original or the transposed) he wishes the song to be played in.

Chorus: For our purposes, the chorus refers to a section of a song also commonly referred to as the "refrain" and not a collective body of singers. The chorus of a song generally occurs after the verse and it typically contains the same melody (but often different lyrics) each time it appears, whereas the verse may or may not deviate upon repetition from its original musical statement.

Coda: Most often the final section of the song that may include slightly or even very different musical material than that which has preceded it. Generally, but not always, the sheet music will indicate "DS al coda," which means return to the DS (Dal segno) sign, which looks like a sideways *s* with a line through it and two dots on either side on the sheet music, and then follow the music through to the "to coda" sign (which resembles a cross with a circle or the cross hairs of a rifle scope). At that juncture, skip to the coda to conclude the song.

Colla voce: Written instruction on sheet music for the pianist, conductor, or other instrumentalist to follow the soloist's musical phrasing. If the soloist chooses for musical or dramatic effect to slow down or move quickly through a musical phrase or part of a musical phrase, then this could be indicated to the accompanist as *Colla voce* (translated in Italian, "with the voice"). The term may also be indicated as *Col voce.*

Diphthong: A term used to describe when one sung, sustained vowel sound becomes (perhaps unnecessarily) two vowel sounds. For example, the word *may* should be, in conventional "correct" singing circles, sustained as:

"Maaaaaaaaaaaaaaaa(y)ee"

Should the singer instead sing:

"Maaaaaaeeeeeeeeee"

and elongate and spread the *e* rather than simply closing the word with it, then this is referred to as a diphthong.

Diphthongs are generally thought to interrupt the fluidity of the "proper" vocal tone, but they are sometimes used to great effect in sung music (particularly musical theatre). Should, for example, the singer wish to engage a Southern accent in the singing or if singing in the rock/pop style, the use of diphthongs may be an effective tool.

Downbeat: The first beat of a bar (measure) of music so named because, with his baton, the conductor places the first beat of a bar from up to down.

Dynamics: Musical instructions on a page of music that direct the level of volume at which music should be played/sung and heard ranging from "ppp" (as quietly as is possible) to "pp" (very softly) or "p" (softly) to "mp"' (somewhat quietly) to "mf" (somewhat loudly) to "f" (loudly) or "ff" (very loudly) to "fff" (as loudly as possible).

Fermata: An indication to hold a particular note or chord until ready to move ahead in the music. Fermatas can serve many means. Like caesuras, they may be used for musical or dramatic effect or for a pragmatic reason. The singer may wish to hold the note (particularly if the note is high and clear in the singer's register) to show off his singing prowess. A tenuto is similar to a fermata, but a tenuto (often indicated as "ten" or a horizontal line over a note) means one of two things: hold the note just beyond its full value or linger on the note (possibly for dramatic purposes), but don't treat it as a fermata (my personal preference of the meaning of the word).

First and second ending: The music usually found toward the end of the song, but sometimes elsewhere that directs the performers (singer and accompanist) either to repeat back to the beginning or somewhere else in the song (first ending) or move ahead in the song (second ending). The endings are always labeled with long horizontal lines and the number of the ending. There may be more than two endings, as is the case with Kurt Weill's "The Saga of Jenny," which has seven (six repeats and a final ending), but the inclusion of this many endings is rare.

Two important points to note: While the use of endings is commonplace in standard sheet music, full piano/conductor scores are typically formatted as straight through with all the repeated sections written out on subsequent pages. If the singer has chosen a song from a full score and wishes to do the first verse, chorus, and then go to the end, he may have to jump ahead a few pages to get to the final ending and indicate the cut marking to the pianist. Second, in musical theatre auditions, the first ending is almost invariably ignored and the second (or final) ending taken. This should always be indicated by a marking for the audition pianist.

Full score (vocal score): An all-inclusive folio of music from a particular show. The full score includes any and all music used when the show is performed (and sometimes even songs that were cut from the show). The full score varies from the "vocal selections" in a number of important ways. The full score is sometimes referred to as the "Piano/Conductor (P/C) score" because it includes the rehearsal piano part and the vocal line as well as indications to the conductor as to which instruments in the orchestration play which lines and when, but may also be referred to as the "Piano/Vocal (P/V) score" that includes the rehearsal piano part and the vocal line only.

Glottal (glottal stop): An interruption in the column of air within a sung vocal line. During this interruption, the singer does not take a breath, but only stops the output of breath, the net effect being akin to a comma placed within a sentence.

In tempo (a tempo): A musical directive that means the reverse of rubato. In tempo means that the music should be performed at a steady and even speed, whatever that speed may be. Most often, this term is seen following a section or a phrase of music that is rubato or after a fermata.

Intro (introduction): In musical terms, and for our purposes here, the intro has multiple functions, but simply put, it is the music that precedes the first sung note of a song. The intro may be as short as a single note (a bell tone) or any duration that the composer or arranger deems necessary and/or appropriate. For audition purposes, musical introductions should be kept brief. They need only establish key and possibly tempo, and the added "air" may not be of use to the singer and may be intrusive.

Key change (transpose): To adjust the key for the singer in order to tailor to the singer's practical vocal range and/or vocal strengths. Unlike in opera, the musical theatre practice of changing keys is commonplace. In the past, to change a key meant writing by hand the transposition note for note, but the advent of musical notation software has streamlined the process considerably. An additional meaning for *key change* is "a change of key" (often raised a half step as in the keys of C to C sharp [or D flat]) that may happen from one section of the musical number to the next for heightened musical effect.

Key and time signature: Appears at the beginning of the piece of music and typically at the beginning of each new line of musical notation (also called "staff" and sometimes "system"). The key signature determines the home base key that the song will be performed in. For the singer, the key is important because it will establish both the highest and lowest note sung.

The time signature indicates how many beats will be designated in each bar of music (top number)[29] and also indicates what kind of note establishes one full beat (bottom note). For example: 4/4 time indicates four beats per bar with a quarter note as the duration of one beat. By contrast, the time signature of 7/8 indicates seven beats per bar with the eighth note as the beat.

Poco and molto: *Poco* is an often-seen musical notation that means "a little" or "not much." Example: *poco ritard* (or *poco rit*) means "slow down the music, but only a little." *Poco* is often seen as *poco a poco* as in *poco a poco ritard*, which means "slow down the music gradually (little by little)."

In contrast, *molto* indicates "by a lot." For example, *molto ritard* (or abbreviated as *molto rit*) means "slow down the music quite a bit."

Rideout: The final musical phrase (frequently the final two to four bars) of the song over which the singer is singing (very often a held note). If the singer is not singing over the final phrase, the rideout may be known as an "air rideout."

Rit (ritard) and rall (rallentando): Both mean "slow the music down," although *rall*, rather than *rit*, is often understood to mean "slow the tempo more gradually." Practically speaking, in the theatre, the two terms are often used interchangeably.

Stinger: A heavily accented musical chord (or single pitch often played in octaves) that is generally played by the pianist or orchestra at the end of the song, signaling that the number is over (and as a cue for the audience to applaud).

Tempo: The rate of speed at which the song is played and sung.

Underscoring: Nonsung music that appears in the musical score to highlight, accompany, or underline stage dialog or stage business.

Vamp: For our purposes, the vamp is a musical device that repeats a certain bar or bars of music over again until it is time for the singer to sing. The usefulness of this convention is very practical: A vamp may be inserted to "buy time" until the dialog preceding the first sung note has concluded and/or the stage business has been wrapped up or for technical matters (such as scene changes) to be completed.

There are two varieties that are often encountered in musical theatre: "Vamp until ready" means that the conductor cues the music to go out of the vamp and the next bar of music is (often) the vocal entrance; and "voice last time," which means that the vamp music is the same as the first bar (or bars) of sung music and the singer's vocal entrance occurs over the *last time* through the vamp music.

Verse: In "old-fashioned" songs (such as those of Irving Berlin and George and Ira Gershwin, for example), the verse is the portion of the song that *precedes* the chorus. The verse, therefore, was expositional information to set up the chorus of the song and this format was virtually invariable. Through the years, as song structure has evolved, the verse has come to mean the portion of the song that precedes the chorus *each time the chorus appears*, particularly in pop music, and the verse may return with different lyrics and possibly different notes no matter the songwriter's wishes. Song format in modern style may well follow this structure:

Verse
Chorus
Verse
Chorus
Chorus bridge (a new musical phrase of a different characteristic of
    the verses and choruses)
(Final) Chorus

The above is the stock example. Songwriters (particularly those for the musical theatre) have varied this structure in innumerable ways.

Vocal selections: The folio of music sold in your local sheet music store or online that contains the principal songs (and occasionally all) from a musical. Vocal selections vary from full scores (which may also be available store-bought or online) in a number of important ways:

- They generally do not include any music from the show other than the songs themselves (e.g., dance music, incidental music, reprises, and overture).

- The songs themselves may appear in a truncated format, eliminating any underscoring that may be included in the song when performed in the context of the show, and intros and rideouts or other material may have been altered.

- The key may be different than the original key as performed in the theatre.

Although today's music publishers often publish the songs in the show key, this hasn't always been true. In vocal selections of older shows, the publishers' objective in choosing the keys the songs were placed in was to make them user friendly for both the singer and the pianist (e.g., not too many flats or sharps for the pianist and neither too high nor too low for the singer).

CHAPTER SEVEN

Coaching Songs Through

What follows are selected excerpts (transcribed and editorialized for length and clarity) from coaching sessions held between myself and professional actors and actresses preparing song material for the purposes of professional auditions. The songs represented here have been judiciously chosen from the widely varying song styles used in the musical theatre so as to represent as wide a cross-section as possible while demonstrating the application of points made in this book. These are presented both in narrative and dialog forms whereby the speaker is referred to by his (or her) initials: (SP) for myself, and the singer's corresponding initials (AB, for example).

"Much More"
(From *The Fantasticks*)

Complete lyric

> A Section:
> I'd like to swim in a clear blue stream
> Where the water is icy cold.
> Then go to town
> In a golden gown,
> And have my fortune told.
> Just once,
> Just once!

Just once before I'm old!
I'd like to be not evil,
But a little worldly wise.
To be the kind of girl designed
To be kissed upon the eyes.

B Section:
I'd like to dance till two o'clock,
Or sometimes dance till dawn,
Or if the band could stand it,
Just go on and on and on!
Just once,
Just once,
Before the chance is gone!

C (or bridge) Section:
I'd like to waste a week or two,
And never do a chore,
To wear my hair unfastened
So it billows to the floor.

B Section (return):
To do the things I've dreamed about
But never done before!
Perhaps I'm bad, or wild, or mad,
With lots of grief in store,

Coda Section:
But I want much more than keeping house!
Much more!
Much more!
Much more!

AR was a young, poised, "legit" soprano who also belted, but
relied heavily on the former because of the types of roles in which
she was usually cast. Her bread-and-butter was Golden Age-era
musical roles that exploited her grace and ability to pull off young
leading lady characters who were not the token belters (or character
actresses) of the show. Having grown weary of singing all too
frequently about love and butterflies, she sought songs shaded with

more dramatic tones and less light on their feet for inclusion in her book of songs. The present song emerged.

SP (*after a sing-through with* AR): "I'd say there's not a lot that's mysterious in this lyric. She explains her fantasies, simple as they are, and tells you what she wants very plainly, save a line or two that we'll have to get to the bottom of."

AR: "Do you think it (the entire song) is too long for an audition? I think I would only use it for auditions when I have more time."

SP: "Still, I think it's too lengthy in its entirety, even for those types of auditions. You can get to the crux of the message, express what you need to here, and show them [the auditors] what they need to see and hear while excising a couple of sections to make it more compact and trim, especially given the repetitive nature of it [the song] A cut-down version will still show off a cross-section of what you do well as long as you include the plum acting moments and the places that show off your voice. And the auditors will appreciate your brevity, getting all that in in under a couple of minutes. They always do."

AR: "Which part do we cut, though, is the question."

SP: "Well, we have the advantage of the entire song as written being in the same key so we don't have to worry with that. My feeling is that the A section is a keeper. I love the vivid language there and that gives you a lot to 'play' [as an actor] with. The first section, which also lays out a succinct statement of what the song is about and a portrait of the singer, frames her very tidily. I also like the bit in the first B section about 'dancing till dawn' 'on and on and on,' but I'm not yet sure if it's the strongest choice musically because we have to tie it to the ending in making a cut if we want to get the powerful vocal ending in, and we should. And cutting from 'on and on and on' to 'but I want much more than keeping house' is a creaky fit lyrically. The C I'm not so sure about either, even though it's lovely, especially the piano arpeggio on the word *floor* that points out her hair cascading to the ground that is probably a metaphor for the song, but we run into two problems if we keep it: The next section [the return of the B] is contingent to some degree on the C, and secondly, the C would have to connect musically to the end of the A, and that's a very awkward choice in this case. Did you get all that?"

AR (*jokingly*): "No, but I trust you."

SP: "All of this being said, I think that we should cut to the return of the B from the end of the first A. The reason is that it makes a smoother transition into the final section, which we know we want to include. You could make a case for a couple of different versions for our purposes, but this just feels better to me, more instinctive, because the lyric is more flowing from section to section, giving it a logical arc and giving the presentation a resolved, clear ending. Also, we aren't forcing any awkward transitions or vocal business in the interest of making a cut."

AR: "So then I can sing 'kissed upon the eyes' and cut out the 'I'd like to dance' and 'I'd like to waste a week or two' sections and cut directly to the 'To do the things I've dreamed about' section and take it to the end from there?"

SP: "You got it. Replace the word *I'd* in the sheet music with the word *to* and skip directly to the downbeat of the bar that starts with 'do the things . . . .' Overall, I think that making a cut is wise because otherwise we get repetitive. Using the same music twice instead of only once doesn't add much in an audition unless fluidity in telling the story is highly dependent on it."

AR: "Perfect. I'm having trouble with the lyric in the 'I'd like to be not evil but a little worldly wise' . . . What do you think that line is all about?"

SP: "It's a good question, and I think this is the one we have to unscramble. The line is really indigenous to the character who sings it in the show and is perhaps most easily understood looking at it in context and, of course, taking into account the vernacular of the show itself. My take on it is that here we get some clues as to what lies beneath her childlike surface and all of this wanting to do this or that. I do think it's a very *human* thing to say and that it's about being empowered, especially the 'worldly-wise' part. You can take or leave my twenty-five-cent interpretation, but it's the only lyric that supports the idea that the rest of the song lyric isn't simply whimsical thinking but is a genuine ache inside of her to punch out of her own life, have some adventures, and be treated as a princess being kissed upon the eyes. In this show, she sometimes has flights of fancy to occupy herself and fantasize about it such as you hear in this number. Of course, we know when Luisa goes out on her own she is gravely disappointed and deceived. The world turns out to be dangerous and sinister, not glittering as she had planned. This is what leads her back to Matt (her love interest in the show). In playing the song even out of context, I think that the line deserves some special attention because it does run a little deeper than much of the rest of the song, and it grants you the opportunity to tap into what's human about the lyric and not simply sing a song about a girl who wants to go places and do things and wear pretty dresses. She wants to live!"

AR: "So, do you think I should use any of the dialog that precedes the singing? There's that long monologue with musical underscoring. Does that help set the song up?"

SP: "I don't know if I'd use all of it because you're not specifically preparing the song for an audition to play the role of Luisa. Maybe we can use a line or two as a setup if you prefer. Using all that dialog, I think, bellies up a little too close to the character in context, and we shouldn't forget that, in a general audition, we want to hide the real *you* as little as possible. The dialog is very 'actable,' but I don't think you need it to jumpstart the song, and it's very long to boot."

AR: "So what should I do for an intro?"

SP: "Oh, I think that the 'bell' tone that's already there in the sheet music is just fine, unless you feel like you need a little more 'air' before you sing."

AR: "Honestly, it doesn't feel natural to me to start this song without a snippet of dialog first. So I think, yes, let's use a piece of the dialog."

SP: "I get it. Okay, so try using the last lines of the written dialog. Take your place in the room, look up, and say what's written there: 'I am special. I am special. Please, God, please, don't let me be normal.' If it's well planned, it will command the room, and in this case, it might make a smoother transition for you, and of course, it supports our story because to the singer being 'normal' is the worst possible outcome. But don't deliver it as arrogant or even as entitled. It's a mantra that you repeat over and over to yourself and it should unfold as just that."

AR: "What I'm really thinking is, 'Please, God, please, I want this job!'"

SP: "So use that. That's a tangible feeling that's close to you and accessible. Wanting that is as valid and as much a truthful want as the wants within the lyric, and above all else, we really have to get at and play the *want* in this song and even exploit it, or the song can fall flat. If you feel committed to using it, I think that the spoken line completely supports the lyric. Isn't the song, after all, about *exactly* what she is speaking to God about?"

AR: "So, am I addressing God throughout this song?"

SP: "This song is one of those 'out front' or 'to the audience' deliveries as internal monologue, although you could make a compelling case for having an invisible scene partner. At its most basic, it's a revelation for the audience or your scene partner, if you choose, into what makes you tick and not just an admission of what you want, per se, but even into your nightmares. By stating that you *want* these things, the subtextual statement is in part that you *don't want* certain things as well. You can place onto the lyric whatever you internalize *your* greatest fears are, what you don't want even if you can't completely relate in literal terms to what Luisa *does* want. This will keep the song personal and alive when you infuse it with your personal subtext. It could go any number of ways. Your deepest fear may well be, like hers, that you'll end up like everybody else you know, if you were from a very small town where nobody ever left, or, more personally for you, that you'll never get a big-time show. In the singer's [your] mind, you refuse to be resigned to that fate. This is your credo in this moment, anyhow, and all songs are sung in the present. It's boilerplate in the song and reinforced over and over again in the lyric. I don't know how much deeper than that the song needs to go, but that's pretty fruitful theatrical terrain."

AR: "What are your thoughts on the vocal approach to this song?"

SP: "It certainly would fall into that 'legit' category, but I
     think the moment-to-moment vocal qualities and approach
     are very much inside the music itself. The accompaniment
     provides you with some very picturesque images and energy
     that you should take into account. The rolling, easy piano
     figurations in the A section are very befitting of the 'clear
     blue stream' and the crescendoed 'rising' musical contour
     of 'just once' and the heavy block piano chords at 'lots of
     dreams in store' seem to scream 'punctuate me with an
     exclamation point!' So you'll want to punch those lyrics up,
     and Harvey Schmidt [the composer] has been very attentive
     to painting that picture for the audience and in making them
     feel a certain way. The music serves the lyric particularly
     well here and reinforces the thought itself. Use what Schmidt
     has given you to dictate your vocal approach. You should
     follow them closely and be very obedient to them and let
     them be your guide both dramatically and vocally. Also, the
     accompaniment figure in the return of the B section changes
     completely from that of the A. Here, the figures are very
     rhythmic and jumpy, surely to underline her own restlessness
     but probably also as a means of saying 'don't sing this too
     legato like the last section.' Schmidt also wrote short-ish,
     clipped phrases here that will naturally keep you from too
     much legato singing. In general, too, in this section the
     rhythmic nature is very tightly wound with brusque piano
     chords that suggest emotions brimming up and fighting their
     way to the surface. So the music here really does paint the
     words and emotional content very vividly, don't you think?"

AR: "I also think it's very telling that she uses the words
     'perhaps I'm bad or wild or mad with lots of grief in store.'
     It's like she is daring to reveal that she is ready to take the
     leap, no matter the outcome."

SP: "And of course, in the context of the show itself there *is*
     heartache ahead for Luisa, and the lyric foreshadows that.
     But you can't *play* that because it hasn't happened yet. You
     can only play the now and your willingness to throw caution
     to the wind to get what you want. I think a sensible
     approach is to play the song like you're revealing not merely
     a big secret but a HUGE one that you know you shouldn't
     reveal but you have to anyway or you'll combust. In the

beginning, the sentiment speaks for itself, but then the floodgates open to another thing, then to another, and then to something else. Your job in playing these things is to keep the descriptions of all that she wants very vivid and to keep visualizing your brass ring. In *playing it* and not just internally *wanting it* being granted and getting these things means no less to her than a theatre career does to you. Her aspirations may seem meek by comparison to yours, but they are hers, and you have to devote the same unrelenting energy to getting them in the playing as you do to getting what you want personally. Always be kicking the investment upward, have a clear sense of what it looks and feels like to get it, and remind yourself that not getting it is the worst thing that could happen."

AR: "Yes. In a way, they do seem so basic, but that doesn't make them any less real. I find the lyric 'go to town in a golden gown' very intriguing that way."

SP: "So each point that the lyric makes, particularly about an 'I want,' has to be personal. For example, I think you have to figure out what your own going 'to town in a golden gown' is in order to make the lyric work for you. Maybe it's how you feel when wearing your Manolo Blahnik shoes."

AR: "I wish I could afford them."

SP: "So there you go. See? You found your 'golden gown.'"

"Separate Ways" (Worlds Apart) (Words and music by Steve Perry and Jonathan Cain)

Complete lyric

Verse 1
Here we stand
Worlds apart, hearts broken in two, two, two.
Sleepless nights; losing ground,
I'm reaching for you, you, you
Feelin' that it's gone

Can change your mind
If we can't go on
To survive the tide love divides

Chorus
Someday love will find you;
Break those chains that bind you
One night will remind you
How we touched and went our separate ways
If he ever hurts you,
True love won't desert you.
You know I still love you
Though we touched and went our separate ways

Verse 2
Troubled times;
Caught between confusions and pain, pain, pain.
Distant eyes;
Promises we made were in vain, in vain, in vain.
If you must go, I wish you love.
You'll never walk alone.
Take care my love,
Miss you love.

(Repeat Chorus)

Coda
No, no

MB was, at 26, a veteran of a number of top-tier casts and possessed an edgy, athletic physical appearance and a top-end vocal range that served him abundantly in contemporary musical theatre. His spot-on, technically supported high As and Bs (above middle C) were decidedly saleable assets and rendered him command and authority over the stratospheric vocal tessituras (the general range) that many male contemporary musical theatre roles require. The present song, recorded by Journey, was a commonsensical choice to showcase his vocal expertise, and MB had an audition appointment to become a replacement for a role in a long-running show sung in the '80s rock style.

At the outset, we established that one verse and one chorus of the song would be adequate on this occasion, and together, we browsed the complete lyric of the song looking for clues and cues as to how to make a prudent cut. "There are two verses, several choruses, and an instrumental break," I noted, "but we need to streamline and not worry with all of those chorus repeats and the instrumental break." I pointed out that such breaks, which sometimes occur in pop-rock, create unusable, unnecessary dead space in the audition room because no scene partner is present to physically interact with and that any musical staging would be inappropriate in that setting. "We know that since the chorus is more or less the same each time, we don't need to make any decisions about which one to use. What are your thoughts," I asked, "on which one of the two verses to sing?"

MB appeared to be indifferent. After a moment I suggested, "If one lays out clearer, more accessible, language about situation, time, and place (givens), then that's the one best used in most cases."

I went on to say that in pop songs, it's especially important to identify (and invent, if needed) the Ws of who, what, where, when, and why because in many cases commercial music lyrics aren't written specifically for the dramatic stage. "We always want to engage as much straightforward, character- and event-driven language as possible to give the audience what is inherent in songs written for the stage," I said. "In other words, clear and unambiguous, explicit information about the story that they are being told."

MB noted that the first verse, starting with "Here we stand," gives the audience that certain (if vague) sense of the current event, and I agreed, but wasn't confident that the lyric that followed moved the storyline along since some of it spoke in hazy generalities.

"First," I said, "you don't have to tell us that 'here you stand' because we see that you're here, present, and in the scene, although 'hearts broken in two' distinguishes this as a 'love affair gone awry' song. But eclipsing that fact in giving this verse the green light is the 'sleepless nights' and 'losing ground' phrase. I think it sounds and plays too much like a pop song lyric, and we want our chosen lyric to dependably sound and play as a theatre song lyric—the less required of us to bend it in that direction the better. Moreover, changing the lyric 'Feelin' that it's gone can change your mind' into 'If we can't go on to survive the tide love divides' points out and speculates on *what might be* instead of what *is*. In this case, it isn't helpful to amplify the circumstances of why you and your scene partner are in this situation, let alone what led you here. Time and content are your currency in auditions, and you must spend them frugally and with discretion. If you include the first verse, you use up half of your allotted audition time with back-story about the effects of the current situation and your speculations about the future instead of stating exactly what the current situation is and discovering the conflict between these two people in the scene right now, right here. This wouldn't necessarily be a bad thing if there was more time to sing an additional verse in order to establish, uncover, and elaborate on what the scene is about, but that's a luxury we don't have time for in auditions." I urged him to remember that "we want to get to the conflict as quickly as possible, identify the dynamics between the players involved, and identify what is currently pending and at stake for the person whom this outcome will affect. Lyrics like this work fine in a pop-rock song, but do they sound like something characters on a stage would say to each other, or even to themselves? This cryptic language does not serve our scene work well, and you're better than that. It will dilute your performance. Sure, your singing will sound great and you'll sound impressive whatever the verse you choose, but that isn't the name of this game. MTV this isn't."

MB agreed, and without my prompting, pointed out that the second verse was far less general and provided a clearer picture, not only of imminent romantic breakup, but also of the internal and external conflict between the parties. "'Troubled times,'" he said, "says it all. Two words get to the point that something bad may be in the offing and sums it up."

"Right," I replied, "it frames the whole setting and sets up what follows, and the lyric 'caught between confusions and pain' gives us an unambiguous, narrow vision of the player's state of mind."

"And that's more playable," he said, "than a lyric like 'losing ground.'"

"And to the point!" I followed. "So let's build this scenario as the playwright would. What's going down here? If we are in agreement that the song is about a romantic breakup and what the stakes are, then we still need to establish time, place, and what's just happened or been happening to set the song and these events in motion."

"It's been a long time coming," MB said without too much thought. "Since I say 'break those chains that bind you' in the chorus,

I think she can't stay in one place maybe because of some long-standing internal struggle."

I pointed out, "She's in love with someone else, an unknown player. It's right there in the text. She's leaving you. Someone else is waiting in the wings or she is going back to her old love—maybe it's her comfort zone. And there's conflict of all kinds to grapple with between the two of you. Then there's your internal conflict, which is what we have to concern ourselves with since there's no verbalized explicit internal conflict from her side in the song lyric, only our supposition of its presence. Who is initiating the breakup, you or she?"

"She is," MB replied without pause, "because of the lyric that I sing 'if you must go, I wish you love.'"

"Okay, good," I replied. "Those are some givens. What about time and place?"

"Middle of the night, my apartment," he shot back.

I thought the time frame seemed apt because that time of night is when we are perhaps most vulnerable and even volatile. Additionally, a private setting locale made sense to me because it granted a freedom of expression unable to be achieved in a public setting where you might tend toward a more mannered and reserved disposition. "Is she there?" I asked. "Is this directed toward her?"

"Yes, definitely," MB said.

"Then no more needs to be said or debated. You're committed," I affirmed. "Now you have a palpable sense of where you are and can play the scene from that perspective and within that given circumstance. Let's take it apart line by line and decide how each line functions in the storytelling. The first two lines are reflective: 'troubled times caught between confusion and pain' sets the temperature and overall mood of the scene, but the second line cements it with 'distant eyes; promises made were in vain.'"

"So it was for nothing," MB suggested.

"If that's your reading of it and your take on the investment, then, yes. At this point you can be as subjective as you want to be in infusing a personal point of view," I said. "Tell me more about how you're reacting to the lines subjectively."

MB thought for a moment and glanced ahead at the lyric and said, "Oh, the usual stuff—disappointment, hurt feelings, damaged ego, inability to believe this really is happening, accepting failure."

"All chapters in the breakup playbook," I said. "So, good. You've managed to tell the story succinctly in making the choice to use this verse and availed yourself of some subtext by pointing out what's underneath the outright saying of the lines. Of course, it isn't so mysterious. Those feelings and sentiments that accompany a scene like this are universal feelings, but how they manifest personally with you alone makes this *your* singular point of view."

I continued by saying, "The next few lines are more active and in the now rather than reflective. 'If you must go, I wish you love. You'll never walk alone. Take care my love, miss you, love.'"

"Not everyday language," MB said.

"Maybe so or maybe not," I added, "but you have to play it as seriously as you would anything else, and you can't comment on the writing within the performance. Be careful about that. If you telegraph to us that you aren't one hundred percent in the moment by not being one hundred percent in the moment, we know you're on the sideline evaluating the material and not living in it. It may not be Shakespeare, but the gig is to make it work. Back to the scene work: Are you fighting for her to stay?"

"No," MB said. "Since this has been going on for a while, I think I'm more resigned than if it was happening out of the blue."

"So you're not begging her to stay and work it out or trying to fight it out, you just let her go. Then what happens?" I asked.

"She leaves, and I'm alone," MB speculated.

"Which opens up the chorus as internal monologue," I said, "because what else could it be if no one else is in the room, right?"

MB agreed and looked ahead. "The chorus is reflective again, thinking on what's down the road for her. I guess I'm armchair-quarterbacking her future love life, hoping she'll get out of those chains," he commented with a half-smile.

With this, we shared a moment of understanding that even as this lyric is what it is, MB wouldn't let on that the topical matter was anything but deadly serious, despite the traditionally nontheatrical language of the text, and would build his performance in compliance with that axiom.

"So what do you want for yourself then?" I asked.

"I want to still be with her."

"Right," I said, "everyone is thinking of themselves even when they're thinking of someone else. And that's not to say that they are thinking selfishly, but of their well-being. So, are you of the opinion that you're better off without her for now, but hopeful for the future?"

MB gave me an I'll-get-back-to-you-on-that look.

"So finally," I said, pressing forward, "we have some uncharted ground to deal with at the end of the song in the coda, and it's a doozy. It turns the scene on its ear. You say . . . "

"No!" MB interjected, "I've changed my mind. I gotta get her back."

"Now you're in a new beat," I said. "Something has changed. The 'boy-gets-girl-back' charge is on. End of scene."

"Another Night at Darryl's" (From *The Witches of Eastwick*)

The portion of the song chosen for audition purposes was:

I get connection,
A bit of fun.
I feel affection where once
I felt none.
And in reflection,
what's done is done.
So why not do it again?
And again . . . and again . . . and again . . . and again
And again . . . and again . . .!
Where life was once cold and sterile,
now it's positively feral,
All thanks to Darryl's guiding light.
(Cut)
Another wrong, another right, another taste,
Another bite . . . (spoken: "Oh boy!")
Another night
Another night at Darryl's!

CE had enjoyed an accomplished career as a concert dancer and was in a period of transition into the musical theatre. Her vocal prowess had limitations, to be sure, but she did possess a natural facility for singing and very good instincts for musical phrasing and delivery. The newest inclusion to her repertoire book was the present song, chosen in part because CE had several specific attributes that the song underlined and highlighted but a proportionate number of limitations that the song didn't disclose. Principal among them were (a) the sung notes were relatively low pitched, which enabled CE to sing mostly in her "chest" vocal register without needing to transition to the upper reaches of her middle[30] (mix) vocal range; and (b) because her breath support was sometimes unreliable and the song included many short sung phrases and ample breathing space between them, she felt a built-in safety net to avoid depletion of her breath.

Our first task was to establish the musical cut. Because the auditions that CE attended were New York[31] chorus calls (ensemble), she needed a song that cut easily to around sixteen bars, which this one did with a couple of nips and tucks. The section we intended to use was still slightly too long, and this needed to be addressed before moving further along.

SP: "We must still make a cut at the end to pare it down a bit more," I said to CE. "Let's hold the six count on the word *night* and then cut directly to the last two bars of the song to finish it out."

CE: "Do I have to hold that note all six beats? I won't be able to think about anything else. It's the place in the song that scares me to death, holding that note."

SP: "It's the one place in the cut where we really get to hear you sing out, so we don't want to lose it—and I wouldn't put you in the position of having to do it if I didn't know you could. Most importantly, it's the crest of the scene as we have fashioned it, and you don't want to miss that dramatic opportunity of gusto singing where the scene is at full tilt. You *could* sing only the first two beats and then cut to the last two bars to finish it. The way the chords are structured, perhaps doing it that way makes a cleaner cut, but doing so is like an open admission that you can't—or don't want to— sing it, and neither do you any favors."

CE: "I'm counting twenty-two bars here."

SP: "Since we don't count the 'air' in the two bars of the intro, we're down to twenty."

CE: "Is that still too long if they say 'sing sixteen bars'?"

SP: "Well, yes . . . but no. Songs as often as not don't cut evenly into exactly sixteen bars. The objective is to get *as*

close to a sixteen-bar cut as is possible so that the cut makes
sense and doesn't end in some peculiar or unresolved way
either musically or dramatically. If it doesn't feel or sound
more or less complete to you with a given sixteen-bar
cutting, then it probably won't to the listeners either, and
that could leave them feeling jarred. Use your instincts.
I don't know any person running an audition who won't
allow you to go over the sixteen-bar limit within reason if
it makes the performance and the song feel more finished.
I know sometimes those stage managing audition
proceedings seem militant about singing only sixteen bars,
but I think this is mostly because people abuse the grace
period and will make all kinds of excuses as to why their
sixteen-bar cut absolutely *needs* to be twenty-eight or
thirty-two bars."

    (I played the first two lead-in bars and asked for CE's
response to what might be happening dramatically during
that air.)

CE: "Well, the music sounds sexy-ish. She's probably thinking
something she shouldn't be thinking."

SP: "The music doesn't lie. It sounds a little mischievous,
doesn't it? So that's probably what's going on mentally
during the introduction air. What's there musically will
inform and prompt your acting the music."

CE: "This is one place where I get stuck—figuring out how
to 'act' the song, how to 'act' what she's thinking and doing.
I'm so in-my-head about how my singing sounds that I can't
think of anything else, especially about becoming her for the
song."

SP: "And that's understandable because of where you are in
your personal process of becoming comfortable with singing.
Let me address one point at a time: I think the first step in
getting past that last hang-up is not to worry about being
in 'her' skin but instead to worry about how to get in *your*
own. Trying to think too much like 'her' in this instance is
going to lead you down a road to representational and
dishonest acting. The key is in your learning and willingness
to externalize your own internalizations pertaining to what
you're singing about. Think, respond, and be stimulated like
CE would and not like 'her.' I'm sure you can relate in some

fashion to her dilemma, and sometimes that takes digging into yourself and always takes a willingness to put it on your sleeve. But I know—and your audience must know—that it's present, and what you're going to find is that when you are attaching a thought and/or feeling to each word and phrase of your text you are just too busy to be nervous or scared! This is what we mean by acting from the inside out rather than on the outside where the self-conscious is driving the performance.

"Now, about 'acting' the air: Let's talk about the song in general so we can make some inroads about how to approach the first beat—the so-called air. So here's this woman having an internal fantasy throughout the song that is pulling her in one direction while simultaneously her common sense and judgment are pulling her in another. Relating all of this to the subject of the air, these points have to show up in the playing as the scene plays out, but the air of the intro can only possess one fragment, one *strand* of the overall, because it's just a *moment*, a beat. In other words, you can't 'act' the entire song in the intro nor would you want to. Choose an impulse that the music directs you to and go with it to fill the air of the intro. The sound of the music affirms to me what you suggested—mischievous little thoughts—and we must see a momentary reaction from you to that stimulation even though the moment, the scene, the thought all move on."

I continued, "What about the rest of the song? What does she want? Where's the scene in this song? What happens once the air is played out and she begins to sing?"

CE: "She's having a civil war with herself, right? This Darryl, this guy, is obviously bad for her, or at least she thinks so."

SP: "Enter inner conflict. Yes, exactly right. The entire number is her, the singer, offering up reasons and excuses to herself to go to the well one more time. One side of her brain is arguing with the other. I hear this number and my mental image is of a matronly, bored housewife having this sexually charged affair with someone who hasn't made her feel this way in a very long time. But you, CE, aren't anyone's wife, and you're anything but matronly, so that negates my preconceptions. It's just as well. Anyone could be having this problem."

(We started the song again to rehearse the "air" and continued into the song for about eight bars, but I noticed that CE, on occasion, would appear to look completely blank, although the singing was mostly intact.)

"So, we have some work to do on feeling confident and singing with vocal power on the extended notes that you certainly can do, but otherwise this is a good baseline vocal performance. What's bothering me is that you're 'checking out' and disconnecting your thought too often. What's going on there?"

CE: "I'm still thinking about the singing too much. I sing a note and it doesn't sound the way I hope it will and I get distracted."

SP: "You get off message. The problem is that even though you stop connecting, the song must not. The scene must not. The performance or audition must not. We notice when you disconnect with your body, eyes, face, or voice, and you lose us. And it's tough to get a panel or audience back at that point. The fact is that *we*, the panel, probably aren't noticing all those little ticks and vocal things that are bothering you and tripping you up. We're engaged in your performance. We're not keeping score. You have to trust yourself, stop beating yourself up, and stay focused on the big picture.

"Your self-consciousness about your singing will subside over time the more you do it and study it. I know that for someone like you, a dancer who is finding your way into the singing and *acting* world, it can be very daunting. As you become more confident, your singing will *be* more confident. We can't worry about that right now. All you can do now is take who you are and what your singing voice is *in this moment* into the room, shine with it, and do so with no apologies. It's important for you to remember that even though you may think that singing auditions are only about singing, that is not true. Now, I don't want to confuse you. Musical directors do need to know that you *can* sing certain notes confidently and hold your own at the type of auditions you go to. No doubt about it. They, and the other creative staff and casting people, may be intently listening to a certain vocal quality and even certain notes. But that fact shouldn't drive or dictate your performances in song delivery unless the casting breakdown specifies those things or you know the show well enough to know the extent of the vocal requirements of it. If the casting breakdown *does* offer specifications, then we prepare to that end. However, in this song we are preparing for a general audition, and we know of no specificities. For now, you've got what you've got with the singing, and the scene's the thing to worry yourself with. If you haven't shown them something vocally that they need to know, they'll ask you to do it. You shouldn't worry about offering something up that you don't even know they want. You're not a mind reader. The truth is that we can tell if you can sing in about four bars of music. Once that's out of the way, all that remains is the *performance* of the song.

"I have seen many auditions succeed *in spite of* a singer's limited vocal ability. I've also seen many *fail* because the singer, although talented, couldn't—or didn't—go beyond just apathetically singing the notes. Connecting to the acting and getting over all these tapes that play over and over in your head about how you 'should' sound is the only fail-safe option.

"Again, instead of taking the singing as your foundation and fixing the acting around it, reverse it. Here, let me show you something, or rather, you show *me* something":

(I played the lowest note of the song.)

"Sing that note."

(She did, and I then played a scale from the lowest to the highest note of the song and asked her to sing it. She did, and well.)

"So you *can* sing all the notes. You just did. And if I asked you to sing them softly, you would have sung them softly; and if I had asked you to sing them loudly, you would have sung them loudly. If I had asked you to sing the first three notes loudly and the rest softly, you would have. You *can* sing the song. You've just demonstrated that. Now everything else has to derive from the acting that the song is telling you to do."

(This helped. CE's outlook changed markedly for the remainder of the session, satisfied that all the raw ingredients of the vocal aspect of singing the song were present.)

"Now we take the acting and the scene work and use it to inform the singing. The first couple of phrases are short and succinct, probably because thoughts are darting around in her head. What this means to the singing is that there's ample breathing room—and you may not even need to breathe. Some of the rests may just be glottal stops, but don't forget to punctuate the commas. Continue to *sing into and through the thought* even though you vocally disconnect or momentarily stop the sound to be obedient to the rests where the commas are. Commas say 'and then . . . and then . . . and here's what else . . .,' so don't forget to link all the thoughts as one long gesture even though there may be a disconnection in the column of breath output. All the while she's having flashbacks and responding to them, so let those imaginings occur as you sing, and shade or don't shade the vocal accordingly."

CE: "How do you mean?"

SP: "The second line, for example. Is the internal impulse that the line 'a bit of fun' generates one of a squeally 'Ooh!' or of a tigress on the hunt who's found the prey? Get it? Make choices about *exactly* what's going on internally, how those thoughts make you feel, and let those feelings inform the vocal inflections. Then we come to 'what's done is done,' and maybe a turning point that ups the ante. Why?"

CE: "If she's giving in . . . and she may feel some guilt for it, but maybe she's gonna do it anyway."

SP: "For much of the rest of the song I think she's bargaining, but I don't think she's made the decision yet."

CE: "Where does she decide to go through with it? At 'Oh boy!'?"

SP: "Sure, that's where she says it outright, but what's more important is what's in-between. She's not there yet. She's in a state of discovery. As the saying goes, 'Don't know the result as you play the scene.' She starts by singing about what makes her feel this certain way and what her life was pre-Darryl (sexually, anyhow). She receives affection where once there was none. And in reflection, what's done is done, I think, and is the indication that she's working through the pros and cons of doing it again.

"Let's start to break this down by replacing the word *she* with the word *you*. The reasons you *should* are all there in the text. The reasons you *shouldn't* are only implied and not expressly stated. Whatever those reasons are have to remain present throughout because they are the force that you're playing or pushing against. With those as your constants, everything else in the scene work will make sense. Without them, the song is just an exercise in words and notes. There have to be *consequences* present in your mind if you do this, but in the end you conclude that what you get out of it is worth the consequences, whatever they might be. So think not so much about the singing here and more about solving her internal problem. When you do that, the singing takes care of itself."

CE: "The 'singing' really doesn't happen until 'again and again and again,' right?"

SP: "By that place in the scene and the music you're in the throes of ecstasy. In each of those repeated words live carnal memories of all that's happened before with Darryl, and the last 'again' is held several beats so, yes, let everything that precedes it build to it. With each one you have to bump up the affirmation, and aren't those feelings exactly what the song is about in the first place?"

(CE agreed, and we sang from the beginning again but didn't feel like the vocal energy was present enough when we reached the "again" section.)

"Don't forget to build up to that last 'again' vocally. With each one you need to notch up the vocal. Crescendo through that whole phrase. It's there in the music, too. Each has to be more affirmative than the last one."

(A second time through rendered a more successful outcome, and CE was happier with how it sounded and "played.")

"Excellent. Now we can move on into the next beat. What's *bridged* the beats, or the moment that something changes, is the memory. The memory has triggered an internal response that moves us ahead in the song. Now you use words like 'feral' and speak of him being your 'guiding light.' That's pretty heavy language. The argument is over at this point. You're completely committed by now, especially having relived how the memory makes you feel."

CE: "So, is 'another wrong, another right, another taste, another bite' the new beat, the resolution to go ahead with it and not be part of the decision making?"

SP: "I think that's a strong choice. The music supports it. The singing of that line all happens on exactly the same note, over and over again. It's like all the monotonous voices in your head telling her 'do it . . . no, do it . . . no, don't do it' that she's casting off. You're tired of those naysayers. Bring on the man. It's almost predatory at this point."

CE: "And that brings us to the long note on the last 'night.'"

SP: "Everything you've done and said in the song so far has led us here. Make 'I' a bright twangy vowel. Use that vowel to your advantage. Sing that 'I' with your whole face. It's congruent with all the scene work up until now. Use the energy—mental as well as physical—that you've generated so far to support the sound."

(CE sang the phrase again and afterward looked surprised.)

CE: "I'm shocked that it came out so naturally!"

SP: "I'm not. You pulled it from what you had been building. It was like a natural occurrence."

CE: "I just hope I can do it again."

SP: "You can, and easily if you build the scene anew each time you sing it. You just have to reconnect each time to the stuff that took you there in the first place."

CE: "My little secret."

SP: "Use it."

"Perfect"
(From *Edges*)

Complete lyric

It's true,
I don't know enough.
Don't really get the stuff they say on C.N.N.
I'll work;
Get so much smarter.

I can try harder.
If I mess up, I'll try again.
People change, People grow.
We rearrange, we let things go.
I could be perfect.
I could be perfect.
Tell me what to do.
I could be perfect for you.
Listen:
You were right.
My friends were bad for me.
Thank God you helped me see how fake they are,
I know.
And look,
Just like you said I should,
I cut them out for good.
I should have done that long ago.
Now it's just you,
And it's just me.
Help me through;
Try to see.
I can be perfect.
I can be perfect.
The other day your meeting ran too late,
I went and ate.
I just sat there on my own.
The waiter watched me as I read my book,
He gave that look like,
"How pathetic, she's all alone."
I don't want to be alone.
Don't let me be alone.
No one else can take your place.
I am yours and you are mine.
So don't tell me we need space.
No, don't use that fucking line.
Now you look me in the face: we are going to be fine.
I will be perfect.
I will be perfect.
I will be perfect.
I will be perfect.

It's not hard to do.
I will be perfect for you.

JC, an experienced actress who had been coaching with me for some time, was attending an audition for which the requirements were to sing an entire contemporary song (something of a rarity as far as duration). She had chosen a song from *Edges* by Jonathan Larson Award recipients Benj Pasek and Justin Paul.

SP: "This one's a lot to bite off. There's a hefty scene here, isn't there? How is the song 'living' in there for you?"

JC: "Good, I think. I'm just having some trouble with a few of the high notes and finding the right arc for it. It feels like 'my song,' but I'm just not owning it enough yet."

SP: "Before we sing it, what just happened here? What do you think the song 'cue' would be? In other words, what has propelled this song into being, forcing the action of singing it right here, right now?"

JC: "He's leaving her. He wants to break up."

SP: "I buy that, but I'm talking about the first line of the song specifically. She says, 'It's true.' What's true?"

JC: (Looking at the sheet music) "Right. I think he's been berating her again."

SP: "Again? So this is not new?"

JC: "Not new. She's done all these things to try to make him happy and make him want her, but nothing's good enough."

SP: "Right. He's told her to dump her friends. She did, but that wasn't enough."

JC: "Nice guy."

SP: "Yes, he's a gem. The fact that she's willing to conform so drastically to 'keep him' tells us a lot about her self-respect. But more to the point, what is the reason the song begins in the first place? What has he said just prior to her saying 'It's true'?"

JC: "You're dumb."

SP: "Wow. What a song cue. How does she answer that horrible thing to say?"

JC: "She's saying he's right—she knows she is and will try to do better—and be perfect."

SP: "Don't jump ahead in the scene yet. Nobody said anything about being 'perfect' yet. So far, all we know is what we know. Perfect comes later. It's a tactical moment to come and a response to something he probably says later on in the song."

JC: "Yes, and the musical interlude and the vocal rests are both him talking."

SP: "You bet they are, and he's giving her—you—the subject matter to sing about. The music is there as underscoring of that dialog. This song sounds like a conversation, and he's in the room. You could go another way with it, as a memory of what he said and as an internalized response to that, but I think it's much more active the other way. I think he's right here. The song is stronger for that choice and so is the delivery. The music in the beginning, as it is in the interlude and rideout, is still and quiet. There's your subtext. You aren't putting up a fight when you say 'It's true.' You are submissive to his words. You could have come back swinging, but you don't. If you were going to fight him, the music might sound wildly different. So, your submission—your temperament—is in the music and your subtext is 'you're right . . . *I know*.'"

JC: "That gives me a good jumping-off point. It lets the scene accelerate. I can hear in the music that it should."

SP: "These things can only be relative to one another in scene work, like music itself: How soft a 'pianissimo' [pp] can be is only able to occur in relation or as a response to how loud a 'forte' [f] is. In the scene that is this song there is a huge 'forte' later, but we know we have to journey a distance to get there, per the content of the scene and the distance it needs to travel in the theatre of our mind. If we know where we have to go, we need a starting point to get there, a 'pianissimo.' Start this scene there and it should feel natural to do so. The music and the words support it. What's the body language here in the beginning?"

JC: "I think the same. Simple. Vulnerable. I probably don't have to do much."

SP: "The less you do the better, I think. I don't know exactly what your version of 'vulnerable' or 'resigned' or 'submissive' looks like, but for most people I would guess that it's a very quiet and actor-neutral body language."

(We sang the first verse of the song, and JC was very
effective and exposed and even defenseless. When done,
I asked her how it felt.)

JC: "Good. I wasn't doing much and that helped."

SP: "Actually, you were doing a lot; it just didn't feel like
much to you. You were reacting honestly to the music and
the imaginary dialog, and isn't that mostly what 'acting' is
about—reacting? It was very effective. The one suggestion
that I have is for you to acknowledge that just because
punctuation is written as one thing doesn't mean that the
subtext isn't another thing. When you sing 'we rearrange,
we let things go' there's a period at the end of the sentence,
but you might be *asking* if he can do just that—let the past
go—in the form of a question. She might be saying 'Can
we just let it ride?'"

JC: "Got it. My notes feel squeaky on 'people change' and
'rearrange.' The notes are high and my instinct is to 'belt' to
get them out."

SP: "In this case, work against that instinct. 'Belting' isn't
congruent with the scene at this point. You're still working
on balance and support in your middle voice, but if you belt
you'll be jumping ahead two sections in the song. Leave
yourself someplace to go—even use that 'squeakiness' to your
advantage. It's okay that those notes happen in your 'heady'
place even if 'placing' the sound there doesn't feel like 'you.'
You should never, as an unbreakable rule, belt *just because
you can*. Remember to always be singing into the same place
that the scene is in, and here that place is absolutely in not
belting, in my opinion. Let's go on: What happens after 'we
let things go'? There's a new beat after that."

JC: "Aha." I say, 'I will be perfect' for the first time. I see what
you mean about using that as a tactic. I'm changing my
tune—upping what I'm offering him."

SP: "Bingo. It sounds more desperate to me. There's been a
line between the sung lines and it's his, as we were saying.
He probably outright rejects her. He says something like,
'We've been through all this before, JC, and nothing
changed. You always *say* you're going to try harder and
do better but you don't, and I can't live with it anymore.'
Gritty, real-life stuff here."

JC: "And the music has a steadier feel to it."

SP: "As subtext, that's your resolve and assurance to him that you will, indeed, be, well, perfect. What happens after the first chorus—right before 'You were right, my friends were bad for me'?"

JC: "I start with 'Listen.' That's something you say when you're trying to direct something a certain way."

SP: "He's ready for the conversation to be over. Maybe he's checking his texts or getting up to leave, who knows? You have to get his attention. He may be finished, but you're not. It's a tactic to get him to stay, in this case, but so is the lyric that follows it: 'You were right, my friends were bad for me,' and so on. You're saying, 'Look what I've done for you so far!' It's very specific. Then you go on to ask for his help and reaffirm your desire to be perfect for him. The next part starts to really get to the heart of the song. It doesn't take much digging to get to what's next, and now the scene starts to ramp up into that belting."

JC: "When I'm telling him about sitting in the restaurant by myself an escalation in the scene begins."

SP: "Moving toward that 'forte,' right?"

JC: "When I sing 'I just sat there on my own,' he probably says something dismissive like 'enough with your pity' and 'what does this have to do with anything?'"

SP: "But it has everything to do with everything. The scene is pitching upward to that place where you're no less than begging him. To get up to that most heightened place—that new beat—there has to be a zinger from him. What could that be?"

JC: "After I say 'I don't want to be alone,' he says, 'Shut up. This conversation is over,' and walks away. I think I'm calling him back on the line 'Don't let me be alone.' He's walking. He's out."

SP: "Probably. As for you, anyone with any amount of pride might acknowledge the defeat gracefully, but instead you keep pressing the issue as if you're saying 'listen to me!' The notes on the word *alone* are long, high, and stout. You gotta keep him here, and you can't let him leave because he might not come back. It's a wail for help and the kind that comes from the gut. One last tactical move to show him you mean business and show him how high your stakes are. Belt your face off there and all through the next section—'No one else can take your place.' The accompaniment is inclusive of a swell, a crescendo, so it's working with you. I noticed also when you sang it last that some of the vocal was a little choppy like 'I-don't-want-to-be-alone.' Connect each of them. Think of each one as a bridge into the next. It will help the fluidity of the line and help you punch it all up. The scene and the singing are both connecting all the way across the room. That's how far the energy has to extend on this line, and you can't do that by chopping it up. Doing it that way also helps your body movement and gesture. Ask yourself what you'd do to make these points physically and use them to accentuate, to drive the points home. Use gestures like the hands going downward in an 'everything is going to be okay and everything's under control' fashion on 'we are going to be fine.' It should and will feel natural and is what you'd do in 'real life' when saying something like that."

JC: "Also say, 'Don't tell me we need space,' so he must have said that. Probably after 'I am yours and you are mine' he exploded."

SP: "He may have used words like *pathetic* and *ridiculous*, and said, 'What part of what I'm saying do you *not* understand? I need to be away from you. I'm done.'"

JC: "So, really, the song is about not wanting to be alone."

SP: "Raise it a notch or two. You are terrified, petrified of what being 'alone' means. It's the worst possible thing that could happen. You'd rather be dead. Being alone means you'd have to face off with yourself. In theory, the song could end after 'we are going to be fine' and you could kick sand over whatever issues there are, bury them, and hope for the best. Instead, you choose reaffirmation of 'perfect.' The song even gets a little creepy there. I also think it bears pointing out that there's sometimes a fine line between eliciting empathy from an audience and them perceiving you as downright pitiable. I think you have to be careful in this number that you never cross that line. Keep yourself likeable and available to us through all this."

JC: "Any suggestions on how?"

SP: "Yes, keep it human. Everyone has *some* sense of pride and self-preservation about them, and you need to keep that in mind and use it. Never take the number too far over the top with the begging. It can make the audience uncomfortable. Your mission is to get him to stay and win him over anew. Use those objectives so that the singer standing before us is never a wretched, deplorable girl who just grates at us and who we want to say 'get a life' to, but rather a mixed-up one with real human failings that we can relate to. We should never feel *sorry* for you either. We should feel some sense of compassion for your situation. I think you can capture that in the last chorus, which really isn't a chorus but more like a fragment of it with a vocal tag. Let that section where you are repeating 'I will be perfect' be self-affirming. Let it be your charge to yourself to now get him back. The vocal quality should be very simple and direct—no vocal pyrotechnics. And keep it real."

JC: "This is not your average happy-go-lucky show tune is it? It's a lot of work."

SP: "For sure. It's weighty, but it's real. And it's what you signed up for."

"Maria"
(From *West Side Story*)

Complete lyric

Verse
The most beautiful sound I ever heard:
Maria, Maria, Maria, Maria . . .
All the beautiful sounds of the world in a single word:
Maria, Maria, Maria, Maria, Maria, Maria,

Chorus
Maria!
I've just met a girl named Maria,
And suddenly that name
Will never be the same
To me.

Maria!
I've just kissed a girl named Maria,
And suddenly I've found
How wonderful a sound
Can be!
Maria!
Say it loud and there's music playing,
Say it soft and it's almost like praying.
Maria,
I'll never stop saying Maria!
Maria, Maria, Maria, Maria,
Maria, Maria, Maria!
Say it loud and there's music playing,
Say it soft and it's almost like praying.
Maria,
I'll never stop saying Maria.
The most beautiful sound I ever heard.
Maria.

JH was called back for a second time for the role of Tony in a high-profile production of *West Side Story*. The creative team and casting director had instructed him to return with the song "Maria" in its entirety at full-throttle performance status, so the heat was on.

My first words to him after hearing the situation were, "So, I'm reading between the lines here (not as a reference to a playability technique but as a figure of speech) and guessing that if they need it again it isn't only to refresh their memories. I think they also want to see how you've gotten your skin around the song, having had more time to process and work a little more assiduously and dig into it a bit more. You've gotten this far so they like what they see, but now they probably need to see if you can make a deeper investment in the material."

"I guess," he said, "but I felt like it was 'there' already."

I said, "Let's take a look and listen to what you have so far."

He sang the song and I played, looking up frequently to take it in. The notes and lyric were indeed entirely accurate and pleasing. JH had satisfied the requirements of the singing of the song. I said, "What you're doing is absolutely right and at times thrilling. The trouble is that my ears are fully sated, but all of me is not. I'm not 'seeing' the song in the same way that I am 'hearing' the song."

JH looked slightly confused.

"Okay," I said, "let's start broadly: What is the song *about?*"

"Her," he said. "Maria. The girl."

I said, "Of course it is, but not only the girl. It's about how the girl makes you *feel*. At the moment when Tony sings this, the entirety of his universe has been turned topsy-turvy, having met Maria at the dance and fallen instantly in love with her. It's not that the song isn't about Maria. The trouble with the delivery right now is that the song is too much about Maria and not enough about Tony. True, Tony is counting the seconds until his next meeting with her, and I get that sense of anticipation from your reading. She seems to have penetrated his every cell and he is immersed in the afterglow of their romantic moment together, and I get that too. What I'm *not* getting is you approaching the song, to put it crudely, like a junkie needing a fix. If the junkie needs it badly enough, he will do *anything* to get it. But it's really not even about the drug. It's about how the drug makes him *feel*. It's *never* about the drug. And here, it's not only about the girl. You've done dutiful work and obeyed the instructions in the music, but the scene work isn't coming off the page yet. Let's start from the principle that there is grave danger in this would-be love affair. Tony knows full well where the line is, and he knows that crossing the line and befriending, let alone having a love affair with, those on the other side is explicitly forbidden because of the long-standing rifts between the two groups. These messages have been drilled into him over and over again by his peer group and probably by his family, too. There's the dramatic tension; it's built in. But like the junkie who *must have* that fix, it doesn't matter that he knows the rules and that they are all but unbreakable. He breaks them nevertheless. At this point, as far as we are aware, he hasn't stopped to think for a moment about the possible cataclysmic implications of the result. This is a visceral and impulsive act that doesn't rely on good sense and reason, which I think is the second problem in your approach: It's too calculated. You're singing it like a twenty-something-year-old who might know better than to break the rules and not enough like a lovesick seventeen-year-old kid who makes snap judgments."

JH said, "I'm thinking too hard about the notes and phrasing, and how my voice sounds, and especially, about the high notes."

"Exactly," I said. "There's an old saying that you can't *think* and *feel* simultaneously. If you believe that, then you believe that the two are mutually exclusive, and that would account for why this material is too dampened coming from you so far. Stop thinking. Forget that stuff. You know that stuff, now let it go. Trust that the musical material is safe on one side of the brain and now let the other side take over. Trust your reflexes and stop reflecting so much."

We sang through again, and the overall performance improved leaps and bounds. "How do you feel?" I asked at the end.

"Liberated!" he said.

"Okay, memorize that and let's break it down even further," I said. I asked him to sing the verse once again and stopped short of the first chorus. The vocal quality was beautiful but quite heavy, and I suggested that he take some of the vocal weight out of the sound. "Leonard Bernstein [the composer] has written only scant accompaniment in the [piano] right hand and the [dynamic] marking is p on the vocal line," I said, "and there are only midrange notes present with no bass, so the vocal weight shouldn't be saddled down but really very delicate like it's just suspended there. We have a long way to go here, so don't forget that point," I cautioned. "Imagine that the lines in this section are aromatic, wafting across the air. Treat it like that sort of sensory experience, but you'll want to punch up and invest more in the telling words like *beautiful* because adjectives are quite powerful when singing praises in song, and obviously give a little vocal nudge to the 'Marias.' Also, don't hold the notes as long on *heard* and on *word*. There's no value in doing that. The words are over in a moment and elongating them only sacrifices breathing room to prepare for the next phrases. You'll need that breath because the next phrases are lengthy and with crescendo. Besides, nonpractically speaking, holding the notes out interrupts and works against the easy stream of the thought process and the music, too."

We reached the final set of "Marias," which led the music into the first chorus after a less weighty repeat of the verse. "Beautiful, so far," I said. "How's it feeling?"

"Better," he said. "It's much easier to sing."

I added that from a vocal perspective it is "sometimes helpful to think of musical lines such as this as pure tone with words sort of dropped over the top of it." He agreed. Going on and having reached the musical passage that leads into the first chorus, the final set of "Marias" in the verse, I pointed out that their presence, and the fashion in which they are conjoined into the first chorus, "creates an inevitability, like a 'burst' into the new segment." I suggested that he "not think of this end set of 'Marias' as the last on the verse but instead the first of the chorus" and that he "let them build" so that they can't not become the chorus.

About this time I noticed that JH was making awkward, unsettling arm and hand gestures while singing. I understood them as being connected to the "acting" but couldn't discern the correlation with any certainty. I immediately intervened, having seen too many singing actors disconnect the physical from the internal in playing songs.

And JH, one step ahead of my query, confessed, "I don't know what to do with my hands!"

My standard reply when an actor feels this way is: "Do nothing until further notice, and further notice will arrive via the music and the text." I instructed him to give himself permission to "act" only from the neck up in the verse and everywhere else in the song where gesture feels awkward. I assured him that sometimes less is more and that actor-neutral can often be a quite powerful nongesture gesture. The places and moments where it feels awkward *not* to use gesture are the moments when gesture is appropriate. "In other words," I told him, "my feeling is that gesture is used to punctuate and for emphasis, nothing more. In the release into the chorus if you feel obliged to use gesture, do so, because, like the chorus itself, you can't *not*."

JH felt more at ease and off the hook to "do something" from that point onward, and his compulsion toward gesture for its own sake was quieted for a moment. But he still wasn't certain *how* to accomplish gesture that looked and, most importantly, felt natural to him. I suggested that he, on the first "Maria" of the chorus proper, try placing her in front of him and asked what he would do if she were. He "looked" at "her" and gently lifted his hands in front of his sternum and said, "I'd hold her face in my hands." It was just right. He was spot-on in letting gesture reinforce what he was singing, and not the other way around.

Moments later, however, he stopped and said, "Now I don't know when to drop them!"

I said, "Well, we've established that gesture is never passive, but you do have to drop them someplace or you'll look silly. Drop them to your sides on 'Maria' of 'I've just kissed a girl named Maria,' and let you and the audience understand it as 'I'm done for,' like a resignation. Then I imagine the next logical place to do something with the hands or arms—if you feel it—would be around 'I've just kissed a girl named Maria' as you remember the kiss."

He retorted with, "I'm not sure I can just do nothing in between," about which I suggested putting one hand on the studio chair beside him as though steadying himself until he could feel "safe" doing "nothing."

We pressed on, and the next spot that seemed in need of some discussion was "say it soft and it's almost like praying." "You're singing it beautifully," I assured him, "very reverent, but in the next line I think there might be an opportunity to take advantage of. Tony may very well be having a moment of do or die decision. It's not in the text, even through implication, but it makes for an interesting choice. It's possible that before Tony exclaims that he'll 'never stop saying Maria' he has had a sober moment to contemplate the gravity of that commitment. He's only human, after all. What may have crossed his mind momentarily are all of the would-be external opposing forces working against this mismatched love. His enthusiasm may recede for a brief moment and linger in hesitation as to whether this is actually a wise idea after all. It makes the choice of deciding to do it all the stronger, but the moment of decision can't be more than that because the structure of the music won't allow it. He has to think, contemplate, and decide in no more than barely two bars of music between 'praying' and 'Maria,' and what follows in the bridge are repeated affirmations of that. Tony isn't merely repeating her name over and over. His mind is consumed with not only the 'most beautiful sound he's ever heard,' but also with subtext of 'what-if,' 'if-only,' and 'won't it be.' Now, vocally speaking, there are other matters to confront." I asked JH what he found most challenging about the section ahead.

He replied, as I predicted, "The high notes and mostly the [high] B flat."

"Yes," I said, "it's that note that makes people neurotic, but I wouldn't isolate *that* note as being *the* note." (I find that for many the vocal thinking on the entire song is built around that single note, important as it is.) I continued, "Remember that every note, before it's sung, should be 'sung' in the mind and readiness for it should occur long before the looming note occurs."

He asked me to be more specific.

"Well," I said, "it seems to me that at the top of the bridge the vocal line begins to 'spin out' once the decision has been made that he'll 'never stop saying Maria,' eventually achieving an independence that is counterpoint to even the accompaniment underneath. I think that you have to accommodate that expansion vocally, too. Bernstein has given you the tools you need; the dynamic marking is *f*, and he asks for vocal accents on the *ri* of *Maria*. He does momentarily demand a *p* leading up to the held [note] G on the fifth *Maria*, but then quickly directs a crescendo."

"It's cruel!" JH said.

"No," I said, "I think it's smart. Bernstein knew writing for the voice well enough to treat the G as a precursory swell to the dreaded B flat, and he's giving you lots of support instead of hanging you out there to dry, which *would have* been cruel, and count your blessings because I've seen many composers do that. In addition to Bernstein's facilitation, this is the one place in the song where you have permission to think about your technique. But don't disconnect from the acting by any stretch, and don't think 'Oh, God . . . here it comes,' because then you really will work yourself into a tizzy. The brain, let alone the muscles, can't operate efficiently under that kind of pressure. Treat the *whole phrase* as the B flat in placement, energy, and expansion, and the B flat has a more likely chance of 'rolling out' instead of 'popping out,' which is how some singers approach it. It might also help to think of each phrase of the bridge as 'terracing up' from the previous one. Bernstein wrote the B flat when there was no place left to go, not just in the music but, more importantly, in the scene. The scene must have swelled in feeling and sentiment at that point so that the high B flat is inevitable, as there can be no more powerful a gesture than that."

"That's for sure," JH said.

The conversation turned to the physical life of this portion of the song. I pointed out that, if there was ever a moment to punctuate with the body, it is the B flat, and added that punctuation would also help propel the note out there. I suggested to JH, "Plant your body into the earth for breath support, spread the ribs and shoulders wide and if you are moved to do so, make no apologies and throw out your arms musical theatre style on the B flat. After all," I said, "you can't 'act' with your torso and legs; they are your support system."

"Also," JH said, "I'm wondering about all the 'Marias' over and over. What's your take on why so many, and what to do with them in the 'acting'?"

"He's speechless!" I quickly replied. "He isn't thinking rationally, right? We've established that so far, and that's the point of the entire song and its dramatic function. He *could* say, 'Maria has beautiful dark hair' or that she has 'round red lips,' or that her father is a milk truck driver, but he doesn't. Ecstasy sometimes eludes thought-out words, and I guess this is one of those times."

He sang the bridge again and then looked blank for a moment. I asked what he felt. "It's true," he said. "Singing the B flat is much harder when you think of it as being an isolated event, and what you said to do with my body made the support feel much stronger."

"Good," I said, "now all this energy that has been generated vocally and viscerally can't go to sleep after the bridge. The song isn't nearly over." I instructed him to sing the second chorus and not to dissipate the energy, even on the *pp* when the vocal is instructed to be very quiet, throughout the caesura and then through the floated "Maria" at the end.

We stopped just before "Maria . . . I'll never stop saying [where the fermata and the caesura occur] Maria," and he said, "Now I'm thinking about the fermata and the [railroad] tracks. How long should I wait between 'saying' and 'Maria'?"

"As long as you need within reason," I said, "but above all, let that duration be motivated by dramatic impulse, not just the need to breathe. How much time does it require to create a reaffirmation, which is what this is? Or how much time does it take to get lost in a moment of reverie at the thought of her name? That's the duration. Don't forget that Bernstein has given you what you need. A rallentando precedes it. Acknowledge that and make it count."

"Now what do you think happens physically on the final 'most beautiful sound I ever heard'?"

"Maybe nothing," JH said. "The sentiment probably takes care of itself. It's like a moment of prayer."

"Good way to look at it," I responded. "Float those high notes in your falsetto and let that last moment be one final affirmation. It's very transparent vocally and very pure. Allow the music to be the gesture." He did, and after returning to the callback, he got the job.

SECTION THREE

Song Presentation

INTERVIEWER: How do you land a job in a Broadway musical?

CASTING DIRECTOR: Come in (to the audition) and deliver an opening night performance.

CHAPTER EIGHT

Your Turn at Bat, Sir

Introduction

Those who ignore that gem of advice on the previous page are likely to join the ranks of the others who didn't get the callback, ruminating over cheap margaritas and wondering whether they should have listened to their mother.

Truth to tell, if everyone got onboard with this million-dollar maxim, far less idle time would pass in the audition room and elsewhere. Instead, auditors too often suffer through the showing of what sometimes seems a parade of singing untouched by much else.

You're smarter. If you've played along at home with all or even some of this book's many directives and suggestions, then by now you probably have, or are on your way to having, dependable, good judgment of the song material that suits who you are and what you have to say and underlines and highlights your vocal attributes. You've begun to astutely select songs that cast light on these, and perhaps, tiptoed around those greatest hits of the musical theatre. You've uncovered cuts that support solid storytelling and mastered the traits of the vocal styles they demand. As the architect of the inner life of your performances, you've meditated on the lyric and personalized the objectives.

Now you're ready to plunge yourself into the waters of the presentation of your song(s), but the trouble is that the places where many of these presentations happen, the audition rooms, are unpredictable places that often appear to have no particular rhyme or reason. Or at any rate, none that you are privy to or can make good sense of.

We'd all like to predetermine the outcome in that volatile bubble, but the truth is that there are only so many variables over which we have any degree of control. How to navigate these and mitigate the rest is the subject of many of the following pages. Moreover, the sections that follow focus on the presentation of the fruit borne of your labors thus far, the place and time where the rubber meets the road. Often, success can be found there not only by the application of the many principles of this book, but by adherence to protocol, etiquette, common sense, and planning.

Sun Tzu might have made for a hell of a fine audition and presentation coach. That is, if the same anxieties of today's musical theatre had been at hand 2,500 years ago around ancient China. The warfare military strategist and philosopher had some inspired ideas that theatre up-and-comers, and even old pros, should take into consideration. He postulated (among other things) that outweighing the importance of real-time tactical application was fine-toothed research and the advancement of a well-honed strategy. The element of surprise weighed heavily in his thinking, too, as did good old garden-variety positive thinking and morale: If you believe you can, then you will. Sage advice, you say, but he didn't have to pull off sixteen bars with a bad pianist and the stony mug of a famished assistant casting director glaring at him.

Even so, singling out and seizing control of the elements that you can are the keys to the kingdom, so to speak, and what is potentially under your control is more plentiful than you might believe. This starts with a plan as to which auditions you not only could, but should, attend and under what pre-existing knowledge.

Who am I anyway (in the show)?

When asking yourself if the role or show is the right fit for you, remember to use the skill set information to lead you from the outset and not solely rely on "type" messages that may repeatedly strum inside your head.

As you are by now aware, more and more in musical theatre roles and even entire shows are cast contrary to an erstwhile norm, whatever that may be or has been. In the last several years, the musical theatre has been occasioned with all types of "color-blind" casting, ranging from Asian Dollys to African-American Aunt Ellers and Nicely-Nicelys, and this casting practice is swiftly evolving. Sometimes, but not always, specifics such as the desire to cast nontraditionally are included in the casting "breakdown" (the printed casting notices that appear in a variety of sources), and you should avail yourself of this invaluable information along with any and all information you are able to ascertain with respect to the skill requirements the role requires as written before you voluntarily place yourself in an audition room.

Your primary objective is to assemble as much specific and pointed casting information about the project as is possible before signing off on the decision to attend, fixing your focus on the above, but also, as one high-powered New York casting director pointed out, the "personality stuff included in the breakdown." This is because, especially with new work, the "vision" of the piece is ever-evolving. As a result, the requisite traits, skill and otherwise, that the casting team is looking for are also evolving and changing.

Casting notices

Printed casting information provided for general perusal on casting websites and in newspapers, and even for agents and managers, is frequently annoyingly general and vague, sometimes on purpose. And, despite the varying protocols of making musical theatre casting happen in different cities and countries, this fact has proven itself to be steadfastly reliable time and again. Auditioners would have a less puzzling time of it if the casting notices contained as much specificity as possible.

> SEEKING: Iris: female, 5′6″ or taller who plays between late teens and mid- (not late) 20s. Self-assured, cool, and not afraid to use her curvaceous figure and Grace Kelly-like movie star allure to her advantage with men. Must have the acting sensibilities to play razor-sharp sardonic humor while maintaining a disposition of commanding elegance. Should possess a classic musical theatre brassy belt effortlessly sustained to a D (an octave above middle C) as well as a legit sound to G above the staff.

Instead, you'll too often see this:

> SEEKING: Iris: female, attractive, mid-twenties with a sense
> of humor and confident air. Outgoing and appealing to men.
> Belt to a D.

Those who compile breakdowns might argue that overspecificity is pointless because the requirements are often quite short-lived owing to the fact that artistic and pragmatic vision and facts evolve. This is understandable.

Nevertheless, is it any wonder that what lies within too many audition halls is an oxygen-depleted phalanx of bodies packed in shoulder-to-shoulder like cattle and they are, therefore, unhappy places to spend an afternoon? The latter character description describes at least half of the musical theatre actresses on the planet. Naturally, the turnout would hardly be light. This would be a more efficient process for all involved if there were more often specific physical and vocal descriptions in the data rather than abstract acting descriptions that most likely induce a collective, "Oh, I can do that!" from most readers.

Regardless, you must prepare the best you can with the information available. If the show you are auditioning for is currently running, go see it, if possible, or if video clips are available on media sites, view them, particularly if the present creative team was also responsible for that production. Through this homework, you may glean useful information about the role, show, and how the team has been known to cast it. However, if the role or show is unknown to you, do the research and draw reasonable conclusions.

Other situations are more easily navigated even if not always reliable owing to nontraditional casting practices, especially when the show is so well known that there are established prototypes. Devotees of musical theatre know well the character type and vocal type discrepancies of Danny Zuko and Mary Sunshine.

Keeping it real(istic)

If you have never danced a step on stage, are you absolutely certain that attending an *A Chorus Line* audition and expecting to win the job is realistic? If you've never sung a principal role and have limited vocal prowess, is waiting six hours to be seen for the role of Jean Valjean probably a waste of time? Is it realistic to think that as a forty-year-old you have a shot at playing Belle in *Beauty and the Beast*? It would be irrational for you to answer "Yes" to any of these questions. It should be obvious that casting these roles is skill-set related, and in the case of Belle, an unambiguous nonfit, no matter your ethnicity.

Even if those responsible for creating and distributing casting breakdowns are sometimes guilty of not providing enough specificity, you not having done your research is the real crime. Being realistic as to the assets and limitations of your set of skills saves everyone time, patience, and money, and allows the volatile casting process to operate with better efficiency, even if it is not ideal.

In short, save your time, talent, energy, and in some cases, money for the shows and the roles that match your expertise. If you are well-rounded and have sufficiently sharpened your talents, then you will find that more than enough audition opportunities are available to you where you can display them. Finally, unless you have been directly requested to attend an audition, but were unable to do so, do not inundate the casting office with postcards and headshots explaining your reasons for nonattendance, although on occasion a casting office gives the okay to do this. The same is true for electronic submissions.

There are a few other strategies that will aid you in maintaining a less stressed and more informed life in those trenches:

- Even though your representation submits you to audition, this does not necessarily mean that the show and/or role is an automatic fit for you. Agents' and managers' offices are hectic places, and at times they depend on their support staff to notify clients about an upcoming audition. No office team has the ability or time to know you and your work as well as you or they would prefer. Due diligence on your part is required to make the final decision as to whether you should invest your time at a particular audition. However, if you have knowledge of an audition that you feel certain is the right fit for you, and your representative has overlooked you for it, bring that to his attention while bearing in mind that it is possible that he tried, but for some reason was unable to get you in. At the very least, in a case like this there will be ongoing open lines of communication.

- If an audition notice asks you to prepare a particular type of musical selection that is not already a part of your audition songbook, it is probably unwise to rush out the night before to obtain and learn something new. Unless you are one of those people with the ability to do the necessary work at breakneck speed (or have been endowed on audition day with an obscene amount of good luck), odds are it won't go well.

- Unless the audition is an out-and-out shoo-in or an important callback, don't move heaven and earth to attend an audition, especially when it involves spending (or probably losing) money to do so.

A first-date guide to dressing for auditions and song presentations

To characterize auditions as akin to first dates is a hackneyed expression that is nevertheless appropriate. Both require active planning and commitment in order to gain a reward. Both can be, depending on one's perspective, white-knuckle experiences that are first steps to whatever may come next along the risk-to-reward thoroughfare. Both require the most presentable and thoughtfully planned versions of yourself to show up. We have spent the greater part of this book investigating the means to take you and your song work to peak performance levels. Now we will devote some discussion to that often overlooked element of making an impression by and because of what you've pulled from the hanger or the drawer this morning.

On your date, you will need not just your wits and your wiles to accompany you, but also, as we are realizing, a fair amount of good judgment in advance of your rendezvous. If dress isn't your strongest suit, you may need to consult a friend or mentor; but a few guidelines are quite helpful in pegging the ideal *haute couture* for the date.

Like your audition material, what you wear for your auditions and presentations should reveal your assets and conceal your less attractive features. Achieving this requires some honest and objective assessments of your appearance and even some superficial observations in order to achieve the goal. Even those of you who are less conventional (and like it that way) should assess and ask yourself "Is there anything about this article of clothing that betrays any part of me that an audience member (date) wouldn't find attractive?" You may be surprised by an answer that may not have a thing to do with concealing spare tires and cellulite.

One common clothing infraction professed by some casting personnel is short pants (in women, attached to an outfit or alone) that stop at mid-thigh. While great legs might grant you favor for some roles and shows, especially for showgirl-type women, generally this much skin is distracting. This is especially true if those legs aren't eye-candy worthy. Fluorescent lighting, the unforgiving kind found in many audition and rehearsal spaces, is unkind enough, but on pale, portly legs it's garish and off-putting.

Large-chested women, and particularly those XL body types, are also common offenders both above and below the bra line. The best advice here is to wear a support brassiere and reveal no more cleavage than you would at a business meeting. Notwithstanding dressing that suggests the clothing of a particular character, men are safe wearing a collared shirt, long pants, and polished dress or semi-dress shoes. Under-dressing in the footwear category is rarely an issue with women.

For both men and women, a bit of attention-seeking color is a good idea. Black, especially all black, tends to portray a vacuum of energy. Conversely, too much white and beige tends to subdue the contrast between the performer and the wall behind him. A tastefully colorful shirt for men, or top, belt, and shoes for women go far toward narrowing the focus for the audience or auditor when the choice isn't a distraction.

On the whole, adherence to the following assures that what you are wearing flatters the product:

- Avoid busy patterns and all logos, especially on shirts or tops.

- Be certain that your shirt or top covers the top of your belt line if worn on the outside. Belly buttons are unattractive and not what auditors are there to see.

- Ripped articles of clothing, whether intentionally shredded as fashion or not, especially jeans, should be avoided.

- Avoid cut-offs or otherwise ragged edges.

And, of course, as mentioned above:

- Use discretion or avoid altogether wearing a top with a deep neckline or short pants whether part of an outfit or not.

Be vigilant to conceal:

- Scabs, birthmarks, body pimples.

- Tattoos and piercings (unless auditioning for a show for which these are appropriate).

- Hair in unusual places.

- Anything else that you might be self-conscious of on a first date.

Dressing (up) for the part?

A delicate line exists between choosing what you should wear for your song presentations that supports the central idea of the number or frames the character and clothing that does not support *you* or is inappropriate for the occasion.

The singer of "I Can Cook, Too" (from *On the Town*) boasts of her abilities to please a man in the kitchen and elsewhere, touting her talents in more than one room of the house even as the line of distinction between cooking and sex becomes metaphorically blurred as the song continues. The song celebrates a certain not-so-subtle sexual liberation within the singer, but makes no overt implications in the reading of the text that should necessarily cue you to think twice before taking her home to meet your mother. And, at face value, the song certainly at no point suggests that what the singer is singing is anything more than mildly naughty.[32]

In spite of this, some of the outfits I've seen females wear when presenting this number (sometimes with accompanying lascivious gestures) have been misguided and inappropriate, and border on the offensive. When this occurs, the confidence, sexual and culinary, that the singer is sharing is instantly upstaged by the panel's impression that she makes her living doing something other than office work. What's worse, solid and playable traits of a character are eclipsed by less-than-interesting traits of a *caricature*.

In the case of "I Can Cook, Too," the attire that would perhaps generate a more desirable impact on the viewer might include a vibrantly colored dress extending to just above the knee with a high-ish neckline and a trendy pair of matching heels (but as a rule of thumb, no character shoes). Perhaps a more attractive choice would be a skirt and top with heels that suggest a triple threat of a woman. Clearly, now she excels in the corporate environment as well as those other venues.

If dressing to (whether intentional or not) overstimulate the viewer is at times the issue for women, men sometimes fail to contemplate the effect of what they are wearing. Anyone who believes that auditioning in Bermuda shorts is appropriate, even if auditioning for a musical set on a beach, is remanded back to Audition Etiquette 101 for a refresher.

Remember that at the end of the day the audition is akin to a job interview. Where the choice of clothing seems to support the direction that you are or are not taking, your song is less relevant than the image that your audience or auditors will see before them.

Then there are those who dress overappropriately to the point of overkill for auditions. Women, never attend an audition dressed exactly like Eva Peron on the balcony, even if auditioning for that role. I have, however, seen the right pair of shoes or jewelry worn beautifully for certain archetypal women's roles. And men, a three-piece suit appears too stuffy, even if auditioning for or singing a number that takes place in an office setting, such as one from *How to Succeed in Business without Really Trying*.

More appropriate would be dressing to *suggest* the character singing the song and the show. The auditions panel may appreciate the thoughtful effort as it may aid them in visualizing you in the role. It is far easier to imagine an actress auditioning for a female role in *The Sound of Music* or *Nunsense* in a simple, dark dress cut below the knees than in jeans and sneakers or a flashy and brightly colored outfit. Remember that your chosen couture should both flatter you and support your product, framing you in such a way that it pleases the panel and gives you confidence.

In addition, I suggest that if you receive a callback, almost without exception you should wear the same outfit that you wore at the initial meeting. The reasoning here is that the auditors were impressed with your overall "package" the first time, and that triggered their wanting to see more of your talents. Never second-guess success. Repeat it.

So many choices with so little time

Singing the wrong song at the right audition can be comparable to discussing biology at a job interview for an accountant. Your prowess may impress me, your interviewer (auditor), and may reveal highly desirable attributes that I seek for my team. However, this is less important than my being confident that you can satisfactorily execute the job for which you are applying. Furthermore, I will absolutely question your ability to follow instructions as well as your wherewithal and willingness to do the requisite homework.[33] You see, I have a producer who has entrusted me with casting his very, very expensive show and is counting on me to staff it with capable and thoroughly reliable personnel. I was certain that in the job announcement I was clear about what I asked you to prepare (e.g., a traditional up-tempo), so I am not just bewildered as to why you are singing a contemporary ballad, I'm also a little miffed. And this does not set a good precedent for us going forward as teammates. One way of avoiding this scenario, as you have been encouraged to do throughout this book, is to diversify your songbook with as many styles as necessary and to have those selections meticulously rehearsed.

Perhaps songbook diversity is not, in fact, the issue, and you are sometimes confused about how to identify and match the musical style of the show being cast with what you have available for presentation. In making your selection, the task is to match the sound (and content) of the show you are auditioning for,[34] vocal and otherwise, with a like-sounding selection from your portfolio songbook. As you recall, a discussion of where to find material occurred in Section I of this book.

We have already established that this can often be accomplished by presenting material written by the same composer or by a composer whose sound resembles the style of the show that you are auditioning for, but most of the truly well-known composers write with a high degree of versatility, so pay attention. For example, there are instances when the music of Robert Marx or Stephen Flaherty is appropriate and acceptable to audition for an Andrew Lloyd Webber show, and sometimes not. Marx's candy cane of a song "Purpose" (*Avenue Q*), or Flaherty's potent "The Streets of Dublin" (*A Man of No Importance*) for a *Jesus Christ Superstar* audition? These miss the mark. Know the musical style and content well before choosing your audition selection.

More obvious are other styles. The music of Bob Merrill (which is vastly underappreciated, in my view), Harvey Schmidt, or Frederick Loewe may be useful and appropriate (pending the textual content, naturally) for Golden Age musicals, and some writers of the post-Golden Age (Jerry Herman and some portions of Adam Guettel's work come to mind). But this is not always so when auditioning for a Stephen Sondheim musical,[35] some of which is indigenous to a Golden Age product, but much of it is clearly not. Golden Age-brand material that may work perfectly well when auditioning for Cinderella (*Into the Woods*) or Johanna (*Sweeney Todd*) doesn't work well when singing for The Witch or Mrs. Lovett in the same musicals. The tone, disposition, and content of these latter two characters are quite disparate from most Golden Age-era roles.

So, song warriors, it is incumbent upon you to extend a selection to the auditors that will allow them an understanding of how you excel in the musical, vocal, and textual styles of the show or shows for which you are interviewing. This choice will sometimes become a more challenging one, such as in the case of principal auditions when there is a specific vocal requirement stated (such as "belt to an F") or with the particular vocal range of the character having been included in the casting notice (such as low G to F an octave above middle C).[36] When this occurs, the more range variety that is already included in your songbook, the better.

In summary, your song choice to suit the needs of a particular occasion should reflect the qualities of that role and show. Textual content should be like-minded, but extending that principle one step further, it is the tone and the spirit of the endeavor that should truly be captured. Singing a leading man ballad to audition for the role of Marcellus in *The Music Man* is as ill-fitting as singing a sultry torch song to audition for the role of Mary Poppins. This might seem self-evident, but in the heat of the moment many singing actors are guilty of forgetting these points (or more likely, simply haven't done enough research on the role at hand). Your task is to test your panel's willingness to suspend its disbelief by transporting its members into the realms of the story being cast, featuring you as the principal storyteller.

Finally, all of this business must reside neatly within a compact cut of a length between short song and eight-bar cut. As a good rule of thumb, always prepare at least a short and trimmed version of your material (if not the entire song, which is preferable) and further establish shorter, more compact versions in thirty-two-, sixteen-, and eight-bar contingencies.

And, to additionally reinforce a number of earlier points, don't lie awake at night fretting about the exact number of bars not being achieved. I have seen much anxiety exhibited from singing actors because their cutting only covered fourteen bars, or more likely, was twenty bars, and therefore, four bars too long. Some have solved the perceived conundrum by cutting off the song without finishing a phrase, completing the thought, or allowing the music to resolve. This is an approach that is unnecessary and not in your best interest.

Keep in mind that the thirty-two-, sixteen-, and in some auditions, eight-bar standards are not hard rules as much as they are guidelines. Finish musical phrases, complete thoughts, and try not to leave auditors hanging there expecting more. Not doing so is like ending a spoken sentence on the word *and*.

Much has been said in this book about the importance of cutting a song that is your presentation package for auditions. The following best sums up what your cuts should accomplish. Your cuts should:

- frame your abilities as succinctly and efficiently as possible, highlighting your strongest assets and playing down any chinks in your armor;

- tell a fluid and accessible fragment of a story that you can portray with a unique, personal, and committed point of view;

- come to a satisfying conclusion, and with a sense of dramatic and musical cadence whenever possible.

Get it done

1   Make a list of roles and shows that are a great fit for you. Does the material in your portfolio book complement your list in stylistic and content terms? Is it time to find more appropriate selections?

2 How might you dress to suggest the roles and shows on your list? What might you wear to a more general song presentation occasion that would be appropriate and complementary and would make you feel great in the wearing?

3 Have a careful look at your song cuts: short song, thirty-two, sixteen, and eight bars. Have you satisfied the specifications indicated in the section above? Might you need to rethink some of the choices?

CHAPTER NINE

Musical Theatre Song and Collaboration

I love a pianist

Why do singing actors too often recall hapless on-the-spot pianist/ singer collaborations? ("That pianist ruined my audition!") Why do audition pianists write and publish books with advice for auditioning singers containing self-descriptions such as "enraged" in the title? This section tells the tale of the chasm that too often seems to exist between these ill-fated Mars and Venuses who might well benefit from a round of couple's therapy. Perhaps the issues that produce the dissonances within what should ideally be a harmonious collaboration can be illuminated in a discussion of effective interaction between the two, one that at the core largely turns out to be about preparation, good manners, and nonpresumptions.

In order to appreciate the perspective of the audition pianist, let us first consider that when this system of a producer-provided pianist to accompany singers at auditions for musical shows began, theatre songs were more straightforward. A simple thirty-two bar, AABA (see Chapter 6) format was quite typical. Even more sophisticated song material held predictability about it, which naturally made for a more or less intuitive singer–pianist alliance. Audition rooms in those days were filled with strains of up-tempo and ballad songs, arias from operettas, blues songs, character songs, waltzes, and patter songs, and all were packaged rather uniformly. If a short cutting was needed for brevity, a sixteen-bar format made sense as the eight-bar musical "thought" (phrase) was standard and the B-A (of AABA) contained two contrasting musical ideas with the last eight (the final A) often containing a "big finish" or "money" note.

Audition pianists today are confronted with anything but that same kind of predictability with what is placed before them. To the contrary, they are frequently seated at the wheel of an unruly vessel and commanded to steer it competently to the finish line, that moment when you've sung your final note and the room is once again silent. If things have gone well, then hold your hat and hallelujah. If not, then you may have been the lone casualty of the shipwreck. After all, it's your audition and not the pianist's.

We must also consider the workday of your audition pianist. Every few minutes and for several hours at a stretch, he is required to spontaneously collaborate on and productively contribute to an event that may determine the future of your livelihood. To boot, he must actively and artistically support an event as delicate and vulnerable as a living song. He has likely not been a part of the rehearsal process that has taken place in your vocal studio and your living room. He has no prior knowledge of the cuts, jogs, jabs, and right-hand turns that the markings on your music may indicate. Then, there is the matter of turning all those black dots, squiggles, and flags into an audibly realized form.

Your abatement of his woes and facilitation of making his workday smoother, if only for the next few minutes, does not begin when your interaction with him does, but rather well before that time. Besides, it should be perfectly obvious that doing so can and will serve to enhance and support your own work and chances of success.

Some judicious strokes of your pencil (I prefer a red one as it commands the eye) will work wonders to ease the audition pianist's daily perturbations and set your relationship on a smooth and clearly charted course. Indications of "start" (the first notes you want the pianist to play), "cuts" (the indication of musical material you wish to exclude), and "end" (the final notes you want the pianist to play) may be discussed at length in audition room training, but are confounding and ineffective if not written properly. Moreover, if additional instructions are required, are they translated into language the pianist understands? And what of verbal indications, such as the tempo, you want the song to be played at?

Ineffectively communicating this could be tantamount to audition and song performance suicide.

Successful preparation and presentation of your sheet music and your musical requirements are outlined below as well as wisdom pertaining to etiquette and comfort for the benefit of everyone in the room. The points are intended to troubleshoot potential hazards of singer–pianist interaction and create a seamless and routine interplay between them that reliably keeps you (and your songbook) at a distance from the ire of that "enraged" pianist.

The entrance

Never

- Saunter from the door to the piano; walk with a purpose.
- Ask the pianist what he thinks the panel would like to hear.
- Hand the pianist loose sheets of music.
- Place sheet music on the piano without the title of the song prominently displayed on the first page even when starting in the middle or at the end.

Sometimes

- Ask the auditors what they would like to hear if you have more than one or two options available or are unclear as to what would best satisfy their needs.[37]

Always

- Greet the pianist and panel professionally with a simple "Hello" or "Good morning/afternoon."
- Carry your music book into the room with a finger marking the page on which you will begin (or have the page tabbed). Flipping to your starting page at the piano is time-consuming and awkward.
- Have your music in a notebook (preferred) or photocopied onto card stock pages taped together.

The explanation

Never

- Ask the pianist if he is familiar with the song.

- Give the pianist a lyric sheet with chords only, or more deadly, a page with the melody line and lyrics but no piano accompaniment such as those found in the back of libretto books.

- Place the "start" marking at the vocal entrance if you want the pianist to begin earlier in the music (intro).

- Require the pianist to flip pages backward as in the case of a DS al coda.

- Drop or ignore rests in the vocal line when giving the pianist your tempo.

Sometimes

- Give the pianist a moment to peruse your music before barreling into your explanation (if he appears to be intently scanning it or appears somewhat confused).

Always

- Understand that the pianist wants to support you and your work, but that he may need further clarification from you.

- Write "start," "end," and clearly mark any cuts.[38]

- When making cuts, think of your music as a road map with definitive start and end points, and most importantly, a clear, clean path between the two.

- Clarify the key you are singing the song in if you or your teacher/coach/pianist has transposed the chord symbols from the written key.

- Clarify where you want the intro to begin (written notes that precede the vocal entrance).

- Point out vamps that need to occur due to dialog and what the cue is for the music to proceed.

- Know if your song is "in 2" or "in 4," and if this is not immediately apparent to the pianist, indicate "in 2" or "in 4" in writing on the music.

- Use a highlighter to emphasize the cuts and other pertinent musical directions, such as (1) coda, (2) colla voce, (3) important dynamic markings that have an effect on your presentation, (4) fermatas, (5) tenutos, and (6) first and second endings.

- Indicate in writing how you want the song to end (like a stinger chord, for example, if not written in the music).

- Tell the pianist your tempo by singing a line or two of the song.

- Organize your music pages so that a forward page-turning trajectory is present.

The presentation

Never

- Make idle chat with the auditors before you begin. Offer a short greeting, announce your name and selection, if you choose to or are instructed to, and begin.

- "Play" or direct your presentation directly to the panel.

- Scoff or look curiously at the pianist if you are not satisfied or are confused with the accompaniment for any reason.

Sometimes

- Use a chair if preferred and available.

- Modify/adjust singing and physical actions when needed to accommodate the space in which you are performing if you discover it to be more intimate or cavernous than you imagined.

Always

- Physically confine your presentation as this is typically a small playing area with a few feet in front and to the left and right of you.

- Drive the tempo train. If the pianist is playing slower or faster than your desired ideal tempo, remain steadfast, predictable, and not nonplussed. Odds are he will find your tempo and synchronicity will occur.

- Assume responsibility if something goes awry with the piano or accompaniment. Calmly stop if the derailment has gone hopelessly beyond recovery. Walk calmly to the piano, confer kindly with the pianist, and start again. No reasonable audition panel will ever demerit you for stopping to fix the issue, but will surely do so if your approach is unprofessional and/or accusatory.

- Have a "Plan B" in the form of at least two contrasting songs should the panel request it, but never assume they will.

The exit

Never

- Ask whether auditors would like to hear another selection (e.g., another song or monologue) once you have concluded your first selection.

- Apologize for anything, including illness, that impeded you singing your best. The panel likely will be aware of your ailment and take it into account.

- Ask when callbacks will be held. If the panel desires a recall, you will be told where and when to appear.

- Take an excessive amount of time to collect your belongings, put on your coat, and so on. Grab your personal effects and exit the room quickly and gracefully.

Sometimes

- At times, auditors will engage you in conversation after your presentation. This is likely so that they can know your personality in more detail before you leave the room.

Always

- Exit graciously with a strategy: Be prepared to perform another selection should the panel request it, answer any questions an auditor has for you, acknowledge "thank you for coming in today" with a reciprocal "thank you" to the panel, thank the pianist, collect your music book from the piano, and move on, keeping in mind that a callback may still be forthcoming.

Setting yourself up for success in spontaneous collaboration

A beautifully crafted songbook, well-appointed in advance, does a great deal of the heavy lifting in your pianist/singer collaborative interactions. It is incumbent upon you to avoid the following pitfalls, and if unsure, seek help and counsel from someone who knows. A few well-informed actions on your part can lighten everyone's load.

- By choosing music that is sight-reader friendly, you allow the pianist to focus on supporting you and your efforts rather than digging through dense accompaniment, unconventional time signatures, and complicated key signatures. Knowing basic music theory is helpful to you in placing yourself in the shoes of your pianist, but if you don't know music theory, consult with someone who can assist you.

- Some older scores never received computerized notation or were never typeset, and the piano/vocal versions (the version sent out as rehearsal materials for productions) remain in handwritten form. In many cases, these make sight reading almost impossible, especially for the weary eye and soggy brain of the pianist in the eighth hour of the workday. Avoid using these versions of the sheet music. First, check your resources online and in print at your library or music store to ascertain whether or not the song was set into print from a publisher, and if so, acquire it. If not, consider paying someone with music notation software to set it for you. If it means so much to you that you simply MUST sing that song, then a computerized printout is well worth the investment.

- In determining the cuts that you will make in your music, ascertain the extent of page flipping required by the pianist to follow your version of the song. If the pianist is required to flip more than once or twice (as in the case of repeats), in addition to ordinary page turns, take note. If he is required to flip around to accommodate a DS a1 coda (see Chapter 6), take note, and should any of the above occur, strongly consider creating a cut-and-paste version of the song whereby the sheet music is entirely neat and sequential.

- If you have photocopied music, be certain that the bottom or top of your pages hasn't been inadvertently cut off.

- Present your music, as ordered above, one of only a few ways (and it bears repeating, never as loose pages!). Music photocopied or pasted onto cardstock is a perfectly acceptable format. Use clear tape to connect the pages so that they fold in and out, accordion style. Notebook binders are obvious choices, but only if they have three rings that prevent the pages from billowing from the top downward as happens when the rings are present in the middle rather than at the top. Finally, the question of glare and nonglare (referring to the presence or absence of a sheen on the plastic that reflects light) page protectors within these notebooks should be mentioned. I can say firsthand, having squinted, crooked, and consequently squeaked my way through many a performance or audition, that reading music encased in these is a very real issue under certain circumstances. Nonglare page protectors are preferred with music sheets inserted back-to-back for turning like the pages of a book.

CHAPTER TEN

How They See Us: Body Language Onstage and Media Online

Now that I'm here, what do I do with my hands (and feet, and hips, and legs, and . . .)?

Those who study such things tell us that over ninety percent of communication is nonverbal. If true, this reinforces the value of accuracy, honesty, and economy of body movement in song presentation.

Several chapters ago I suggested that a singer of a song, while singing it, must be in a spontaneous and ongoing state of discovery of the current and the following lines, thoughts, and the underlying sentiments therein. This is useful not only because this strategy provides trajectory of action (a song must never be in neutral and must always occur in real time), but also because the song is given a reason to keep going beyond the first line, which must be a response to an event or events that preceded it and set the song in motion.

Physical responses are motivated by mental and emotional ones, and the internal reactions that the singer has to this constant state of discovery dictate physical responses manifested through body movement.

Consider the following (imaginary) line: "When I wear this dress I feel sexy!"

If the singer delivering this line were delivering it after having already made this discovery (offstage before the song began, for example), and therefore before this very moment, then it is old news and no longer a moment of real-time discovery. The resulting delivery might not elicit much surprise and might rather send the message of a second-hand dose of excitement.

On the other hand, an at-this-moment discovery of this fact is something entirely different. The singer first has an emotional response that, in turn, triggers a reactive, impulsive physical one (eyes wide in disbelief, a devilish smile, a hand that reaches to touch the garment as though to be sure the whole thing is real).

This is not only an appropriate example of a truthful, active response to these thought impulses, it is also a testament to the fact that body movement, in song performance as in life (although on stage all is ten times larger in scope), is the result of moment-to-moment discovery and thoughts feeding into our motor system.

Discovery feels good and buttresses the right-here-right-now immediacy in the many tenets that this book has set up: staying active, responding to outer and inner forces, solving the problem at hand, and even overcoming obstacles of one kind or another. Overall, it is another useful device that allows you, the singer, to "do" rather than just "be," the latter tantamount to just telling us about it rather than allowing us to witness you, the singer, experience what you are singing about now and in real time.

In short, it is best to, whenever possible and logical, sing in a state of moment-to-moment personal discovery rather than a premeditated state in which the singer (you) has already experienced the flush and surprise brought about by fresh realization. Appropriate reactive physical responses will naturally follow. As a singing actor, how would you physically react to the following lines being sung for the first time?

- "I finally found it!"

- "I will never do that again."

- "He might ask me!"

- "That was a close call."

- "I had the time of my life!"

- "Please come home."

- "How could you have left me like that?"

- "I will fight this injustice!"

- "Now that (X) has happened, things will never be the same."

The above are all common themes of musical theatre song lyrics, and you can probably easily comprehend how singing these lyrics as in a state of immediate discovery will elicit honest reactions likely to encourage genuine and honest physical sensations that do not appear staged, preplanned, or artificial.

Gestures should only be used as a physical reaction to some internal or external stimulus that has triggered it (and as a punctuation tool), encouraging some part of the body, often the face, hands, and arms, to reinforce the verbiage. Use caution, however, to ensure that you do not devolve into acting and gestures of the kind where the singer sings of the moon and then points to it as if to reinforce the obvious. Use your physical gestures sparingly and economically, and always be prepared to drop all of them, singing gesture-free with only your voice, face, and heart when requested as will sometimes happen as an adjustment in an audition room.

See and be seen on Facebook, YouTube, and everything else

And then it hits you, the inevitability of it all. Half a generation ago, at the genesis, it didn't occur to most of us that it would eventually, like an Orwellian foretelling, grow to be the key marketing instrument of the future, whether for a plumber, potter, or performer.

But personal websites, social media, and sharing sites are the no-brainer go-to answer to mass projection of the hawking of your message to heaps of consumers, specifically that overtaxed theatre-biz demographic known as the creatives and casting directors. Straight from the mouths of these decision makers comes the edict to get yourself (through a well-produced video of your work) on the

Internet, as many affirm that the business of casting is being done, in part, electronically.

Seizing these opportunities also offers another advantage: If you are vigilant, they allow you a much greater degree of control over the product your buyers are perusing in ways that aren't possible in the rushed, volatile audition room or live performance setting. This is due to the fact that you can record as many takes as it requires to get the performance to your liking prior to posting. In the audition room, asking to do it again is unheard of in a first audition meeting. Here, do-overs are encouraged. Maintaining control over what others record and place on social media (a cabaret performance, for example) is more difficult, and this is where vigilance is required to keep the best version of your work front and center, but I have seen many do it with a high degree of success.

So what of a strategy to ride on the back of the world's largest audition and performance room?

- Post on your personal website (get one if you don't have one), social media pages, and video-sharing sites a video of your best, most recent work. Audio tracks alone are not recommended by many in the casting business.

- Keep these clips succinct, and preferably, of the material you use to audition and perform. Be cautious when using clips from a live performance as they are often shot too far away and are unfocused. (That scene of you playing Rizzo in high school that was shot with your dad's first-generation iPhone probably won't come off well.) Be sure to include several contrasting styles (e.g., a traditional, contemporary, and pop/rock selection).

- Hire a professional videographer who also edits, a rehearsal room with a pleasing backdrop that won't distract, and an accompanist.

As for evidence that casting personnel are screening your work on video at 3:00 a.m. in their pajamas, I offer the following: A student of mine, now living abroad, was contacted out of the blue by a London-based casting office that had seen a video of his work on YouTube. At that time, this particular office was seeking a replacement for a leading role on an international tour of a popular musical. After forty-eight hours and an in-person meeting, he signed his contract.

Being tolerant of the sour along with the sweet, you must accept that there do exist some unseemly woodpeckers out there who'd like to peck down your tree house in the comments section of sharing sites. For the sake of your sanity, my best advice is to post it and forget about it, but don't post it before you assure yourself (and possibly have been assured by trusted mentors/representatives) that it accurately and favorably represents the product (you) that you wish the buying public to see. Another cautionary note: If your intentions are to use social media for professional purposes, be certain that you do your utmost not to allow, through being tagged or otherwise, unflattering photos or videos of yourself. Don't post or allow yourself to be tagged in photos of that night at the pub when you lost your wits, or worse.

CHAPTER ELEVEN

Finale

If I had a dollar, euro, or pound for every coulda, shoulda, and woulda

Sometimes there is (understandably so) a good bit of fretfulness associated with song performances, prompting after-the-fact do-overs on the stages and in the audition rooms of our minds. This is true, in particular, if singing isn't your primary discipline, as is the case with dancers and dramatic actors new to the craft of *singing* the dance or the monologue and not merely moving or speaking it.

Some portion of this nervous worry about singing must be driven by your intrinsic fears of being judged harshly, and why shouldn't it be? In the audition process, for example, you need a job, and the panel will assess your skills relevant to the requirements of the position(s) that they have available. Much of that decision (although sometimes less than you might think) will be predicated on how skillfully you demonstrate your wares during your time before them. Although audition room pep-talkers often like to remind you that the panel is rooting for you to be the perfect fit and does not sit in harsh judgment, this makes little difference when you feel subpar to the competition. Worse, there are so many variables outside of your control (a shaky pianist, acoustics of the room, illness that affects your voice) that you might feel overwhelmed and unable to overcome it all.

But there is happy news. Crafty and diligent preparation of the kind recommended in this book coupled with repetition will abate the fear, cast away the "I can't!" demons, and allow the best version (or a close facsimile) to arrive for the song presentation.

When traveling the road from preparation to repetition, it is important to understand that this is the period when the muscles in the body are memorizing the commands that will later become routine. If a song performance is sometimes not all that we'd like it to be, it often means that the body doesn't know it as well as the intellect and that more repetition is needed to cement the performance. Militaries run soldiers repeatedly through simulated battlefield experiences with good reason—so that when the time comes to perform and the pressure spikes, the performance becomes automatic. But, of course, even then things can and do go amiss: The high note wasn't well supported, the focus was foggy and indirect, or a lyric was fouled up. So be it. I have never heard of anyone being removed from the running because one of these very human snafus occurred.

By now, a regimen of selection, preparation, and presentation has been offered for your consideration. As mentioned, I further advise frequent and methodical reiteration of what the first two have generated. Your mission is to cloak yourself with certainty and confidence that leaves no doubt in your mind as to what will come out of your mouth when you sing or how you will physically respond in your song performances. Of course, this must appear spontaneous and effortless, leaving room for the jewels of discovery that sometimes appear in the heat of the moment. I have never seen nor heard of anyone who adopted these strategies being failed by them. Does constant perfection exist? It is foolhardy and unreasonable to believe that it does or to attempt to attain it. It is best to deliver a performance expecting one hundred percent and realizing that eighty percent is a very impressive showing. Perhaps less means that there is more work to be done, but theatrical actors aren't in the business of quantification. It is better to fully and innately realize that there is always more to be done because we can never, by our own nature and temperament as performers, be wholly satisfied.

If things go well in a song performance, celebrate the victory because it likely has not occurred by accident. But realize that you must not rest on your laurels and that what was good today must be nurtured, maintained, and refined for tomorrow. Furthermore, if things did not go well (outside of those factors over which you may have no control), then try to understand the experience as a call to action. Some energies, emotional or physical, have not yet been crafted, harnessed, or repeated enough and your process is yet to be complete. Let the day go, but keep the experience active and use those notions of coulda, shoulda, and woulda as your personal palette of *possibilities* instead.

Thank you and goodnight

And so it is: Musical theatre song has a trunkload of diffuse yet cooperative moving parts. It has a lifeline that begins well before the first notes are sung and an exigency to resonate well after the singer has sung the last of them.

At its most fruitful, it both entertains and opens the ears, mind, and heart with a jolt, a trigger, an awakening. Perhaps to the hardened, reticent naysayer or the pure entertainment seeker this is an unexpected surprise. Yes, I say again at the last as I did at the first, the theatre is indeed full of surprises.

As revealed in these pages, the yeoman's work of the musical theatre songster involves scrupulous planning, soul-scavenging rehearsal, and premeditated recital. When viewed through the long lens, these are not the burdens, but rather the pleasures of your lifework as a singer, as efforts are too soon hamstrung by the rigors and realities of living in the professional world. Viewed statistically, I regret that (and this is not news to many of you) a shockingly small number of those who *aspire to* it ever *get to* put their labors onstage as an employed professional of the craft in the "big time." The plummiest of jobs are hard won and can be heartbreakingly short-lived, leaving those who choose this fickle and finicky profession to do a great deal of dancing between raindrops, so to speak. Nevertheless, I implore you to press forward and never allow your craft to become stymied as a result. Too many worthy ones have been led astray, and the theatre is the poorer for it.

In closing, musical theatre song aficionados, warriors of your present and stewards of your past, I offer a tidy assortment of final advice. Revere yourself as a practitioner of a great art form, respect those who continue to resolutely carry it forward, and venerate those who invented it. As you do, make all efforts to be a teller of your own truth and truth of the songs you give life to. Paint vibrant and effervescent pictures as you tell the stories and be well remembered for them, but above all, reveal *your self* within. You have been endowed here with a great amount of the necessary alchemy to make those aforementioned too-wonderful-for-words moments materialize. So be the pot of gold. Be the inexplicable "it."

Be the surprise.

NOTES

1 The use of the word *Broadway* here and throughout this book should not always be understood as a geographical reference (e.g., New York or the USA), but sometimes as an all-inclusive one, a musical play on whatever the stage in whichever the country.

2 It is appropriate here to point out that, for example, if you were delivering a narrative of the evolution of the automobile, America would also be the logical setting. The story of opera, however, would be entirely rooted, and, therefore, set within European soil, with references and strands of narrative set outside of those confines when necessary and appropriate.

3 This is so because, although this volume is not one entirely dedicated to the craft of auditioning per se, but rather to song performance in general, a great deal of song selection occurs for audition purposes.

4 The songwriters listed here are a sampling of those whose work I have become familiar with and admire. There are many other worthy inclusions, I am certain, and as I become more educated, I shall certainly include them in future editions.

5 This practice has raised a fair amount of debate over where the "line" stands. Is an audience expected to suspend disbelief to the extent that they should be asked to get onboard with a casting choice or scheme that is counterintuitive? My personal belief is that, if the casting choice is so ludicrous because of a physical or a skill set issue that it becomes unreasonable for an audience to suspend disbelief, then we do have a collective problem.

6 The traditional types referred to here are the standard issue molds set forth in yesteryear and based largely upon superficial traits of age, height, weight, and overall physical appearance, particularly looks: the leading lady and leading man, the juvenile and soubrette, the ingénue, the comic relief character man and woman, and so on. In musical parlance, titles such as "comedienne belter" often mean that the character woman and character man would sometimes be assigned a patter number, whereas leading lady and leading man are often associated with soprano, mezzo, and baritone roles,

respectively. The juvenile, soubrette, or ingénue would often have vocal ranges and musical material in the tenor, soprano, or belting ranges, respectively. Moreover, quite often roles were devised as varying combinations of these traits.

7   Do not make the mistake of advertising *only* that fact or by choosing a song or vocal approach that blasts the auditors' eardrums unrelentingly. Save the big guns for the appropriate text at a strategic dramatic juncture.

8   Perhaps one of these songs may emulate this particular sound although the song may have been written later than the Golden Age.

9   The majority of the work of John Kander and Fred Ebb as a songwriting team and a significant portion of Jerry Herman's and Charles Strouse's output was produced following the conclusion of the Golden Age, commonly thought to have ended circa the mid-1960s. Nevertheless, much of their music suits the old-fashioned, habitually lyrical, and recurrently snappy show tune genre of the age perfectly well.

10 This mix and match is anything but exact science. Although many songwriters' stylistic tendencies to write in whatever the style that held sway at that particular time and shows written by their contemporaries may frequently cross-pollinate nicely, this isn't always the case. For example, Frank Loesser's *The Most Happy Fella* and Lionel Bart's *Oliver!* share little musical style in common outside of both being Golden Age musicals. In making your selections, common sense and homework are required to be certain the match is well-suited. In addition, many shows overlap (mostly the more old-fashioned musical comedy kind) in that their song characteristics are both Golden Age-like as well as Great American Songbook-like (see Item 3). Overlap is perhaps more common in the contemporary era listings. Finally, the savvy steward of musical theatre might quibble that certain show titles have been omitted, and he would be quite right. This list has been pared to represent musicals that receive at least a small number of productions each year worldwide. For example, *Call Me Madam* and *Applause*, great shows though they might be, receive next to nil in numbers of productions, and they have therefore been excluded from the list of shows that you might be auditioning for.

11 One of those most awkward audition room moments occurs when the singer, after winning the panel's interest through a snappy up-tempo, sheepishly answers "No" to the query. Now, with swiftly vanishing interest in the singer's work, the casting personnel, having heard the up-tempo and with no place left to go and the clock

ticking, reply with the anxiety-inducing "Thank you for coming in today." These moments can be avoided if the singer has at least one of these particular varieties of selections in his book.

12 The distinction of "mix-y" is used here for clarification primarily for female singers who must negotiate the blend of their "chest" and "head" registers as a "mix" of the two in the area of the female voice that lies "in between."

13 Women may recognize this area of the voice as the area above the chest register where the voice is, in many cases, markedly weaker until trained. Some call it the "hole" in the female voice.

14 By way of example, I've seen productions of *Sweeney Todd* where the "Epiphany," the title character's soliloquy song (during which his entire life plan alters and radicalizes before his and our eyes), was sung with such weight, control, and attention to minute detail that it could be easily transferable to the operatic stage. In this environment, primacy is placed upon note-perfect musical formulations with respect to obedience to the written score and vocal quality. By contrast, I've seen and heard other versions of the song in other productions that were equally effective where these elements were far more relaxed.

15 In vocal sound quality terms, as has been previously stated, many songs written in the Contemporary Era nevertheless *sound* interchangeable with previous eras (the Golden Age, for example).

16 Again, for our purposes, since the conclusion of the Golden Age.

17 The sheet music itself will rarely provide exclamation points and will rely on dynamic markings and accompaniment to provide musical direction.

18 Are there many exceptions to this guideline? Absolutely, depending upon the universality of the song. For example, songs such as "Small World" from *Gypsy* or "What I Did for Love" from *A Chorus Line* are easily transferable to many varieties of singing actors. In the case of a song such as "Small World," however, you must consider identity not so much with type, but with iconic character, show, and situation.

19 I have occasionally seen and heard of the time limit method, especially in auditions outside of the United States.

20 These auditions assemble large numbers of auditors, representing numerous theatre companies, who gather in one room, often a theatre, and hopeful actors audition for all en masse.

21 I have deliberately chosen the term *often-heard* and not the term *overdone* because I believe the latter to be (a) far too subjective and (b) irrelevant if the song is done exceedingly well.

22 However, to the publishers' and editors' credit, some of the more recent editions contain less well-known and well-traveled songs.

23 A distinction must be made here between "pop" and "popular" music. Popular music has, of course, been a mainstay on musical theatre stages as long as there has been musical theatre. For purposes of this discussion, however, "pop" music refers to a style of singing outside that of what is sometimes understood as "typical" musical theatre.

24 It bears emphasizing here that when auditioning for a specific character, as is most often the case with a callback, the audition panel is "seeing" the character, and you are playing within that specific context.

25 Taking the song out of context and at face value, we know nothing of Clara's mental and emotional challenges in the musical itself, which is the plot lynchpin within the show but not relevant to our purposes in this context.

26 Questions must be stated (sung) *as questions*. Too often, the singer will forget to punctuate, and therefore the line becomes indirect. If a line is written as a question, then the person singing it *really* wants an answer.

27 Although it certainly still exists everywhere, particularly in pop music.

28 I, personally, use this term very rarely, but many still do. Therefore, it is included here.

29 The exception being "actual" beats and "felt" beats.

30 Generally, the area of F4 and Eb5 is referred to as the "middle" vocal register of females.

31 Calls of this nature in London are often more generous, allotting the singer more time/bars.

32 The reader is reminded that, although the role of Hildy, the singer of this song in *On the Town*, is often played in a brash and aggressive fashion, out of context, the song requires no such approach and can be played any number of ways.

33 There may be several reasons why this has occurred, one or two not your fault; but you alone must bear the brunt of the song choice error, for I will have no knowledge as to why it occurred.

34 In the case of a casting authority present who is casting multiple shows in varied styles (as in a season of several diverse musicals) or in combination with more than one authority present, choose the material that *best* represents your offering.

35 With Stephen Sondheim, because the nature of the material is unique
    and unmatchable, casting authorities will often instruct those
    auditioning to prepare a Sondheim song directly.

36 The more accurate method to identify the notes in this description is
    G4 to F5, but understanding that most singing actors might find this
    confusing and unfamiliar, stating it the long way is the usual method.

37 But not generally in a chorus call, where they are only looking to
    assess you and your vocal essence.

38 The most efficient way to do so is to place an *I* marking with an
    O through it at the place you are cutting from to the place you are
    cutting to.

SELECTED BIBLIOGRAPHY

Ardoin, J. (Ed.). (1998). *Callas at Juilliard: The Master Classes.* Portland, OR: Amadeus Press.

Berger, G. (2013). *Song of Spider-man: The Inside Story of the Most Controversial Musical in Broadway History.* New York: Simon and Schuster.

Craig, D. (2000). *On Singing Onstage* (revised ed.). Milwaukee, WI: Applause Theatre and Cinema Books.

——. (2000). *A Performer Prepares: A Guide to Song Preparation for Actors, Singers and Dancers.* Milwaukee, WI: Applause Books.

Filichia, P. (2011). *Broadway Musical MVPs: 1960–2010: The Most Valuable Players of the Past 50 Seasons.* Milwaukee, WI: Applause Books.

——. (2013). *Strippers, Showgirls and Sharks: A Very Opinionated History of the Broadway Musicals That Did Not Win the Tony Award.* New York: St. Martin's Press.

Gilbert, D. (1963). *American Vaudeville: Its Life and Times.* Mineola, NY: Dover Publications.

Gottfried, M. (1990). *All His Jazz: The Life and Death of Bob Fosse.* New York: Bantam Books.

Kasha, A., and Hirschhorn, J. (1987). *Notes on Broadway: Intimate Conversations with Broadway's Greatest Songwriters* (revised ed.). New York: Simon and Schuster.

Kayes, G. (2004). *Singing and the Actor* (2nd ed.). London: A & C Black Publishers Ltd.

Kenrick, J. (2010). *Musical Theatre: A History.* London: Bloomsbury Publishing.

McCoy, S. (2004). *Your Voice, an Inside View: Multimedia Voice Science and Pedagogy.* San Francisco, CA: Inside View Press.

McKinney, J. C. (2005). *The Diagnosis and Correction of Vocal Faults: A Manual for Teachers of Singing and for Choir Directors.* Long Grove, IL: Waveland Press.

Maslon, L., and Kantor, M. (2010). *Broadway: The American Musical.* New York: Bulfinch Press.

Rutherford, N. (2012). *Musical Theatre Auditions and Casting: A Performer's Guide Viewed from Both Sides of the Audition Table.* London: Bloomsbury Methuen Drama.

Sondheim, S. (2010). *Finishing the Hat: Collected Lyrics (1954–1981) with Attendant Comments, Principles, Heresies, Grudges, Whines and Anecdotes.* New York: Alfred A. Knopf.

Soto-Morettini, D. (2006). *Popular Singing: A Practical Guide to: Pop, Jazz, Blues, Rock, Country and Gospel.* London: Methuen Drama.

Stanislavski, C. (1989). *An Actor Prepares* (reprint ed.). London: Routledge.

Suskin, S. (1990). *Opening Night on Broadway: A Critical Quotebook of the Golden Era of the Musical Theatre, Oklahoma! (1943) to Fiddler on the Roof (1964).* New York: Schirmer Books.

——. (1997). *More Opening Nights on Broadway: A Critical Quotebook of the Musical Theatre 1965 through 1981* (2nd ed.). New York: Schirmer.

——. (2006). *Second Act Trouble: Behind the Scenes at Broadway's Biggest Musical Bombs.* Milwaukee, WI: Applause Theatre and Cinema Books.

——. (2010). *Show Tunes: The Songs, Shows and Careers of Broadway's Major Composers* (4th ed.). London: Oxford University Press.